PLATO'S *CHARMIDES*
AND THE
SOCRATIC IDEAL OF RATIONALITY

SUNY Series in Ancient Greek Philosophy
Anthony Preus, Editor

PLATO'S *CHARMIDES*
AND THE
SOCRATIC IDEAL OF RATIONALITY

W. THOMAS SCHMID

STATE UNIVERSITY OF NEW YORK PRESS

For Catherine

Published by
State University of New York Press, Albany

© 1998 State University of New York

For information, address State University of New York
Press, State University Plaza, Albany, N.Y. 12246

Production by E. Moore
Marketing by Patrick Durocher

Library of Congress Cataloging-in-Publication Data

Schmid, Walter T.
    Plato's Charmides and the Socratic ideal of rationality / W.
Thomas Schmid.
        p.   cm. — (SUNY series in ancient Greek philosophy)
    Includes bibliographical references and index.
    ISBN 0-7914-3763-9 (hc : alk. paper). — ISBN 0-7914-3764-7 (pb :
alk. paper)
    1. Plato. Charmides. I. Title. II. Series.
B366.S35 1998
184—dc21   97-27154
                                                                CIP

10 9 8 7 6 5 4 3 2 1

CONTENTS

PREFACE

*Think of Greek antiquity as a festival, carried out by
Greek contestants, poets and players, surrounded by
Greek spectators. In a larger circle around them are the
spectators of the subsequent centuries of Western history, to which we belong. . . . Then suppose that out of
that half-observing, half-performing Greek crowd a single individual were to step forward, take hold of us and
draw us into a conversation. In that conversation we
would forget the division between us and the Greeks,
and the platform would suddenly become the stage of
our own life, our own self-understanding. It is only after
we have been spoken to in this way by Socrates—concerning our very lives—that we might permit ourselves
to say that we know him.*

—Helmut Kuhn

The study of individual Platonic dialogues is viewed with
skepticism by some philosophers. What value might there
be to a commentary on just one early dialogue, and such an
inauspicious one as the *Charmides*, at that? For inauspicious and
often neglected the *Charmides* certainly is. Despite the fact that its
subject matter is *sophrosune*, defined in the middle of the
Charmides as "to know what you know and do not know"
(167a6–7)—a definition that points unmistakably to Socrates' own
self-description in the *Apology* (21a–23b), and that suggests this
dialogue, *perhaps more than any other*, focuses critically on
Socrates himself, and on the values and practices at the center of
his life—the *Charmides* is seldom referenced in contemporary
books on Socratic philosophy, and does not have anything like the
position in Plato scholarship that one might expect.[1]

Part of the problem would seem to be the difficulty of placing the work. Scholars have asked whether it was written early, middle, or late in Plato's career. Although most have taken the *Charmides* to be early, others have assigned it to the middle period of Plato's philosophical development, and some even to the late period.[2] The reason for this is found in the text: the dialogue is aporetic, but it is also highly suggestive of themes developed in later dialogues, such as the nature of soul, the concept of knowledge, and the ideal of utopian community. I shall argue that the *Charmides*, while Socratic, is not easily categorized in terms of early, middle, and late Plato. It is unquestionably Socratic—it reflects an intellectual world that is more open than the intellectual world of the middle Platonic dialogues seems to be—but it conveys a pattern of ideas that are highly advanced, and in some ways philosophically more attractive than the ideas of those works. The treatment of the Socratic dialectic, the relation drawn between it and the Socratic notion of self-knowledge, the Socratic ideal of rationality and self-restraint, the norm of wholistic and moral health, the interpretation of the soul as the rational self, critical examination of the concept of knowledge, the connections drawn between dialectic and autonomy and moral community—all of these ideas are explored in the *Charmides*, making it a kind of microcosm of Socratic philosophy. Or so I hope to show.[3]

I am also interested in persuading the reader—student or professional—of the merits of the methodological approach I have taken to the dialogue, which supposes that there is a far-reaching and intimate relationship between the drama and argument, the *logos* and *ergon* of the dialogue.[4] While the view that the dramatic elements in a Platonic dialogue should be taken into account to determine its meaning has come to be widely accepted in recent years, there is still considerable disagreement as to how that insight should be implemented. Radical adherents of the principle, like myself, offer very different interpretations of the dialogues from those found in most Plato scholarship, which basically still confines itself to the analysis of arguments, without interpreting them through their dramatic contexts. The kind of reading I offer here may seem to take the literary aspects of the dialogues as more important than the philosophical. I do not believe this to be true, but by contrast to the prevailing modes of scholarship the charge is understandable.

The broader case for the interpretive approach I champion has been made by Rosemary Desjardins in an important recent article.[5]

Desjardins shows that the quest for definition in the early dialogues is characterized by ambiguity, and that the function of the dramatic elements does not lie essentially in charming the reader, but rather in providing the necessary parameters that allow the reader to cut through the ambiguity at the discursive level. This is a point of view on the Platonic dialogues with radical implications for their interpretation. It implies, for example, that we cannot take the refutation of a definition at its face value; what may be refuted is only that definition under a certain interpretation, but not under another interpretation, which may be indicated by the drama, but not addressed in the argument. The effect of this approach is to create two different levels of meaning, as we read the dialogues. There is a surface level of meaning, in which definitions are put forward and refuted; and there is a depth level, at which, through various means but especially through the use of dramatic elements, the same definitions, interpreted differently, may be recovered. The contrast between these two levels of meaning is essential to the Platonic art of philosophical writing, and to the pervasive role of irony in that writing.[6] I hope to show how such a contrast functions in detail in the *Charmides*. This kind of argument cannot be made, except through the interpretation in depth of individual dialogues.

This is not to say, however, that the findings of such a study may not be important to the overall interpretation of Socratic thought. Just to give one example, albeit a significant one: a chief question in the study of Socratic philosophy concerns his intellectualism—why he denies *akrasia*, moral weakness of will, and claims that virtue is knowledge. I shall argue that the *Charmides* answers that question, not in its words, but in its deeds, by showing how Socrates employs the elenchus to lead his interlocutors to a moral choice. That choice concerns not only their relation to dialectic, but their self-determination and future self-knowledge. If made rightly, it may lead in the direction of rational virtue. If avoided or made badly, it leads in the direction of self-deception and a diminished self. These themes are developed in the central part of my study, chapters 3 through 5.

My study follows the structural pattern of the *Charmides* itself (see appendix A). I begin in chapter 1 with the prologue, which depicts the complex political and educational culture in which Socrates engages his philosophical inquiries, and suggests the radical difference of outlook and manner characterizing Socrates and the philosopher-type he represents, as opposed to his contemporaries. The discussion with Charmides and Critias leading to the definition at 167a shows how the inquiry into the definitions of a virtue can constitute a social and historical, as well as personal dialectic, and how moral ideals and social values interact (chapter 2). The next two chapters examine the relations among knowledge, virtue, and dialectical engagement in such a way as to redefine the ancient Greek ideal of self-knowledge in terms of the Socratic ideal of rationality: it is now to be understood as something achieved *in* rational inquiry, through a particular kind of self- and other-relation tied to such inquiry. The *Charmides* also introduces a metaphysical framework for conceptualizing the self, and suggests an understanding of psychology that in some ways is Plato's most advanced and sophisticated (chapter 5). Further articulating the basic themes of Socratic philosophy, the dialogue explores alternative conceptions of knowledge, rejecting one epistemic model of self-knowledge and suggesting, if somewhat obliquely, another, Socratic model (chapter 6). Finally, the dialogue also shows how a utopian vision of social relations may degenerate into dystopian fantasy, if the underlying moral and epistemological principles are flawed. This part of the dialogue anticipates criticisms leveled against the *Republic* from a perspective which, if not explicitly democratic, is at least conducive to and supportive of democratic political relations (chapters 7 and 8). Thus I shall argue that the *Charmides*, in which the two chief interlocutors are men who later become members of the Thirty Tyrants (including in particular the infamous Critias), will provide evidence in support of a Socrates who, if not an unreserved admirer of *demokratia*, is more a loyal friend than enemy of the Athenian constitution.

The *Charmides* is Plato's most sustained reflection on the Socratic insight that human wisdom consists not only in knowing what we know, but also, and even more crucially, in knowing what we do *not* know—on the implications of the Socratic knowledge of ignorance. In sum, the depiction and account of *sophrosune* in the *Charmides* adumbrates Plato's vision of the life of critical reason, and of its uneasy relation to political life in the ancient city.

I am not claiming that the *Charmides* offers Plato's final account of moderation or virtue and knowledge. His mature theory depends upon the idea of justice, and this topic is investigated only in the *Republic*. (For comparison of the two dialogues, see appendix B.) This study, however, focuses on the *Charmides*. I am concerned to explore its depiction of *sophrosune*—human moderation—as an attitude that must be dynamically brought to each new situation, and dynamically reachieved in that situation. As we shall see, *sophrosune* on Plato's account is a quality that can be retained or lost, affirmed or denied. It is a function of insight, but also of choice. It is sustained by wariness toward bodies and appearances, by principles governing our relations to other persons, and by an intellectual discipline of critical rationalism that does not rest satisfied with unexamined opinion, no matter who or what the source. The absence of any of these elements implies the absence or corruption of moderation, of rationality, and of self-knowledge. These insights are of perennial philosophical value.

ACKNOWLEDGMENTS

The hermeneutic philosophy I have brought to the reading of the *Charmides* was influenced by many people, especially Robert Anderson, Robert Brumbaugh, Hans-Georg Gadamer, and Morris Kaplan. Anderson, Brumbaugh and Kaplan taught me to read Plato dialogically, in terms of the relation of drama and argument. Gadamer convinced me that the goal of interpretation consists in a "fusion of horizons" between the past and the present, and that this fusion cannot occur unless one conceives of the work in its historical context.[1] My approach has also been influenced by the generosity of Gregory Vlastos, since I first attended his National Endowment for the Humanities (NEH) seminar on "The Philosophy of Socrates" at the University of California, Berkeley, in the summer of 1981.[2]

As regards the *Charmides* itself, I have drawn freely on both Anglo-American and Continental traditions of scholarship. I have found each of the commentaries on the *Charmides* in English, by T. G. Tuckey and by Drew Hyland, to be valuable.[3] I have benefited from the studies of Socratic philosophy in the recent scholarly literature, particularly the work of Michael O'Brien, David Roochnik, Kenneth Seeskin, and Gregory Vlastos.[4] I have also benefited from what amounts to a local tradition of study of Socratic self-knowledge at St. John's College and at the Pennsylvania State University, which began with Jacob Klein and Stanley Rosen, and continued with their students, including Charles Griswold, Drew Hyland,

David Lachterman, David Levine, and Thomas West.[5]

My citations are from Thomas and Grace Starry West's fine English translation of the dialogue, though I have have not taken over their rendering of *sophrosune* as "sound-mindedness," but have left it in the original or given it as "moderation" or "self-knowledge," depending on the context.[6] The other English translations of Plato are taken from the Loeb Classical Library editions.

I use masculine pronouns in contexts refering to interlocutors in the dialogues (all of whom, apart from Diotima in the *Symposium*, are males), inclusive language in modern contexts.

At the institutional level, thanks are due to the National Endowment for the Humanities and to the University of North Carolina at Wilmington, my teaching home for the past eighteen years. I am most recently grateful to the NEH and to Diskin Clay and Michael Gillespie, organizers and directors, and to the participants, including Joseph Cropsey, Doyne Dawson, David Depew, Michael DiMaio, Peter Euben, Charles Kahn, Richard and Cynthia Patterson, Donald Nielsen, Malcolm Schofield, Evanthia Speliotis, and Zev Trachtenberg, for the 1994 Summer Seminar on "Plato and the Polis" at Duke University, which proved crucial to the development of my thinking on this topic and on Plato in general—thinking that is different in certain important respects from that found in my previous study, *On Manly Courage*.

I am also grateful to the State University of New York Press, especially my editors, Clay Morgan, philosophy editor, and Anthony Preus, editor of the series on Ancient Greek Philosophy. I would like to thank my readers for the Press, including Tony Preus, Gerald Press, David Roochnik, and an anonymous reader, and also Martin Andic, all of whom read and offered helpful advice on the manuscript. I would like also to thank all the people at the State University of New York Press who have or will contribute to the publication, marketing, and distribution of this book.

On a more personal level, I would like to thank a number of friends for their help and support of this particular study, including Bob Anderson, Morris Kaplan, Kim Plochmann, and Ken Seeskin, who read all or part of the manuscript in draft form and helped save me from many errors. I would also like to thank them and other friends and teachers for the many conversations I have enjoyed with them on the themes of moderation and self-knowledge over the years, including Ferenc Altrichter, Joan Bayliss, Seyla Ben-Habib, Belinda and John Buescher, Susan Finsen, Emily Fischer, Chris Gill, Bob Haywood, Hope and Jim Lanier, John Lemos, Dale

McCall, Jim Megivern, Linda and Reid Murchison, Eli and Ray Norton, Lorenzo Simpson and Marsha Abrams, Peter Storey and Carol Moore, and Jim Walsh.

Finally, I am deeply grateful to my mother, Frieda Schmid, and to my children, Karl, Leo, and Mary Beth, for their love and support of all my endeavors, scholarly and otherwise. And I am uniquely grateful to my wife, Catherine Hooe Schmid, to whom, with love, I dedicate this study.

ONE

⋑◈⋐

PROLOGUE

Do you see how erotic Socrates is with beautiful young men, how he is always hanging around them and is taken with them? And on the other hand how he claims that he is ignorant of everything and knows nothing? . . . His outside is like a Silenus, but when he is opened up, my fellow drinkers, you cannot imagine how he teems with sophrosune *within.*

—Alcibiades

T he idea that moral concepts can be better understood when they are discussed in the context of human lives and actions has come to the forefront of philosophical thinking in recent years, perhaps especially through the influence of Alasdair MacIntyre's *After Virtue.* Of course this idea is also expressed in the Platonic dialogues, which through narrative and drama in historical context give to the meaning of moral terms a depth they otherwise would not have. It is clear that the prologues to the dialogues often have a special role in this function of framing, through drama and narrative, the ethical and cultural context of the philosophical inquiries Socrates conducts with his interlocutors. And yet the prologues are often ignored in the scholarly literature on Plato's dialogues, presumably because they fall outside the inquiry itself, in which concepts are examined and arguments developed, and therefore may seem not to contribute to the substantive, philosophical part of the works. If the interpretive approach I outlined in the preface is correct, however, this dismissive attitude toward the prologues is mistaken.

This matter is particularly relevant to the *Charmides,* which enjoys one of the most richly textured and fascinating among all the prologues to Plato's works. The prologue thematizes four issues that are of interest not only for understanding the *Charmides*, but for understanding Socratic philosophy in general: (1) the theme of war in relation to moderation; (2) the theme of *eros*; (3) the theme of Charmides and Critias and the aristocratic tradition in *sophrosune*; and (4) the theme of Socrates and his self-portrait as a moral therapist. But despite its importance, the way in which the prologue prefigures the understanding of these themes prior to the inquiry has not been appreciated in the scholarly literature on the dialogue. Many scholars, including Tuckey, Taylor, Guthrie, and even Friedlaender, devote relatively brief or no attention to the prologue, while Hyland, who offers a more complete account, admits that he does little more than raise issues rather than elaborate on them.[1] I wish to suggest that a fuller appreciation of the prologue will prepare the reader for a deeper understanding of the later inquiries and of the dialogue as a whole. Unless these themes are recognized in the introduction, their later functions in the dialogue may be ignored, undervalued, or suppressed.

In this chapter, I will show how the prologue characterizes the cultural setting in which the ancient Greek ideal of *sophrosune* was situated. I will argue that that setting displays the problematic character of the ideal in relation to conventional Athenian attitudes toward military and political life, and toward *eros* and education. There is a profound relationship between violence and a certain kind of erotic attachment thematized in the prologue and dramatized in the later work which is important for understanding the psychology and political philosophy of the *Charmides*. There is also a profound relationship indicated in the prologue between the problematic of *eros* and its relation to *sophrosune* and to the very idea of rational self-identity, which must be appreciated to make sense of later developments in the argument. In relation to the third topic mentioned above, the reader is introduced in the prologue to the notorious figures of Charmides and Critias, who are fated to have such an important role in the Athenians' judgment of the historical Socrates' influence on public life. Their depiction in the dialogue in general and in the prologue in particular has been widely misread in the scholarly literature on the *Charmides*, with a distorting effect on the interpretation of the entire work. Finally, there is the thematization of Socrates himself, of his role in Athenian intellectual and moral life, and of the nature of his claim—after all the qualifications and denials—to some form of wisdom and virtue-inducing therapeutic power through dialectic. Now, there is a sense in which every Platonic dialogue named for a character in it chiefly concerns the central value of that character. But obviously they are all about Socrates as well, and, as I indicated in the preface, the *Charmides*, much more than other dialogues, amounts to a kind of critical self-examination, or examination by Plato, of Socrates' philosophical enterprise. We run the risk of failing to understand the extent to which this is the case, if we rush past the prologue on our way to "the real philosophy." The prologue is part of the real philosophy, though it involves no arguments.

WAR, POLITICS, AND MODERATION (153a1–d1)

The *Charmides* begins with the fact of armed conflict between Athens and Sparta, and the intense involvement of those present in that conflict. It is around the year 429 B.C.[2] Socrates has been away from the city for an extended period of time, and has just returned to a "familiar haunt," the palaestra or athletic school of Taureas, from the war camp of the Athenian army at Potidea, after that army was engaged in a fierce battle.[3] While he was away, the plague may have struck Athens for the first time.[4] On entering the gymnasium, he encounters the excitable Chaerophon, who would have Socrates tell him and the others, who include Critias, news of the battle.[5] They are tremendously eager to hear him, and we can well imagine why, since many friends and relatives may have been killed or injured. They would also want to know who fought well and who poorly, and how Socrates himself fared—as Chaerophon blurts out, in the opening question of the dialogue: "How did you survive the battle, Socrates?" (A question that will reverberate throughout the dialogue, as we reflect on its possible different meanings.) With masterly brevity, the initial scene projects the reader forward to the entire tragic story of the Peloponnesian War, beyond that to the tyranny of the Thirty, and beyond that to Socrates' own trial and execution.

Almost immediately, Socrates' narrative serves to contrast his own attitude toward the war to that of all the others present. They, like Chaerophon, if only barely less so, are caught up in its excitement and energy. (The word used to describe the battle, *ischuros*, "fierce" or "intense," is used later in the dialogue as the contrary to a term used for moderation, *hesuchos*, "calm.") To the others, the war and everything related to it is the focus of their interests and concerns. But Socrates characterizes this interest with a dismissive phrase, and says that "after we had enough of that," he was able to turn the conversation to what interested him (to what brought him to this familiar, pleasant place), namely the young men of Athens and their education. He wanted to know who was well reputed for beauty or wisdom or both. Thus Socrates is made to stand out, by his own words, as someone who specifically is not concerned with the values of the others, the values of politics and war, but rather as someone concerned with the things of peace, philosophy, and the education of the young.[6]

This contrast between Socrates' evident lack of passion with respect to the war-fever—associated with his love of philosophy and the young—and the marked passion of his contemporaries is underscored by something else, which informs the narrative though it is not directly expressed. For we know from Alcibiades in the *Symposium* that Socrates not only survived the battle, but he performed with exemplary courage in it, saving Alcibiades' own life (220d–e). Thus Chaerophon's question, which he impulsively failed to consider might have been a cause of intense embarrassment to his friend (e.g., had Socrates saved himself by dropping his armor and running), might have tempted Socrates to embark on a tale of his own heroism. Instead, Socrates' reply is a model of modest reserve; we hear nothing of his courageous deeds, and his silence would seem to underscore the fact that he, unlike the others, simply does not care about those things. But this does not imply that he is not capable, when duty calls, to be courageous. Socrates' moderation is not incompatable with deeds of great physical energy and fearless resolve.[7] For him the one does not imply the absence of the other. This fact will prove especially relevant, when we come to consider the argument in which the first definition is refuted.

The life and death struggle alluded to in the opening lines of the dialogue relates to the political coloring the ideal of moderation/restraint had come to have in late fifth century Greece. As Helen North has shown in detail, *sophrosune* was a virtue characteristically (and propagandistically) identified with the conservative aristocratic tradition in Greek political thought, and with Sparta in particular—in marked contrast to Athens, which was viewed by many as a deeply immoderate regime.[8] This tradition is represented in the *Charmides* by the title character and his guardian and uncle Critias, whose individual significance will be discussed shortly. The classic statement of the conservative view is found in Thucydides' *History*, in the passages where the Corinthian delegates to the Congress at Lacedaimon at the beginning of the war contrast the relentless energy and daring of the Athenian people to the phlegmatic conservatism and caution of Sparta (I.68–71).

To this description, which he does not deny, the Spartan king Archidamus replies that what the Corinthians disparage is in fact a quality of wise moderation, which tempers everything the Spartans do, and which renders them more able than other peoples to deal judiciously with both good and bad fortune (I.84). *Sophrosune* in the conservative tradition of Greek thought was a quality of temperament and mind rooted in sound laws, strict educational discipline, piety, and the sense of shame. It was a quality they believed most lacking in the Athenians, who were excessive, bold beyond measure, and excitable in everything they did, much like the democrat Chaerophon (cf. 153b2–3). On Thucydides' account, the Spartan virtue of *sophrosune* was the product of a repressive culture and training not found in fifth-century Athens.

But of course this was the Spartan, not the Athenian perspective. In the Athenian view, expressed in the Funeral Oration, neither Spartan moderation nor even Spartan courage (which Archidamus had said was rooted in their moderation and sense of shame) are virtues, for the simple reason that they are unfree. Genuine virtue, Pericles argues, must arise from choice, not from habits driven by coercion and fear, and it must be informed by intelligence.[9] These are themes to which we will return in chapters 2 and 3.

Despite Pericles' remarks, it must be acknowledged that moderation was not held up as a *manly* ideal in his Athens, and that elements of the kind of immoderation for which Athens was condemned are present in the Funeral Oration as well. Thus Pericles boasts to his fellow countrymen that they have "forced every sea and land to be the highway of our daring and have left everywhere imperishable monuments of our good and evil deeds behind us" (II.41), and he urges them to conceive a passionate love (*eros*) for Athens in their hearts, that they might emulate their fathers' achievements and add to Athens' glory (II.43). This was the kind of ambition that caused Athens to be charged with tyranny and tyrannical *eros*, both in the pages of Thucydides' *History* and by Sophocles in his *Oedipus Tyrannus*.[10] It was also the kind of ambition that would later be associated with Pericles' egotistical young ward, Alcibiades, and with his scheme to seize Sicily, which led to Athens' eventual defeat; see especially VI.24, where Thucydides says that the Athenians conceived a passion (*eros*) for the adventure and for the beautiful island they thought it would bring them. It is no accident, I suggest, that immediately after Plato has depicted the kind of passion the Athenians, particularly Chaerophon, show about the war, he goes on to depict a striking intensity of passion about the beautiful young Charmides. The drama of the dialogue will recur to this theme of the desire for beautiful or noble things (*ta kala*) and the willingness to use violent means to obtain them. In fact, the erotic intensity attaching to Charmides' beauty in the prologue will be defused in the course of the discussion, and transferred to Socrates' beauty in the end. But there we shall again see how immoderate desire spills over into violence or the threat of it.

Now all of this is related to the widespread chauvenistic or "phallocentric" Athenian attitude that moderation was more a woman's virtue, or that of a youth such as Charmides, rather than a manly virtue, the virtue of a free citizen and warrior.[11] Thus Charmides, who is acknowledged to be *sophron* (or at least his uncle claims that everyone regards him so), is clearly not regarded by the others as fully virtuous. (The word *arete* occurs only once in the entire dialogue, at 158a1, and there innocuously.[12]) That attribute would call for other qualities, such as courage or prudence, but no one claims Charmides possesses either of these (his uncle admits the boy is lacking in *dianoia*, i.e., thinking ability, and his actions will not prove him either thoughtful or brave). Thus the prologue shows us an Athens in which the focus of attention, for almost all of those present, is on what Aristotle calls "the life of action," namely the military and political life of the adult male citizen. This is a way of life in which moderation, at least as it is understood in Athens, is deemed to have a relatively minor role. But this is somewhat puzzling, too, since the Spartans share the Athenian admiration for the life of action, but they nonetheless believe that moderation is an important, indeed central virtue. Clearly the reader will not be able to fully appreciate the arguments of the dialogue, unless the meanings of its terms are considered in relation not only to the context of war and the life of action, but also in relation to the cultural/political context and the way in which the virtue may be structured differently in different societies.

EROS AND SELF-CONTROL (153d2–155e2)

A second function of the prologue is to situate the ideal of moderation in relation to connections in ancient Greek thought and culture between *paideia* and philosophy, *eros* and beauty. The theme of the relation between education and *eros* is developed through the depiction of the beautiful young Charmides and the effect he has on the others present, especially the grown men. Here again, the initial effect of the prologue is to contrast the Socratic to the conventional attitude, represented by the others present. But the narrative then also offers an internal view of Socratic moderation in *eros*—a view literally without parallel in the Platonic dialogues.[13] This event will prove to be of crucial importance for understanding the later inquiry, when Socrates and Critias reflect on the nature of self-knowledge.

After the brief opening scene and its allusion to the war, Socrates asks concerning "affairs here," that is, affairs having to do with the young and education (153d3). To his question who among the young are the most renowned for beauty or wisdom or both, Critias answers that he will soon meet the most beautiful, and Charmides makes his electrifying entrance. Socrates:

> In my opinion all the others were in love with him, so excited and confused had they become as he came in. Indeed, many other lovers were also following among those behind him. Now this was not wondrous on the part of us men; but turning my attention to the boys, I noticed that none of them, not even the littlest, looked anywhere else, but all were contemplating him as if he were a statue. (154c2–8)

This description is followed first by Chaerophon's quip that as striking as the boy is, Socrates would think nothing of his face, were he to see his naked body (*eidos*, 154d5), and then by Socrates' rejoinder, that they then need to consider only one little thing, to see if Charmides is truly perfect: whether his *soul* is lacking in any respect (154e1).

Chaerophon's remark reflects the fact that moderation did not conventionally attach as a virtue to the grown male lover in ancient Athens, or at least not as contemporary readers might expect.[14] It certainly did not appear as a voice of moral censure; the *erastes* normally had no qualms about wanting to have the beautiful young lad. On the other hand, moderation did conventionally attach to the beloved, who was expected, within the framework of Athenian sexual morality, to protect his reputation and not let himself be seduced (like the high school girl, in the age of double standards). There is a decidedly "feminine" quality to the conventional virtue of moderation in the context of sexuality in fifth century Athens, in the sense that it is supposed to attach to the passive object of masculine pursuit and be reflected in behavior that neither submits to that pursuit, nor takes advantage of it to behave in a domineering manner toward the lover.[15] Charmides fulfills this norm; despite being the object of intense sexual pursuit, he is "moderate" and "restrained" in his behavior and demeanor. Thus he is the opposite of the young Alcibiades, who slept with whom he pleased and moreover used his sexuality shamelessly to pursue his ambitions, as we also learn in the *Symposium*. This suggests another dimension of the moderation expected of the beautiful young *eromenos*, a dimension Plato also subtly reflects in the prologue—the relation between *eros* and tyranny. Just as the beloved may in his eagerness for conquest ignore the well-being of the beloved, so the beloved, accustomed to the fawning behavior of his lovers, may take for granted his domination of them (cf. 156a1–3; also *Lysis* 206a, *Meno* 76b).[16] But it is not clear that moderation in this conventional sense is ultimately beneficial to the one who possesses it—at least not if virtue is primarily a function of action and conquest, rather than of resisting such conquest or refraining from taking advantage of another's weakness.

A second aspect of Charmides' entrance scene is to contrast once again the attitude of Socrates to that of all the others present. They are stunned by Charmides' beauty, and the men at least are openly eager for his body; but Socrates is not taken in by the erotic fever for Charmides in the same way, and he remembers to be concerned for the boy's soul, which they in their passion momentarily forget (cf. Aristotle, *Nicomachean Ethics* VI.5, 1140b12–20). We soon learn that even Socrates is not entirely immune to Charmides' charms, however. For he goes on to relate that shortly after Charmides approached him, he happened to see inside the boy's cloak, with the result that

> I was inflamed, I was no longer in control of myself, and I held Cydias to be wisest in erotic matters, who, speaking about a beautiful boy, advised someone that "a fawn coming opposite a lion should beware lest he be taken as a portion of meat." I myself seemed to myself to have been caught by such a creature. (155d4–e2)[17]

Socrates then proceeds to recount the dialogue he shared with Charmides, and how, in the course of that conversation, he regained his composure and "was rekindled to life" (*anezop-uroumen*, 156d2–3).

The chief value of this remarkable narrative is to depict the inward struggle for self-control in such a way as to link Socrates' success in that effort with his practice of rational inquiry and with the reachievement of his personal identity.[18] It is as though Socrates *himself* is extinguished by the impulse of his sudden passion for Charmides, and is not reawakened until that passion has subsided and the familiar Socrates, charismatic teacher/philosopher, is back in charge.

Viewed from the outside, Socrates' behavior toward Charmides is that of a man whom Athenian fathers can trust with their handsome young sons. He is not stunned by Charmides' beautiful physical appearance, in vivid contrast to Chaerophon and the others, who forget Charmides' soul in their absorption in the boy's looks (154d1–e1); and he acts in an altogether seemly manner with the youth during their whole conversation. He is perfectly, naturally moderate.

The personal narrative reveals more. Socrates' moderation is no mere disposition of behavior, natural or otherwise. It is a dynamic, voluntary habit that can require controlling his impulses and enacting his deeper sense of himself, his identity as a lover of wisdom. It includes an element of moral wariness in dealing with beauties such as Charmides, who have a dangerous innocence about their charm. It includes principles with regard to how the other should be conceived and treated—with respect, as a "rational soul," not as a mere means to the satisfaction of his desires.[19] And it is achieved through the process of dialectical engagement, for it is through reasoning with Charmides that Socrates reestablishes the common ground on which their interaction can proceed in a manner appropriate both to his deepest desire and to his and Charmides' rational selves. The connections between Socrates' erotic moderation and his philosophy are complicated and reciprocal. While his practice of philosophy seems to depend on the ability to restrain impulses he perceives as alien to his deeper purposes, in fact that restraint is itself grounded in his love of wisdom, his awareness of "how wise Cydias was." Socrates' erotic quest, stimulated by the beautiful, is nonetheless oriented most of all to wisdom and the potential for it in others. His love of wisdom is in turn dependent, as he will explain and demonstrate later in the dialogue, on his realization of what he does not know. These are themes to which we will return later, when the argument will seem to disconnect self-knowledge from desire.

The depiction of Socratic moderation presented here is also relevant to the concept of the self or rational soul, which is also a focus of later discussion. It is apparent from this example that the rational soul relates implicitly to the impulses of a potentially unruly body. Clearly, a person must become aware of those impulses and of the nature underlying them; but just as clearly, she must distinguish herself from them. They are not simply alien; but they are also not "her own," unless she succumbs to or embraces them.[20] The structure of the self depicted in the prologue involves a hierarchical relation between the second-order desire of the rational self and the first-order desire of immediate impulse. To "know himself" in this situation, Socrates must preserve his rationality in the situation of erotic temptation; but he must also realize his lack of perfect substantive rationality, his need for wisdom and its relevance to his relations to others. His success here suggests the larger pattern of the whole: the love of the beautiful is moderated and transformed by the rational pursuit of wisdom.

Note, however, that the public events of the dialogue do not reflect Socrates' inner drama at all. They simply display Socrates in easy conversation with Charmides. Perhaps a close account of Socrates' behavior would reveal something different (the "I was inflamed" may imply that he had an erection), but that would not have been observed by anyone else present, and at any rate there would be no suggestion from an outside observer that *Socrates* had somehow lost his identity, only to regain it later on. The narrative contrast between the objective and subjective points of view, and the relevance of that contrast to the nature of personal identity, is crucial to the meaning of the dialogue. Lacking this perspective, we might not be aware of the elements of self-consciousness and self-determination in the moral situation; we might view it merely from the perspective of behavior, rather than agency. Plato presents the reader with a depiction of a familiar moral experience, one part of which is easily suppressed in thought, because it does not have the significance in the world of public action that it has in the world of moral life. Narrative, however, allows the reader to move between the objective/behavioral and subjective/reflective points of view, somewhat as we may in real life, and thus be reminded of the dynamic, self-reflective, and self-formative character of moral life, which is easily forgotten, and of which the other participants in the drama seem not to have any intimation.

CHARMIDES AND CRITIAS

A third purpose of the prologue is to introduce the interlocutors, whose opinions inevitably shape the direction of the conversation, and who would also, if they were well known, raise specific questions in the minds of Plato's ancient readers. Now, this brings up an interesting point that is relevant to all of the aporetic dialogues. It is obvious that Socrates' interlocutors are especially selected by Plato for the particular virtue under discussion, and the strange thing is that they appear so often to be uniquely ill-suited to it. Why, for example, did Plato select Euthyphro, such an unorthodox man, for the dialogue on piety? Why a pair of defeated generals, Laches and Nicias, the latter accused by some of cowardice, to examine courage? Why begin the discussion of justice with a resident alien? Why discuss friendship with a pair of mere boys? Why choose Charmides and Critias to talk about moderation?

Plato would appear to have had two main reasons for selecting these individuals to be Socrates' interlocutors in a dialogue on *sophrosune*. The first has to do with the above-mentioned association of this ideal with the aristocratic class in ancient Greece. Charmides is a character-type of the Young Gentleman, and one of the clearest representatives of this type in the dialogues.[21] As a young gentleman, Charmides was expected to be *sophron*, self-restrained in his moral behavior, and we learn in the prologue that he so well fulfills this expectation that he is regarded as the most moderate (*sophronestatos*, 157d6) of the young men of his generation. Critias, his uncle and guardian, was a character-type of the Laconist or Oligarch: of aristocratic lineage, critical of Periclean democracy, closely associated with Spartan values, and excluded from the mainstream of Athenian political life. Moreover, he upheld conservative moral values, and particularly the ideal of *sophrosune*, in his writings. Both Charmides and Critias would appear to have been well qualified to discuss the virtue. There is even Athenian political history at work here, since both could trace their ancestry back to Solon (cf. 157e6), the great statesman of political moderation and legislator of the republican form the Athenian constitution took until the installation of the participatory or "radical" democracy of Pericles and Ephialtes. Both were relatives of Plato, Charmides being the brother of Plato's mother, Perictione.

But Plato clearly also had another reason for selecting these particular individuals for this conversation. Charmides and Critias were not only associated with the "conservative" virtue of moderation, they were also associated with its opposite, the vices of *hubris* and tyranny, and it was thought by many that they came by these qualities through the influence of Socrates.

Charmides appears to be a youth of unusual promise, morally upstanding, noble of lineage, and physically beautiful and charming. Tuckey calls him "the perfect raw material for a true statesman," and Friedlaender goes even further: "His inner being seems to correspond to his outward appearance, for he has both philosophical and poetic talent. This combination must be Plato's own image; it is the stuff of which he wished men to be."[22] As we shall see, this impression of Plato's depiction of Charmides is *very* misleading, but it must have been a common view in Athens, which would have made all the more troubling his later failure. We learn also in the prologue that Charmides may be deficient in regard to his thought, and this is what Critias hopes Socrates might help him improve (157c7–d1). Somehow the Socratic method of teaching would seem relevant to the educational task of shaping the mind of this young gentleman of Athens so that he might become a leader in a democratic society. But as we know, this will not occur.

The figure of Critias raises even more sharply the question of Socrates' political and educational influence. Critias is one of the most contradictory figures of his age. He was known to have written poetry in praise of the Spartan constitution and Spartan customs, and the central virtue of his encomia is *sophrosune*. At least one historian of ideas (Doyne Dawson) believes Critias was instrumental in the creation of the "Spartan myth" of the excellence of Lacedaimonian social institutions and values.[23] Yet Critias embodied, by other accounts, the very opposite of the virtue he praised so highly in speech. This is brought out especially by Xenophon, who in his history of Greece depicts Critias as the most politically immoderate and violent of the Thirty (*Hellenica* II.iii–iv; cf. also *Memorabilia* I.ii.12), and who in his Socratic writing depicts Critias as sexually immoderate and hubristic (*Memorabilia* I.ii.29–31). Furthermore, Critias would become infamous in antiquity as the author of the *Sisyphus*, the first Greek play to articulate explicitly the idea of atheism.[24] This idea is reflected in his speech on self-knowledge in the *Charmides*, as we will see later. "A curious mixture of *Junkerduenkel* and sophist" (Tuckey), the historical person Critias was at once a poet of traditional aristocratic values, and an atheist and sensualist; a spokesman for hierarchy and stability, and a bloodthirsty reactionary; a student of the Sophists, and—this is the key point—a companion of Socrates.[25]

Both Charmides and Critias are associated, each in his own way, with the notion of moderation and especially with the Laconizing notion of moderation, and both are famous companions of Socrates. But the political ideals associated with Sparta were deeply authoritarian, and it seemed to many of Socrates' Athenian critics—as it has seemed to contemporary critics such as Ellen and Neal Wood, or popular writers such as I. F. Stone—that it was Socrates who must have induced in these men their antidemocratic, authoritarian, and self-aggrandizing attitudes.[26] If Xenophon is right, it was perhaps primarily for reasons of his association with Critias (and that other immoderate pupil Alcibiades) that Socrates was condemned (*Memorabilia* I.ii.12; cf. also Aeschines, *Against Timarchus* 173). It will turn out that the definitions of *sophrosune* offered by Critias in our dialogue may derive from Socrates himself, and he and Critias seem at the end to be about to take over the education of Charmides—who will turn out to be his guardian's henchman in the Thirty! This raises urgently the question, whether Plato can show us that his teacher was *not* responsible for the future crimes of these, two of his most famous companions.

These factors make it likely that Plato intended to examine Socratic *paideia* in the *Charmides*, both with regard to his method of education he employed (the elenchus) and with regard to the doctrines he advocated, especially the ones that seemed to valorize rule by an educated, dictatorial elite over rule by persuasion and majority consent. If Socrates was in fact the positive influence his admirers claimed him to be, why did he not have a more benign influence on these two future tyrants, who spent so much time with him and seemed to be so taken with his thought? And what was the content of that thought, to which they were so attracted? Did he not advocate the possibility of a political statecraft, based on wisdom and operating through coercion rather than persuasion? Socrates does speak, in the *Charmides*, of his "dream" of a society run by knowledgeable experts, and it appears that Critias is not only familiar with, but deeply attracted to this notion. Was Socrates not the defender of a Laconist, authoritarian model of the ideal society, albeit one based on a slightly different concept of rule in which "knowledge" was the justifying criterion? Did he perhaps teach this authoritarian ideal to Critias, who later in his life sought to impose it violently on Athens? Is there not solid evidence that the Socratic circle was "surrounded by an atmosphere of authoritarian elitism, which nourished the most reactionary, aristocratic, even crypto-oligarchical views"?[27]

The *Charmides*, by the choice of its theme and characters, is *the* Platonic dialogue to explore and defend Socrates against the charges against him, and to raise the question of his educational influence. As we shall see, it does this in a way that reflects on the very puzzling fact that Critias could exhibit such a striking contradiction between his words in praise of moderation and his immoderate deeds and life. The *Charmides* will suggest a reason for this contradiction, and for Socrates' failure to effect a positive influence on Critias and Charmides. It will show why Charmides could not break free of his uncle's influence, and why Critias was immune to Socratic education. In particular, it will identify Critias as a student not of Socrates, but of the Sophists. This is the quality linking Critias to the other most puzzling characters in the aporetic dialogues, and to the general question of what is most deeply wrong with Athenian cultural life. For the defining characteristic of Plato's depiction of Socratic philosophy in the early dialogues is to show him struggling intellectually not only with the traditional Greek ideals and values that have come under attack, but also with Sophistry in all its manifold and subtle forms. Again and again, as if wrestling with Proteus, Socrates reveals Sophists beneath their outwardly deceptive guises—the self-certain Critias, the self-pious Euthyphro, the self-admiring Ion, the self-protective Nicias. The overall effect is to display Sophistry as a "disease of the soul" in Athenian public life, a disease that renders its victims unable to know themselves and live a life in harmony with their ideals. The drama of the *Charmides* will take us a long way toward understanding Plato's view of the relation between Sophistry and Critias' future tyranny, and of why Socrates did not have a more benign effect on him and his ward.

SOCRATIC PHILOSOPHY AND THE SOUL (155e2–158c4)

This brings us to the final purpose of the prologue, namely, to introduce the ideal of philosophy that Socrates represents in relation to the scientific context of Athenian life, as the background in relation to which the definition of *sophrosune* at 167a1–7 and the arguments involved in the examination of that definition should be understood.

On Socrates' request that they examine the young man's soul, Critias reports that Charmides has been suffering of late from headaches.[28] To draw Charmides into letting Socrates question him, Critias suggests that Socrates pretend to be a doctor (155b1–7).[29] Socrates gladly agrees to the game, but he tells Charmides that before he can give him the drug for his head, he must be certain the

boy is already healthy in his soul. For he has learned from a certain
Thracian priest-physician, during his sojourn with the army in
northern Greece, that one ought not attempt to cure the body without the soul. The Thracian physician taught him that the soul must
be treated with certain incantations—"beautiful speeches" (*kaloi
logoi*, 157a4–5)—and enjoined him not to treat anyone with the
drug for their head before that person first submits to be treated by
the speeches for their soul. There is something playful in all this,
but something serious as well—and no doubt something attractive
to the young man, who now finds himself involved in conversation
with the famous, dangerous Socrates, but who also finds himself
entralled by a wonderful story of Thracian priests and a charm for
the soul. It is when Socrates says that he must first apply the charm
to Charmides' soul before he can apply the drug to his head that
Critias observes it would be good for Charmides to be treated, if he
might improve in his thought (*dianoia*, 157c7–d1). As regards moderation, however, Critias says that Charmides is already the most
moderate of all the young gentlemen of his age, and blessed in every
other respect as well. Socrates appears to confirm this high opinion
of Charmides and of the noble station he is expected to fulfill, but
he will not let the young man go without first putting him to the
test. To determine whether or not Charmides truly is healthy of
soul, he must examine him. The dialogue leaves it ambiguous
whether the "beautiful speeches" that induce *sophrosune* in the
soul are the same or different from the speeches/arguments used by
Socrates in his method of examination. Possibly it is those very
same speeches, which test someone and their beliefs for soundness,
which induce moderation itself. Or possibly those speeches do not
have that effect, but other, more beautiful speeches are needed.

This self-representation offers a distinctive perspective on
Socrates' philosophical practice.[30] If it is not meant ironically, it
suggests that Socrates is a "diagnostician of the soul" who can test
the moral health of his interlocutor, which seems to imply that
Socrates knows what it is to possess that virtue. The stronger
implication would be that Socrates is a "physician of the soul" who
can induce moral health in the interlocutor. This stronger claim is
of special interest in relation to the later inquiry, where moderation
is defined as the "knowledge of what you know and do not know,"
since if Socrates can bring the interlocutor to that state it would
seem he rendered him *sophron*. And this of course is Socrates'
claim to moderation and wisdom in the *Apology*, that he alone
knew what he knew and did not know, whereas his fellow citizens

thought they knew what they did not know about moral matters (cf. esp. 21a–23b). If Socrates possesses such an art, he would seem to possess the very thing the dialogue will later seek under the title of *sophrosune,* namely a science (*episteme*) that would somehow both constitute and produce or reproduce the virtue in question (assuming that he would re-create it in himself as well as in others). That is to say, he would appear to possess a *techne* of moral virtue; he would appear to possess moral expertise.[31] Socrates seems to claim something like this in the *Gorgias,* where he presents himself as the only "true statesman" in Athenian life, on the grounds that he alone aims at the formation of virtue in his fellow citizens (521a f.), and where the elenchus is portrayed as a tool of psychic surgery and cathartic punishment (cf. esp. 475d, 505c, 521e). But Socrates also characteristically and expressly disavows possessing anything like a moral *techne,* with all that that implies of rational mastery of its subject-matter and the capacity to teach it to others (cf. e.g. *Apology* 21a–23b, *Laches* 184d–187b, *Protagoras* 319a–320c, *Gorgias* 509a, *Meno* 71a–c). At any rate, it is hardly clear why philosophical inquiry of whatever sort should impart *moral* value to the participants.

A first question arising from Socrates' self-depiction in the prologue to the *Charmides,* then, is whether he really is a "psychic physician" and practitioner of a craft of moral health—whether we are to take his playful self-depiction seriously. At first reading, it might seem that the aporetic ending of the dialogue casts serious doubt on the value of Socrates' "art." Consistent with this impression, I will argue that Socrates does not possess a *techne* of moral virtue. But I will also argue that the *Charmides* is meant to explain and justify the claim that dialectic has moral import. It shows how the interlocutor may come to deeper self-knowledge by means of the elenchus, and begin to attain the Platonic equivalent of the moral point of view; it also shows how the refusal of cognitive moderation and self-knowledge is a first step toward tyranny and moral vice.

The other idea suggested in the prologue and distinctively associated with Socrates is the notion of the soul (*psyche*). He introduces it in his characteristic, story-telling manner, offering a *mythos* in which he associates this idea with a mysterious cult he encountered during his sojourn away from the city, whose practitioners "it is said, even immortalize people" (156d6). He goes on to contrast the view these Thracian physicians have regarding virtue and health to that of Athenian medical science. The Athenian physicians, he says, have a deficient appreciation of the causes of sickness and health, and of the overall structure of human life. Their science *ignores the whole*, and treats the body as if it were separate from the soul, but in fact *everything good in the human being derives from the soul*, so that if the soul is in good health—if it truly possesses *sophrosune*—the well-being of the body will follow readily thereafter.

> For he said that everything starts from the soul, both bad and good things for the body and for the entire human being, and they flow from there just as from the head to the eyes. (156e6–157a1)

But if this part can be brought to health, then everything else will be well also.

There is a tension built into Socrates' description of the relation of body and soul in these passages. On the one hand, he suggests (1) the body is a part or instrument of the soul, and to think of it as anything else is to misunderstand or ignore the whole (156d8–e6); but he also indicates (2) the soul is the most important part of the person, namely the part that can make it whole, and make all it does or suffers be of value to it (156e6–157a3).[32] This tension is relevant to a later discussion in the dialogue, where the question arises as to how one ought to conceptualize the human being. Is *psyche* somehow the distinctive category for conceptualizing the human being, but if so, how is it to be related to the body and to the whole person? Do we translate *psyche* correctly, when we use terms like "mind" or "soul," or is another term sometimes more appropriate? The novel perspective on human life which Socrates has introduced here—deriving from a quasi-mythical origin—suggests that the conventional Athenian ways of conceptualizing the relation of body and soul are inadequate, a theme the *Charmides* will develop in greater detail as the dialogue unfolds. The poetic mode in which Socrates presents these ideas does not gainsay the fact that he appears to call for a new understanding of human life, the relation of appearance to reality, and the relation of body and soul.

Socrates' description of the relation of body and soul is also relevant to Socrates' act of erotic moderation, depicted earlier in the prologue. There, as we saw, Socrates' rediscovery of who he was—his rational self, his identity as a lover of wisdom—enabled him to resist Charmides' charm until he was further able, as their conversation renewed, to reclaim his identity and restore calm to his body, as well as to his mind. Might the philosophical physician need to practice his therapeutic art not only on others, but also on himself? In other words, might it be the task of philosophy to cure a constitutional defect or excess in the human being, by applying the *logoi* that bring or return both physician and patient out of a condition of unhealthy desire, back to the moral health attendant on rational inquiry?

Socrates' playful, but dramatically and conceptually important story of what he learned (*emathon*, 156d4) from the Thracian physicians adds an ethical, and possibly even a metaphysical dimension to what he has suggested about his dialectical-therapeutic practice. At any rate, it implies a substantive moral vision comparable to the one Socrates proclaims at *Apology* 28b–30b, where he contrasts his own care for the good of the soul—how it stands with respect to reason and virtue—to his fellow citizens' concern for wealth, honor, and power. Here, too, Socrates uses the term *psyche* for the moral center of the person; contrasts the good of the soul to every other good the person might enjoy; suggests that virtue is sufficient for happiness; and implies that virtue is, if not a function of knowledge, at least directly related to being informed by the right *logoi*. Socrates' use of the term *psyche* suggests, therefore, that he has a particular object in mind when he speaks of self-knowledge later in the dialogue, namely "knowledge of one's rational soul." It also suggests that that knowledge may consist at least in part in the recognition of the absolute priority of the rational soul over the body or other aspects of the soul. To "know oneself," on this view, would require that one know one's rational soul and its needs, as compared to the other things one might be concerned about. By implication, the judgment of secondary or trivial importance might be extended to everything that falls in the realm of appearance, including the things that distinguish the young Charmides, such as his physical beauty and his noble family name (discussed ironically by Socrates at 157d9–158b4).[33] From the standpoint Socrates has introduced here, such things are mere accidents, in no way essential to the kind of self-knowledge he is challenging Charmides to display. For Socrates to know Charmides, and for Charmides to know himself, it would be necessary to determine whether he possessed something of real value, namely *sophrosune*. Even if he possesses all the other good things, but not this, he would from the perspective of this kind of self-knowledge or self-estimation have nothing of value. Even if he knows himself in all his contingencies of historical relations and physical aspect, he would still not know himself, if he did not know how he stood with respect to this universal human virtue. It is from this radically unconventional perspective that Socrates says he must test Charmides, to see if he has a sufficient share in moderation, or if he is still in need (*endees*, 157c4).[34]

The prologue displays an Athens in which politics, private life, and even science is inordinately attracted to appearances. It introduces a young man who seems to have surpassing promise, but who will become a traitor and tyrant. It introduces another man, Critias, who seems to be a close associate and follower of Socrates, but who will become the most violent and immoderate man in Athenian political history. The dialogue will examine the beliefs and values of these two men, and they will be found wanting. But it also introduces in word and deed the Socratic idea of the *psyche*, as a moral reality in comparison to which the merely outward aspect of things must be understood. This idea, and the correlated idea of a moral-rational therapy, applied somehow both to disorderly *eros* and disorderly thought, hold out the possibility that the dialogue might present us with a true understanding of moderation and its place in a good human life.

TWO

TRADITIONAL MODERATION

We can translate the Greek word for courage used in the
Laches and the word for friendship used in the Lysis, *as*
the two dialogues prove, but the subject of the
Charmides *is, What is* sophrosune?—*and that word can-*
not be translated by any one English word. The truth is
that this quality, this sophrosune, *which to the Greeks*
was an ideal second to none in importance, is not among
our ideals. We have lost the conception of it.
—Edith Hamilton

Quietness or peaceful orderliness (*hesuchia*), shame as a
form of moral consciousness (*aidos*), doing one's own and
not invading the affairs of others (*ta heautou prattein*), and
self-knowledge in the religious sense enjoined by Apollo (*to heauton gignoskein*)—these four conceptions are all deeply associated
with *sophrosune* in the tradition of Greek ethical thought.[1]
Nonetheless, most scholars have regarded the definitions offered by
Charmides and Critias as incidental to the interlocutors and not of
general significance. Gerasimos Santas, who has contributed much
to the understanding of the *Charmides*, is representative of this
view. He observes that the list of the definitions offered in the dialogue is "striking for its variety and apparent lack of rationale," and
concludes that "we must take this diversity at its face value and
not search in vain for unity or a continuous line of development."[2]

I believe this interpretation is mistaken; that we should
attempt to relate the definitions to the traditional concept, and that
if we do, we will discover the outline of a dialectical progress in
Socrates' inquiry. This progress is relevant not only to the personal
contexts out of which philosophizing about the moral ideal of

sophrosune emerges in the dialogue, it is also relevant to the question of the relation of Socratic inquiry to the social and historical context. It would be rather strange, after all, if definitions of virtues examined in a Socratic dialogue were not centrally related to the Greek tradition of thought about that virtue. What could be the philosophical and moral value of examining a series of unrelated notions that were no more than the idiosyncratic speculations of a particular individual? How could the inquiry be of ancient Greek, much less universal human interest, if somehow the decisive alternatives for understanding the virtue in question were not included? This is not to say that Plato would necessarily want to make this inclusion self-evident: part of his artistry lies in creating characters whose representations are deeply personal to themselves, yet also carry a broader import.

In fact, the traditional ideal of moderation was composed of four chief elements, all of which are reflected in the definitions examined in our dialogue: (1) a norm of outward behavior (corresponding to definition 1), (2) a norm of inner conscience and emotion (definition 2), (3) a norm of social function or role (definition 3), and (4) a norm of religious self-knowledge (definition 4). These norms were the defining ingredients of the traditional virtue, and it is no accident that Plato presents them in the *Charmides*. By examining what Charmides and then Critias say in regard to them, Socrates examines the ideal as it was and came to be understood in ancient Greek, especially ancient Athenian history. By revealing the inadequacies of these definitions, he reveals the limitations of the traditional ideal, and how it was transformed. In the process, he points toward a new understanding of the old meanings.

The reading I offer of this section of the *Charmides* is, then, different in important ways from that found in other scholarly discussions of the dialogue, because I shall argue that the dialectic constitutes an ascending treatment of features that are part of the idea of *sophrosune* as it functioned in ancient Greek history. If I am correct, the definitions are intended to represent the multidimensional meaning of that moral ideal, and also to represent the way in which it was superseded, in Athenian life, by a very different mode of thought. The fact that the ideal is represented in this manner is itself philosophically interesting: by its very structure the dialogue invites us to think on the complexity of ways in which a moral ideal functions and how its meaning may change in social life. This is not to say, however, that the primary focus of Socratic dialectic is not on the meaning of the concept for the interlocutor(s). As was made clear in the prologue, Socrates' leading concern in the inquiry is to determine if Charmides indeed possesses *sophrosune*, as his guardian and uncle Critias and the others allege. The philosophical inquiry, which may have a general significance reaching even into our own times, is thus made to supervene on a personal inquiry that centers on one individual; dramatically, at least, the discussion is chiefly concerned with the welfare of one human being. But of course the dialogue is being retold by Socrates to his unnamed auditor—and to us. And for us, the inquiry concerns not just the particular definitions, but the Socratic encounter with the ethics of moderation in ancient Greece. To appreciate this encounter as it is dramatized in the *Charmides*, we must recognize that the traditional ideal is represented by Charmides; he not only defends it with his speech, but exemplifies it personally. Critias, on the other hand, presents us with what has become of the tradition—how it has been appropriated by a man decisively influenced by Sophistry.

THE BEHAVIORAL DEFINITION (158e6–160d4)

As we have seen, the inquiry begins because Socrates is unwilling to accept the received opinion that Charmides is truly *sophron*, but rather wishes to test him on this issue. To do this, Socrates has suggested that if Charmides is moderate, he will have some perceptive basis (*aisthesin tina*, 159a2) within him to form his own opinion concerning its nature. They will then be able to use this notion to determine if the young man in fact possesses the virtue. It is not Charmides' first definition, however, but his second, which conforms to Socrates' suggestion.

Charmides' first definition is as follows:

> doing everything decorously and quietly, not only walking in the streets and conversing . . . in sum, a certain quietness (*hesuchiotes tis*). (159b3–5)

Why does Charmides define moderation in this way? Socrates suggests the reason: this is what "they" say it is, how his tutors and guardian, who monitor his behavior, have defined it for him, as he is growing up. And yet it does not tell us what it is within him, which makes Charmides behave this way and makes others think he is *sophron*. Even so, the first definition is still perfectly consistent with his possession of the virtue. For a young Greek gentleman would have first learned what moderation is by having its corresponding behavior defined for him by his superiors (cf. *Lysis* 207d–208e, *Protagoras* 324d–326e).

The first definition presents the most obvious element in the traditional understanding: whatever the social station, the *sophron* person is expected to exhibit behavior that is bounded, restrained, temperate. The opposite of such behavior—behavior that is extreme, impulsive, and violent—is prohibited, if the traditional virtue is practiced. As we have already seen, there is much in the prologue corresponding to this definition.

In the first place, there was the intense excitement about the war, particularly on the part of Chaerophon, whose unrestrained behavior led Socrates to call him a "madman" (*manikos*, 153b2–3). A most striking instance of "immoderation," of course, is the war itself, and the term used to describe the battle, "fierce" (*ischura*, 153b9), is later used by Socrates as one of the qualities opposed to quiet or peacefulness (cf. 160c2). But in the midst of the turmoil about the war, there is a center of calm: Socrates, whose concerns are centered on *sophia* and the young. The other vivid exhibition of immoderate behavior occurred in relation to *eros*. Thus the confusion when Charmides walked in, Chaerophon's self-forgetfulness in praising his bodily form, the turmoil when Charmides took a seat (154b8–c8, c8–e1, 155b8–c5). Even Socrates, who had retained his presence of mind during that entrance, was "inflamed" and disquieted by the boy, though he restored himself to calm with some effort.

It is no mere accident, then, that the inquiry begins by focusing on orderly behavior. It is there that moderation appears, and it is in relation to the outward norms of the virtue that it is learned.

To refute the first definition, Socrates invokes an extremely complex and interesting argument, which has been subjected to considerable scrutiny in the scholarly literature on the dialogue.[3] The discussion involves three stages. In the first, Socrates shows Charmides that with respect to the things of the body, not quietness and slowness, but swiftness and energy seem to be more beautiful (159c1–d12). In the second, he does the same with the things of the mind (159e1–160b2). He then summarizes as follows: "Either nowhere or, if at all, in very few places did quiet actions in life appear more beautiful to us than swift and fierce ones. But even if, my friend, no fewer quiet actions happen to be more beautiful than are vigorous and swift ones, not even in this way would *sophrosune* be acting quietly rather than vigorously and swiftly, not in walking or speaking or anywhere else at all; nor would the quiet life, a decorous one, be more *sophron* than the one that is not quiet . . ." (160b9–d3.)

There are several points that scholars have noted concerning this argument, all of which reveal it, on critical reflection, to be different from what it otherwise seems.

First of all, Socrates' logic is doubly fallacious. Whereas he concludes that the quiet action is less beautiful than the vigorous one, in fact his argument typically only implies that the quiet *and* slow action is less beautiful than the vigorous and swift one. Furthermore, Socrates generally does not prove that the quiet action is ugly, but that it is *less* beautiful than the opposite—which does not prevent it from also being beautiful. It is interesting, then, that the contrast between a process understanding of the act involved and an achievement understanding is built into some of his examples, for this is where the presumed superiority of swiftness to slowness no longer applies: just as with the argument itself, too quick (and careless) a mind will often imply failure to appreciate or understand what is at issue, while the slower, calmer one will take the time and make the effort to succeed. Thus the action of the dialogue subverts its overt speech.

The summation at 159b7–d3 reflects the doubts Plato intends the careful (quiet) reader to entertain regarding the argument. Socrates says that moderation would then not be "a certain quietness," as if to suggest it might be another; he says that neither would the quiet life be moderate, "at least from this argument," again suggesting it might be from another; he says that nowhere or "in very few" places did quiet actions appear more beautiful than swift and fierce ones, but he had not mentioned this possibility before; he concedes that even if "no fewer" quiet actions are more beautiful than vigorous and swift ones, still moderation would not be more the one than the other, thus for the first time raising the possibility that, contrary to the argument, *some* quiet actions might be equally or even more beautiful than the vigorous; and he introduces the concept of the quiet life (*ho hesuchios bios*, 160c7), concluding that it would then not be more moderate than the one that is not quiet, because moderation was posited as one of the beautiful things, and swift things have *appeared* no less beautiful than quiet ones.

When analyzed in this critical manner, the argument yields two results. The first is simply that both behaviors that seem *sophron* and those seeming the opposite may or may not be *kalon*.

This is itself an important conclusion, especially when we consider—as mentioned in the discussion of the prologue—the political connotions of these terms. On the surface, Socrates' argument seems to reflect the widespread Athenian conviction that their intense life of action was more noble and beautiful than the slow, conservative Spartan way. But at a deeper level of understanding, the argument reveals the possibility of deeds of body and mind and even of a way of life that would be both intellectually active and quietly beautiful, though it might not appear so compared to the fierce and vigorous life of public action, which finds its foremost manifestation in war. This is a second implication of the argument, which Charmides does not even begin to recognize—he is too "slow," too "quiet" in thought. But Plato certainly intends the reader to discern it. The basic point is, appearances can deceive.[4] Neither quiet behavior nor its opposite can be judged virtuous, but the account of virtue must be sought at another level. This conclusion conforms to Plato's conviction in the *Statesman*, incidentally, where he treats the opposition between quietness and energy as a function of nature, which must be transcended by reason (305e–311c). A chief task of the statesman is to weave courage into the naturally restrained nature, and moderation into the naturally bold one; virtue is found in both together, guided by reason, not in either one by itself.

THE EMOTIONAL DEFINITION (160d5–161b4)

The quality of moderation cannot be determined at the level of behavior alone. It must be found at another level. But what might be more appropriate than the quality *within* the person, which would cause him to behave of his own in a manner that is regarded as moderate?

The second definition is also illustrated in the drama of the dialogue, in the very way I have suggested. For immediately prior to Socrates' injunction that Charmides formulate his opinion based on the perception he had of the quality in him, Socrates had asked the youth if he was, indeed, moderate, and Charmides answered with a blush (158c5–7). Socrates goes on to recount that this behavior made the boy appear more beautiful (*kallion*) than ever to him. Thus from the narrative we learn that Socrates' attraction to Charmides is enhanced by his natural moral beauty, perhaps even more than by his physical beauty. It was from Charmides' own perception (*aisthesin*, 159a2) of that blush, we may suppose, that Socrates would have expected the boy to form the second definition to which he has now been led, that *sophrosune* is:

> [what] makes a human being have a sense of modesty and feel ashamed, . . . [the sense of] shame (*aidos*). (160e3–5)

This second definition of moderation has not always been appreciated in the scholarly literature on the dialogue, and has often been taken to mean nothing more than youthful modesty.[5] It is true that Socrates will soon criticize the definition in a way that is directly relevant to this point, that youthful shyness is not appropriate for one who would become a man.[6] This is obviously also a concern of Socrates toward Charmides, who in his hesitation and reserve has shown himself to be shy in the pursuit of truth (compare Xenophon, *Memorabilia*, III.vii). But there is another dimension to Socrates' treatment of this definition than its relation to this particular individual.

The notion of *aidos* has a central place in the system of values surrounding traditional virtue. In fact, it is identified throughout the aristocratic Greek ethical tradition as the psychological core of *sophrosune*—and not only for youths. Here, for example, is E. R. Dodds on the subject, as it pertains to the Homeric hero:

> The strongest moral force which Homeric man knows is not the fear of god, but respect for public opinion, *aidos*: *aideomai Troas*, says Hector at the crisis of his life, and goes with open eyes to his death. . . . In such a society, anything which exposes a man to the contempt or ridicule of his fellows, which causes him to "lose face," is felt as unbearable.[7]

Nor is this understanding of the role of shame in the psychology of traditional Greek virtue confined to Homer. We recall the definitive statement of traditional Spartan virtue by Archidamus in Thucydides: "We are warlike, because moderation (*sophrosune*) contains shame (*aidos*, i.e., the sense of honor and shame) as a chief constituent, and shame bravery" (*History* I.84).

The concept of shame, then, identifies the traditional form of moral conscience, namely that form which corresponded to the traditional virtue of *sophrosune*. It was a form of conscience that did not discriminate between moral principle and social rules, but rather the two converged in the notion of the *kalon*, the "noble and honorable." To act in accordance with this was to enhance one's *persona* in the moral-social world. To violate it was to "lose face" and diminish or even destroy that identity. *Aidos* in this sense is actually very similar to the emotion of self-assessment we call "pride," such pride or self-esteem being linked into a social system of appropriate behaviors, roles, and so on.[8] Interestingly, Critias is also a representative of this emotion, albeit in his case it is not the negative, restraining element which is active, as it is with his ward, but the positive element of ambition for honor. This becomes evident in his responses to Charmides at 162c1–d6 and to Socrates at 169c3–d2.

Thus Charmides' second definition is directly relevant to the logical progression of Socrates' examination of the traditional ideal. Charmides is regarded as moderate not merely because his behavior is—he might have acted in a self-restrained manner out of fear of punishment—but because he is self-governed from within by his own sense of honor and shame. It is this inner regulator, inner presence of *sophrosune* in the form of *aidos* that causes Charmides to behave with noble self-restraint, and it was this which manifested itself in the self-revealing blush alluded to by Socrates, when he elicited this second opinion about the virtue.[9] Charmides is moderate because he has his eye on how he will look to others, and he wants to fulfill the standards he has been taught. It is this moral but heteronomous quality that is the inner essence of his moderation and the psychological essence of the traditional ideal.

In stark contrast to the argument he uses to refute the first definition, the argument Socrates uses to refute the second is surprisingly brief. But just like the first argument, this one also turns on the contrast of appearance and reality, and the point he makes is crucial to Plato's overall treatment of the traditional virtue.

Socrates asks Charmides whether he does not regard Homer as an authoritative guide, and Charmides of course agrees he does. But then does he not also agree with the advice given by Telemachus to the disguised Odysseus, that "Shame is no virtue in a needy man"? For if shame is not good, it cannot be virtuous. Charmides has no reply, but must admit that his definition is inadequate (160e6–161a4).

The refutation is interesting in several respects. For one thing, it rests on the authority of Homer, which Charmides cannot question, but which it is the cultural task of Platonic philosophy to question (though not on this point).[10] In the prologue, Critias had praised Charmides for his poetic gifts, but admitted he might be somewhat lacking in thought, and we have seen a demonstration of his slowness in this regard. Here we see another. For with this definition, Charmides has not been expressing a mere opinion, what people say or he had heard, but one founded in his own experience and reflecting his own opinion. As Socrates says, he has had to "look within himself" (*eis seauton blepsas*, 160d6). This takes focused attention and intellectual courage, and Charmides has done this—not swiftly, but beautifully nonetheless. As a result, he is engaged in the argument in a manner different from the way he was earlier. Now *his* experience, his truth, his self-knowledge, is at issue.[11] In refuting it, Socrates refutes him. And this is the existential basis of the *elenchos*, for with the expression of a definition rooted in his own experience, rather than the mere words or injunctions of others, Charmides has the dawning idea of knowledge— which is the very thing that Socrates refutes! In this way, and in this way alone, "the irrational and accidental individual is brought to the appreciation of universal science, out of his individual arbitrariness into the common world of reason" (Richard Robinson).[12] So it is crucial to our assessment of Charmides and the dialogue bearing his name to determine why he cannot question Homer and defend himself in this situation.

The answer would seem to lie not merely in his own youthfulness, but in the relationship Plato is depicting between the traditional virtue of *sophrosune* and the inability to take a critical perspective on the demands, authorities, and horizons of that virtue. As we have seen, the second definition presents the psychological core of the traditional notion. The person governed by the sense of honor and shame, albeit appropriate to his age and station—we will see further, in coming to the third definition, how this is relevant— acts in accordance with the *kalon* and avoids, at all costs, the *aischron*. The sense of shame is the inner form of traditional moral self-consciousness, and to violate it is to suffer the loss of one's most precious possession, "face." But then the social psychology of the traditional virtue does not, in essence, permit the kind of contrast Socrates is asking Charmides to reflect on. The Homeric warrior and the Spartan citizen—the man who lives morally within a shame-culture—simply does not consider whether he must violate the noble or beautiful, in order to preserve his own good, much less his moral self-respect.[13] If he violates it, he suffers the loss of the good that is most precious to him, his public identity. And this restriction goes deep into his relation to his moral life. For it also entails that he cannot question the cognitive grounds of the emotions of shame and pride defining his social connectedness, or the standards of the society of which he is a part. He cannot ask the question: Is the *kalon*, as my society defines it, really what I ought to do? Or again: Is the emotion that I now experience what I ought to feel? And he cannot reflect on whether he should not do something his society says is beautiful, because it might not be good for him. The world of traditional *sophrosune* is one in which these questions—the kinds of questions that the Sophists and Socrates ask—cannot be asked. It is a world in which there is no room for specifically *moral* thought, for principles that may conflict with the *nomoi* of the society, for deliberation concerning a conception of the good that is not coextensive with what society says is noble, or for an autonomous, rational relationship to such a good. (Compare Socrates' relation to the matter of honor and shame, expressed at *Apology* 28b f., and in the *Crito*, esp. 46b–49b.[14])

THE DEFINITION BASED ON
SOCIAL FUNCTION (161b4–164d3)

Socrates' refutation of Charmides' second definition—of the definition expressing his real belief and personal experience—is so swift and surprising that the youth is taken aback. He had just been complimented by Socrates for his effort to define the term (160e5–6); now he is even more abruptly refuted. He is shaken by this experience, as well he should be: Socrates has called into question his deepest self-understanding, not only of the pride he takes in himself (a pride reinforced by his many admirers), but also of the values and even the society supporting that pride of self-evaluation. But rather than pursue the matter further, persevering in what he believes is true and in that way entering the fissure Socrates has momentarily created between his "knowledge" based on experience and the "noble belief" based on the authorities he has been taught to accept, Charmides retreats to a third definition, which he admits he has heard from another, that *sophrosune* is:

doing one's own things (*to ta heautou prattein*). (161b6)

Thanks again to Socrates' narrative, we learn that this definition derives from his uncle and guardian, Critias (161b8–c1, 162b10–c6).[15] The latter will himself soon intervene, to defend his definition against Socrates' criticisms. So Plato's treatment of this aspect of the traditional virtue will be conducted on two levels, first in relation to Charmides, then in relation to Critias.

Charmides *(161b4–162b11)*

The third definition adds a further dimension to the discussion of the traditional virtue, the dimension of social station or functional role.[16] It is clear that this element was already reflected in the critical attitude Socrates had asked Charmides to bring on his own shyness—appropriate for a mere boy, but not for a man. Even in the adult station, however, it was not open for Homeric man or the Spartan citizen to question the rules governing his conduct. As Bruno Snell remarks concerning Odysseus' deliberations in a moment of crisis before Troy (*Iliad* XI. 404–10), the Homeric aristocrat determines his course

> by concentrating on the thought that he belongs to a certain social order, and that it is his duty to perform of the "virtue" of that order. The universal which underlies the predication "I am a noble" is the group; he does not reflect upon an abstract "good" but upon the circle of which he claims membership. It is the same as if an officer were to say: "As an officer I must do this or that," thus gauging his action by the rigid conception of honor peculiar to his caste.[17]

In this way, the third definition reflects the manner in which the traditional Greek ideal of *sophrosune* functioned through the institutions of social role and social responsibility, albeit in an ethic that was essentially heteronomous.

And yet, despite its abstract relevance to the progress of the inquiry concerning the traditional virtue, Socrates is playfully angry with Charmides at this definition. Why? The answer seems to involve the kind of complex relation between word and deed that we will see again in relation to Critias. Charmides offers here a definition of moderation as "doing one's own." But it is not his own definition; it derives, as he admits, from another. In fact, Charmides, thanks to Socrates' intervention, *could* now call into question the system of beliefs and values that have bounded his life to this point. But he does not. Having displayed sufficient intellectual courage to articulate his own innermost belief regarding *sophrosune*, but having seen his belief suffer refutation and the limits of his own powers of reasoning exposed, he takes flight and does not persist in what has been shown to be the difficult, risky path of thought. So he is not doing what is most truly "his own" in this situation; he is not doing what he has been called on to do, not thinking for himself, not using his speech to test his own beliefs and experience with Socrates. This is what disappoints Socrates so sharply that he calls Charmides a "wretch" (*miare*, 161b8, literally one who is defiled with blood, a very derisive term; cf. *Euthyphro* 4c1). Charmides is giving up, abandoning the path of personal-intellectual inquiry, in order to see his uncle and guardian put to the test. (For a completely different response—one that demonstrates his moral courage and willingness to acknowledge his need—see Alcibiades' response to Socrates' refutation of him in the *Alcibiades I*, 127d.) In a sly, somewhat cowardly act of youthful rebellion—the rebellious aspect of which is encouraged by Socrates— Charmides puts forward the words of another, so that he will not have to be questioned himself. In a lesser way, then, Charmides is "doing his own" by withdrawing and having his guardian tested. For Charmides' role or station is subordinate to that of his uncle, whom he accepts as his moral and intellectual superior. *Charmides' "own" is to be—at least for now—the dependent of Critias.*[18]

Charmides exhibits one of the more important respects in which one can fail to engage rightly in the process of dialectical inquiry: he stops thinking for himself and merely puts forward the opinions of others. This action amounts to a withdrawal from the opportunity Socrates is giving him, through the self-revealing and thus potentially liberating process of the *elenchos*, to develop his own autonomy and capacity for rational agency. Instead he confirms his own moral-intellectual heteronomy or better, heterarchy, in proposing Critias' definition.[19] Nonetheless, if that definition is refuted, Critias' authority would be undermined, and Charmides might be encouraged to try again some other time with Socrates, who might yet help him to improve his thought. It is not implausible that Socrates might regard Charmides, rather than Critias, as the person more likely to benefit from his dialogue with the latter.

These observations concerning Charmides are relevant to the teaching of the dialogue. For what is wrong with his conception, what makes it less than truly noble and good, is the fact that *the traditional virtue is not a function of freedom and reason.* Odysseus in the *Iliad* accepts his social role, and the rules binding on it, no less than Charmides accepts his role here in our dialogue. It is not Charmides' "place" to question Homer, or his guardian Critias, or to think for himself. But so long as he feels this way, he will remain trapped within the blinders of his own "individual arbitrariness . . . and not enter the common world of reason."

Socrates' argument at 161d1–162a9 against the third definition addresses the social and political dimension of the traditional virtue. He does this in a strange way. He begins by asking Charmides about the arts of the mind, of writing and reading. Is each person to learn to write only his own name, or is he not to learn to write everyone's name, even those of his enemies? Were the boys meddlesome (*epolypragmoneite*, 161d11) and immoderate when they did this? Charmides agrees they were not, and Socrates goes on to ask regarding the arts in general, whether they are not all instances of "doing" and again Charmides agrees. Having thus established the equivalence of doing or acting (*prattein*) and making (*poiein*), Socrates extends the domain of *sophrosune* to the level of the city as whole. Would a *polis* be "well-managed" (*eu oikeistai*, 161e10) under a law that had each person weave and wash his own cloak, make his own shoes, his oil flask and scraper (used by the ancient Greeks after bathing), and in short do everything for himself alone? Charmides admits such a city would not be well-managed, but that if it were managed moderately, it would also be be managed well, so doing one's own "in this way" (*houto*, 162a7) must not be moderate.

The idea of moderation on the level of political order is found in many conservative-aristocratic Greek thinkers, where it is expressed in terms of several different ideas, including *eunomia, eu oikeisthai,* and even—*hesuchia*.[20] But on reflection, we cannot but be struck by the narrowly economic and apolitical conception of the city Socrates utilizes to push the argument through (without objection from the too quiet Charmides). He begins by identifying making (*apergazesthai*) and doing (*prattein*, 161e8, 162a2), thus blurring a distinction fundamental to the Greek conception of political life.[21] Then, in discussing the well-managed city, he limits his discussion to arts very narrowly concerned with the body, and none related to political life, such as strategy or rhetoric. Finally, his conception of the well-run city is explicitly apolitical, since he imagines for Charmides a city that has no rulers—in marked contrast to the ideal of the moderate city Socrates and Critias discuss later in the dialogue (171d1–172a5, 173a7–d5)—but is governed by a law (*nomos*, 161e11). This is an apolitical conception of the city and of human life. It is a notion of moderation leaving no room for political activity, even the activity of consent as to who should rule. In short, it is the point of view of a person such as Charmides, who makes no claim to political rights and has no conception of how moderation might be a political virtue. It is the point of view of someone who does not appreciate the distinction between making and acting, because he is still morally dependent, still someone who does not, in the full ancient Greek sense of the term, *act*—that is, someone who does not flourish as an autonomous person in a community of his own cooperative creation.

Critias (162c1–164d3)

At the end of the refutation, Socrates mocks the definition in such a way as to embolden Charmides to raise the question whether its author himself knew what it meant. This affront provokes Critias' abrupt entry into the conversation. Socrates explains in his narrative that, being competitive and desirous of honor (*agonion kai philotimos,* 162c1–2) and unable any longer to contain himself, Critias could not endure the suggestion that he had been refuted, and was angry with Charmides, "just as a poet is with an actor who recites his poems badly" (162d2–3). When Critias demands to know from Charmides whether, simply because *he* does not understand what the author of the saying meant, the author himself does not, Socrates takes this as the opportunity to invite Critias to take up the defense of the definition, which he does. (Critias' remark would be particularly ironic, if he himself had heard the phrase discussed by Socrates in another context.[22])

Again the drama, reinforced by Socrates' narrative, is revealing. Critias is more concerned about his own reputation and "poem" (the definition under consideration) than he is about Charmides, whom he rebukes harshly and humiliates in this ugly scene. Critias' concern for "his own" does not extend, in a loving and educational manner, to his ward. He cares for him in an instrumental manner only, as the "actor" representing his ideas (and honor), not lovingly, as a son. This shows vividly a way in which the traditional ideals have been corrupted in the person of Critias.[23]

Critias' initial defense of the definition underscores the impression that the traditional meaning of the virtue has been lost, replaced by a new, sophistic perspective. Critias begins by citing a famous dictum from one of the great poets of the archaic tradition, Hesiod, who declared that "work is no disgrace." In Hesiod this phrase affirms the value and dignity of honest labor, and belongs to an overall scheme of thought concerning the division of labor in society, in which all classes are seen to contribute to the common good.[24] On Critias' interpretation, however, the phrase takes on an entirely different meaning, in which it is not bound to the notion of social service, to a "work" within the community. He claims that Hesiod meant to distinguish works and doings from mere making, since the former are never disgraceful, but the latter can be, such as the makings of shoemakers or salt-fish sellers or prostitutes (162e7–163c2). The lumping of shoemaking with prostitution indicates Critias' disdain for common labor—just the opposite value to the one Hesiod extolled. In this regard, Critias betrays himself as precisely the kind of arrogant aristocrat Hesiod criticizes, as a man who *lacks* political moderation.[25]

Critias' further interpretation of the saying indicates that he has fully abandoned the traditional aristocratic point of view. For he says that "works" are those things that are made beautifully and beneficially (*ophelimos*, 163c3), and these are the things that are kindred to oneself, while the harmful things are alien. Thus anyone who is prudent (*phronimos*, 163c7) will have to agree with Hesiod, that the one who "does his own things" is the one who is moderate.

Critias' underlying thought is clear: the true meaning of *sophrosune* does not consist in making or even doing what is beautiful; it rather focuses on the idea of procuring benefit for oneself and avoiding all harm as "alien" (cf. *allotria*, 163c6).[26] Socrates does not miss this point in his summary: "You call things good that are kindred to oneself and one's own, and you call the makings of good things doings" (163d2–3). It is not that Critias identifies himself with the good (as Socrates does in the *Apology* and *Gorgias*, in the sense of an enlightened egoism that centers on justice and *paideia*); it is that Critias identifies the good with what benefits himself, in the sense of a calculating, narrow egoism. The notion of the noble or beautiful, as that which is beneficial to the society but possibly harmful to the individual (such as the requirement that he face death in battle, which Odysseus in the *Iliad* had to accept as "his own," his duty of station), is no longer the orienting principle of the virtue. Critias is an aristocrat only accidentally, in a society in which no one, including himself, lives by the principles of naive aristocratic life: he is a decadent aristocrat.

On the interpretation of the virtue that Critias offers, *sophrosune* is no longer tied to the good of the society as a whole; it is focused solely on the good of the individual, who takes the good for himself and regards the bad as "something fit for others." This is not a man who acts in accordance with honor and social station, but a player, skilled in the wiles of self-gain—which is what *he* means by "practical wisdom" (*phronesis*). It is not someone who has learned his virtue through the process of social identification and imitation of noble exemplars. For him, virtue is not conceived of as a matter of moral conscience and action, but as a matter of individual desire and reason (making)—as actualizing superiority, rather than nobility. Socrates underscores the sophistic nature of Critias' attitude by adding that he had heard Prodicus (the Sophist) make "ten thousand" such distinctions.[27]

THE RELIGIOUS KNOWLEDGE
DEFINITION (164d3–165b4)

The transition from Charmides as interlocutor to his guardian Critias is a transition from the world of traditional values to the world of contemporary Athens, a cultural world decisively influenced by Sophistry and nonaristocratic values. It is also a transition from a moral world bounded by the concept of the beautiful or noble (*to kalon*) to one bounded by the concepts of the prudent (*to phronimon*), the beneficial (*to ophelimon*) and the good (*to agathon*). The category of the noble and the ideal of social welfare is crucial to the traditional ideal, but those values have not carried over entirely into the world in which Charmides now finds himself, where they may appear to clash with the value of individual advantage. Thus *sophrosune*, long the virtue of moral/social rationality and fair practice, may come to appear to be less than a virtue in this new context, unless it is a calculating, dominating rationality, a winning attitude of mind and will that operates with skill and contempt for its opponents to attain its ends. Critias, the representative of this sophistic notion of *sophrosune* (his literary counterpart is Euripides' Jason), eschews what is noble and beneficial to society for what he thinks benefits himself and is good.[28] But in doing this, he turns away not only from the traditional notions of the place of the individual in society, he also turns away from the traditional notion of the human being in the cosmos—the religious horizon of the traditional ideal, the image of man in the moral center of the universe, between the beasts and the gods.

In moving to this point in the dialogue the inquiry takes a somewhat unexpected turn. Socrates has brought Critias into the conversation, and he has led him to another feature of his definition, the notion that *sophrosune* is "doing good things." Now, it is Socratic dictum that the good is that concerning which we are unsatisfied with the mere appearance; we want the real thing.[29]

When Critias identifies *sophrosune* with achieving the good, we are not surprised that Socrates indicates he may be telling the truth (164a1). But we expect Socrates to lead the dialogue to consideration of what is good. He does not. Instead, he leads Critias to consideration of whether the artist who performs his art well must also *know* that he is benefiting. The argument is obscure: must the artist, to perform as he should (*ta deonta prattein,* cf. 164b3, 5), know that he is benefiting the other in terms of his technical duties or in terms of the person's life as a whole? Or must he know that he is himself going to get a "profit" (cf. *onesesthai,* 164b9), either in terms of being paid for his services or in terms of improving his own life? Is it then possible that the doctor who benefits his patient or harms him does not know that he did it? Or that even if he did it beneficially, but did not know it, he was nonetheless *sophron* in so acting (as Critias now seems to suggest)? Might the *sophron not* know his own *sophrosune?* Socrates does not argue here, as he does in the first book of the *Republic* (341b–342e), that the artist qua artist is essentially oriented to the good of the other, only accidentally to his own good, nor, as he insists in his dialogue with Callicles in the *Gorgias* (511c–513c), that the artist must distinguish the immediate service his craft may convey from the larger question of benefit and harm, but the questions and distinctions underlying those arguments are reflected in this discussion, too.[30]

The effect of these questions is to raise the characteristic Socratic concern regarding an art or practice of virtue. Is there, in fact, a skill at "doing well"? And if there is, what is the knowledge associated with that skill? Does the man who "does good" then also know that he is doing good? Is he a *self-knowing* practitioner of good? Unnerved by Socrates' questions, Critias abandons his own definition quickly: *he* cannot conceive that the *sophron* might not know his own *sophrosune.* Instead, he proclaims himself unashamed to correct his previous remarks, rather than saying that someone who did not know himself was *sophron.*[31] But what does Critias mean by self-knowledge?

Critias again attempts to base his position on the authority of traditional values and institutions, this time Delphi. He launches into a long rhetorical display, intended to reassert his wisdom. But in the process, while offering his first formulation of the fourth definition, he completely inverts the meaning of the traditional ideal:

> For I assert that this is almost what moderation is, recognizing oneself (*to gignoskein heauton,* 164d4); and I go along with

the one who put up such an inscription at Delphi. For this inscription in my opinion was put up as if it were the greeting of a god to those entering, instead of "hail," in the view that this greeting, "hail," is not correct, and that they should not exhort each other to this, but to be moderate [or sound-minded]. Thus the god addresses those entering the temple somewhat differently than do human beings. Such was the thinking of the one who put it when he put it up, in my opinion. And he says to whoever enters nothing other than "be moderate," he asserts. He says it, of course, in a rather riddle-some way, like a diviner. For "know yourself" and "be moderate" are the same, as the inscription and I assert. Yet someone might perhaps suppose they are different, which is what happened, in my opinion, to those who put up the later inscriptions "Nothing too much" (*Meden agan*) and "A pledge, and bane is near." For they suppose that "Know yourself" is a counsel, not a greeting by the god for the sake of those entering. And then, so that they too might put up counsels no less useful, they wrote these and put them up.[32] (164d3–165a7)

This is the longest speech in the inquiry, and second only to Socrates' opening speech in the dialogue as a whole. It occurs more or less in the middle of the dialogue, which may also be meant to signal its importance. But it has not fared well in most of the discussions of the work; some commentators have even identified what Critias presents here with Plato's own opinion.[33] In fact, their views are almost diametrically opposite.

The real meaning of Critias' speech begins to be made clear when it is compared to the actual religious tradition he invokes. In fact, the contrast between the Apollonian ideal of self-knowledge and what Plato has Critias represent could hardly be greater.[34] The Apollonian ideal was the revelation of the god, of divinity, to human beings in their limitedness. It was an injunction to religious recognition of oneself as living in a divinely ordered world—a world in which one could not attain happiness except through the moral appreciation of those limitations and of human community as bounded by them. The Apollonian ideal is no greeting of equal to equal, and it cannot be separated from the moral injunctions with which it is associated. It is the normative voice of revelation, one which addresses the mortality of the person and yet nonetheless calls him to a life of dignity, respect for others, and moral wisdom.

Critias' account of the inscription, however, does imply that this "beautiful speech" is of merely human origin, invented by a clever man who ascribed it to a god, and he goes on to imply that it functions not as a norm for morally rational, *sophron* human beings, but as a greeting between equals, that is, as if to say that the man (such as Critias) who knows what it really means is himself like a god.[35] Perhaps most important, Critias separates the "greeting" of self-knowledge, addressed to godlike men, from the "moral counsels" of lesser men, who failed to see the point. *For Critias, self-knowledge is separate from moral virtue.* Thus in several crucial respects, Critias, still under the guise of seeming to embrace the traditional ideal, actually offers a counternotion to it: (1) whereas the traditional ideal represents the truth as deriving from a divine origin, Critias attributes it to superior humans; (2) whereas the tradition represents moderation and self-knowledge as a norm for all humans alike, Critias asserts it as the self-recognition of an elite convinced of their own superiority; and (3) whereas the tradition counsels the inseparability of moral virtue and true self-knowledge, Critias claims this is due to misunderstanding. Critias' wisdom—his "opinion," as Plato has him say no less than three times—is the amoral human praise of self-certainty, not the divine moral counsel of self-restraint.[36]

With Critias' atheistic interpretation of Delphic self-knowledge, Plato's treatment of the traditional Greek ideal of moderation comes to an end. He has considered it in all four of its principal respects: (1) as a norm of restrained behavior; (2) as an emotion of social conscience and self-regulation; (3) as a standard for social order; and (4) as a mode of religious awareness. He has shown, through the course of the drama and argument of the *Charmides*, the inner structure and limitations of that ideal. As a norm of behavior, it clashes with the counternorm of swiftness and bold action; neither is adequate in itself, but the two must be found together, governed by reason. As a form of social conscience, it fails to provide guidance for how to relate the beautiful and the socially beneficial to personal benefit and the good; again the dialogue suggests that these two must be rationally harmonized, not split apart. As a principle of social order, it is profoundly apolitical, and has in fact given way to a new, sophistic understanding, according to which "doing one's own" is no longer a function of social station, but of self-gain and self-assertion. And as a counsel of religious self-understanding, the traditional ideal has also given way to a new, sophistic conception of life, in which the gods have faded and been replaced, at least in the minds of some, by notions of human superiority and wisdom.

The world of Charmides—the world of noble conduct and concern for the *kalon*—has given way to the world of Critias—the world of sophistic skill and concern for gain, and this transition is not unrelated to the "sickness" infecting Athenian life as a whole. This transition is not, however, entirely unfortunate. For the world of Charmides and traditional moderation is innocent to the life of reason, weak in thought (*dianoia*). The cure to the troubles of the present day cannot be a return to the past; it must involve a new ideal of moderation, oriented to the life of reason, but somehow also reclaiming the moral values of the old ideal—values of peace and calmness of mind, of concern with the noble and shameful, of social function and contribution, and of moral and religious self-understanding. It will be Socrates' task in the remainder of the dialogue to suggest such a notion of *sophrosune* to Critias and to Plato's readers. In the next chapter we shall consider how his definition of that ideal arises, and to what it is opposed.

THREE

SELF-KNOWLEDGE

If an eye is to see itself, it must look at an eye, and at
that region of an eye in which virtue is to be found; and
this, I suppose, is sight? Yes. And if the soul too, my dear
Alcibiades, is to know herself, she must surely look at a
soul and especially at that region of it in which the virtue
of a soul occurs—wisdom—and at any other part of a
soul which resembles this? True. And can we find any
part of the soul that we call more divine than this, which
is the seat of knowledge and thought? We cannot.

—Alcibiades I

The next section of the dialogue culminates in a definition
that characterizes *sophrosune* as "the knowledge of what
one knows and what one does not know" (167a7). This definition occurs in the center of the inquiry and constitutes its high
point: the inquiry ascends through the three prior stages to this definition, and then descends in three stages in which it is criticized
on metaphysical, epistemological, and moral grounds, each stage of
criticism moving further and further away from the ideal proposed
at 167a1–7. (See the discussion of the structure of the dialogue in
appendix A.) But the definition serves not only to organize the
dialectical structure of the dialogue as a whole, it also gives rise to
the most important problem regarding its overall interpretation.
For this definition of *sophrosune* in terms of self-knowledge and its
subsequent criticism poses an interpretive dilemma, beginning
with the question of whether the definition is Socratic. If it is not
meant to be Socratic, why is it so clearly analogous to the classic
Socratic self-description at *Apology* 21a–23b? But if it is Socratic,
why is it refuted?

Many discussions of the *Charmides* have failed to articulate, much less resolve this dilemma.[1] Those who argue that the definition is not Socratic have failed to explain why it embodies at its core the Socratic ideal of human wisdom as the "knowledge of what you know and do not know." Those who argue that it is Socratic have failed to explain why it is refuted. Is Plato here, already in this seemingly early dialogue, developing a critical perspective on his teacher? But this would be very strange, if only because of the presence of Critias and Charmides. The implication of criticism of his teacher in their proximity might suggest that Plato agreed with the common judgment against Socrates—a very unlikely prospect!

A second problem in the interpretation of this part of the *Charmides* is the relation of the prior discussion at 165b3–166e10 to the formulation of the definition and to the criticism made of it in the final segment of the inquiry. On the one hand, it is clear that Critias, with Socrates' apparent approval, is intent to distinguish self-knowledge from other modes of knowledge, in particular from (1) *techne*, technical-productive knowledge or art, and from (2) what Aristotle terms *episteme*, theoretical-objective knowledge or science. On the other hand, Socrates seems to revert to the technical understanding of self-knowledge/*sophrosune* later, when Critias is finally refuted on ethical grounds at 172d–175a, especially at 174e–175a. This conflict within the *Charmides* has consequences for the assessment of the overall question of the role of the craft analogy in Socratic philosophy. If the definition is somehow genuine and Socrates accepts both that self-knowledge or *sophrosune* thus conceived is virtue (or a virtue) and that it does not have the cognitive form of a moral *techne*, the *Charmides* would appear to offer strong evidence that Socrates does not, finally, accept the craft model of virtue.

These interpretive controversies cannot be resolved, I suggest, unless we bring a different approach to the reading of the dialogue than the "analytic-doctrinal" method that still dominates Plato scholarship.[2] It is necessary above all to appreciate the role of the drama—of action—in clarifying the ambiguities of the arguments—of speech—and ultimately of the text as a whole. This methodological principle is relevant both to the question of understanding the ambiguities in the definition at 167a1–7, and to sorting out the attitude of the dialogue to the ideal of a moral *techne*. What we shall discover is that there are two different conceptions of "the knowledge of knowledge" at work at 165b3–167a8 and in subsequent passages in the dialogue—not one, but two ideals of self-knowledge represented in the *Charmides*.[3] One is properly associated with Socrates, and will prove to be a plausible candidate as a moral as well as cognitive ideal. The other is associated with Critias and as he represents it constitutes a form of cognitive and moral vice. The difference between these two conceptions of *sophrosune* is brought out only indirectly, however. It is a chief task of the reader of the dialogue to discern the two concepts, and follow their role in the drama and argument. What we shall also discover is that the Socratic concept of self-knowledge does not conform to the model of *techne*. We shall have to await the later discussion for explanation as to why he reverts to such a model in the final argument of the dialogue.

SOPHROSUNE IS A FORM OF SELF-KNOWLEDGE (165b3–c6)

Critias begins the investigation of his new definition by asserting that he will defend it, if Socrates does not agree that it is "oneself recognizing oneself" (*to gignoskein auton heauton*, 165b4). Socrates' answer sets the frame for the following discussion. For he insists that this is precisely what he does not claim, to *know* about these matters, and it is not a matter of his will or wishes at all; rather, he is inquiring because he himself *does not know*—he will only be willing to answer if he agrees or not after he has investigated; Critias must be patient on that (165b5–c6).

Socrates does not claim that he cannot know, only that he is not willing to rest his agreement or disagreement on what he believes *prior* to investigation. What is at issue is not merely his beliefs; it is the habit and attitude he brings to the cognitive situation, the habit of rationally testing his opinions in the practical situation where they have become relevant. This habit of reason is, it seems, more important to him than the habits of belief that he has formed as a result of his previous testings or whatever else in his experience would have caused him to hold his beliefs. It is a principle of cognitive self-restraint, by means of which he reachieves his moral beliefs in the immediate situation, and through the process of testing them reachieves awareness of the reasons underlying them (or rejects them, now knowing why he does not believe them any longer to be true). It is in fact nothing less than the means by which he systematically comes *to know what he knows and what he does not know.* Thus the drama of the *Charmides* makes evident, at the very beginning of the inquiry into the possibility and benefit of self-knowledge—an inquiry that will end aporetically—that some form of knowledge of knowledge and ignorance *is* possible. The drama will also soon make evident that it is beneficial, by contrast to the harm caused by its absence.

Socrates then asks Critias if *sophrosune*, since it recognizes (*gignoskein*, 165c4) something, is not then clearly a kind of science (*episteme tis*, 165c5), and a knowledge or science of something (*tinos*)? This is the first controversial move in the exchange between Socrates and Critias in this section.[4] The *Gnothi s'auton* of Delphi is correctly translated as "Recognize oneself," that is, become aware of your place, your role in the scheme of things. It has no connotation of scientific or technical wisdom. But this is not the case with *episteme*, which belonged to the set of knowledge-terms associated with the Sophistic Enlightenment in late fifth-century Athens.[5] Critias, in his eagerness to equate *gnosis* and *episteme*, blurs an epistemological difference of no small significance. He wishes to claim for his notion of self-knowledge a level of expertise the ancient religious ideal did not include and he will later prove unable to defend. And this is perfectly consistent with what we have seen of him throughout the dialogue thus far, as suggested by Socrates' linking of Critias' thought to that of the Sophist, Prodicus. But it is also this claim that makes Critias interesting to Socrates, since it implies that he can give a rational account of his beliefs. It is this latter perspective on knowledge that can explain Socrates' own willingness to connect self-knowledge with *episteme* rather than *gnosis*, if he believes it is not a mere function of intuition, but is mediated by rational investigation and justification.[6] This is not to say that Socrates regards self-knowledge as a form of "theoretical-objective knowledge" or science in the Aristotelian sense, as will soon be made clear. But it is to say that Socrates here accepts, in the process of inquiry leading to the definition, the principle that self-knowledge involves something *more* than mere intuition—it involves the relation of the self to reason. This is a chief point for the interpretation of the dialogue, and for understanding Socrates' contribution to the Greek ideal of self-knowledge. If Socratic self-knowledge were, as some interpreters would have it, mere *gnosis*, then it would be as susceptible to the later criticisms of "the knowledge of knowledge" as Critias' understanding proves to be. But this is not the case.

SELF-KNOWLEDGE IS NOT A
TECHNICAL-PRODUCTIVE SCIENCE (165c7–166a2)

Critias' response to Socrates' question is that *sophrosune* is the knowledge "of oneself" (*heautou*, 165c7). Again Socrates does not object to his answer, but it leads to the next line of inquiry, for he points out that medicine is the science of health, and it produces the benefit of health, and architecture is the science of building houses, and it produces the benefit of houses. What beautiful work (*kalon ergon*, 165e1) then is the product of this science?

Given what Socrates has said in the prologue, we might suppose Critias could answer, "moderation," but he does not, for how could a science or virtue have itself as its own object? And yet, exactly some such self-relation must be involved, if moderation is a dynamic habit that somehow reachieves itself in each situation that tests it—though perhaps not by aiming *at* itself. Or we might suppose that he would answer, "one self," that is, the rational unity or identity of the self (cf. *Gorgias* 482b–c). But this cannot be the case, since surely the self exists as agent and not as its own product. Yet this too is not as absurd as it seems, if we consider how in the prologue Socrates was able, by means of his self-control and recollection of Cydias' wisdom, to reunify his momentarily fragmented self and reidentify with his rational interests. Somehow it will be necessary to understand the complex way in which the self and its virtue is the product of its own actions, is a "formed" or "socially constructed" rather than a "given" or "natural" reality, if the suggestions of the prologue are to be integrated with a notion of self-knowledge which is practical and not merely theoretical, rational and not merely intuitive; but of course Critias does not take that direction here. Instead, Critias says that Socrates is not inquiring correctly, for he is examining *sophrosune* as if it were similar to the other kinds of sciences, but neither it nor they are similar. For there are no products in arts such as logistic and geometry in the way that there are for others, such as architecture and weaving. (This remark may be compared to Critias' previous comments on productive work at 163b3–164c7 f.[7]) His point would seem to be that self-knowledge does not have an external product, an *ergon* separate from the craftsman and his art, in the way that weaving aims at the production of an item of clothing, or architecture at the construction of a house or a temple. Somewhat belligerently Critias concludes: "And you can't say otherwise" (165e3–166a2).

This additional remark is typical of Critias' defensive-aggressive attitude throughout this section of the dialogue, in contrast to Socrates' own attitude of patient inquiry. On the one hand, Socrates' relation to his dialogic partner is that of questioner, seeking to uncover and test the reasons for the others' views. Critias, on the other hand, presents himself and Socrates as knowers who already share the same knowledge. Thus he believes Socrates is questioning him merely to refute him before the others. Whereas for Socrates the dialogue turns on the truth concerning the beliefs under discussion and the relevance of those beliefs to his own and others' welfare, for Critias the dialogue turns on the question of the recognition of his (superior) person: Socrates does not show him the respect he is due, and he is getting mad. Socrates has before his mind an epistemological distinction that Critias seems not to appreciate—*knowledge versus opinion*. Critias has before his mind a political distinction that Socrates seems to disregard—that of *authority versus disgrace*. Socrates will have to resolve this tension in the conversation soon, or Critias may withdraw in anger. As it turns out, this difference is related to their very different conceptions of self-knowledge.

Critias has distinguished the theoretical from the productive sciences and assigned self-knowledge to the former or at least not to the productive arts (thus exhibiting himself a knowledge of the sciences according to their kinds). Clearly, if Socrates accepts his distinction here, then he would appear to move away from a technical model of virtue—thus setting up the second dilemma mentioned above and undermining the overall interpretation of Socratic virtue as modeled on a craft. Terence Irwin argues in *Plato's Moral Theory* that this passage has no such implications:

> We might think that 166a5–b3 recognizes that *logistike* can be *tou artiou kai tou perittou* (about the even and the odd) with no product. But the phrase *plethous hopos echei pros hauta kai pros allela* (the multitude they make with themselves and with each other) suggests the product—the right answer is a result of the calculations distinct from the calculations themselves. Socrates then does not recognize Aristotle's distinction between *poiesis* (production) and *praxis*.[8]

However, this argument has been refuted by David Roochnik, who shows that Plato allows in several dialogues for the distinction between productive and theoretical arts, and that the dialogue admits of a very different interpretation than the one Irwin assigns it.[9] Rather than supposing it is the craft-model of self-knowledge that Socrates accepts, which is then subjected to refutation, Roochnik, following Hyland, suggests that it is Critias'—not Socrates'—understanding that fails to adequately distinguish self-knowledge from productive knowledge, and that this failure causes the downfall of the definition later in the work: "By here employing *techne* as a model of knowledge Socrates brings about the downfall of Critias's definition, as well as his public humiliation."[10] Thus whatever confusion may exist in the *Charmides* concerning the relation of self-knowledge to technical-productive knowledge is not due to Socrates, but to Critias—though in fact Critias in this passage rejects such an assimilation, even if he later allows it.

SELF-KNOWLEDGE IS ALSO NOT A THEORETICAL-OBJECTIVE SCIENCE (166a3–c6)

In contrast to Irwin's claim, then, Socrates does not dispute the rejection of the technical-productive sciences as a model for *sophrosune*—suggesting he agrees that self-knowledge does not simply have an external product as its object. But this should come as no surprise, given what he had argued at 163d–164c concerning the knowledge an artist (e.g., physician) might have or lack regarding the benefit of his art to himself or his patient: self-knowledge must somehow encompass the good of one's activity, and the technically productive arts do not do this. If this is the case, self-knowledge also cannot simply be of itself, it must be of oneself in relation to one's own good.[11] Nor is Socrates' rejection of the *techne*-model surprising in the light of what he will say next, concerning the role the knowledge of ignorance plays in *sophrosune*. There is a self-critical dimension to Socrates' conception of self-knowledge, the possession of which is not measured simply by the ability to achieve its ends, even if that ability is accompanied by a rational account of the means to do so.[12] So Socrates continues his questioning, asking if Critias does not say that in all of these cases, the knowledge is of something different than the knowledge itself. Thus logistic is of the even and odd in regard to multitude, in their relations to themselves and to one another, the art of weighing is of the heavier and lighter measure, and in each case the object—the even and the odd, the heavier and lighter—is different from the respective knowledge of the object. Again Socrates wants to know what it is that *sophrosune* is the knowledge of, which is different from itself (166a3–b6).[13]

In response, Critias insists that moderation is unique in precisely this regard, for whereas the other knowledges are of something else and not themselves, *sophrosune* alone is a "knowledge of the other knowledges and of itself" (*he de mone ton to allon epistemon episteme estin kai aute heautes*, 166c2–3). This objection would again seem valid, insofar as self-knowledge, if it is to encompass self-benefit, cannot simply be theoretical, cannot be of something simply *other* than itself. But again Critias is angry with Socrates for questioning him further, as if Socrates were merely unwilling to agree with him, and this time he accuses him directly of arguing eristically and not caring about the *logos*, that is, the truth of the matter (166b7–c6).

Critias' replacement of the knowledge (or science) of oneself (*heautou*) with the knowledge that is a knowledge of itself (*heautes*), is the second of his moves in this discussion that is highly controversial.[14] How can the knowledge of *oneself* be transposed into the knowledge of *itself*? Critias would appear to assume that self-knowledge takes the form of knowing that one knows a science, that is, self-knowledge is of oneself qua knower, qua cognitive self—not of one's particular, contingent traits of personality, or particular abilities or interests, as self-knowledge generally is understood in a modern context.[15] This approach to self-knowledge compares to its treatment as the knowledge of the "self-itself" (*auto to auto*) in the *Alcibiades I*.[16] As we have seen already, in discussing the prologue, Socrates' own concern with self-knowledge does not focus on the particular contingencies of family history or physical appearance, but on the self in relation to moral ideals and universal human interests. Thus Socrates may well agree with the transition, even if he understands self-knowledge differently than Critias. For there remain his questions from 164b11–c3: Might not someone know that he knows a science but still not know himself, for example, might not a physician know that he knows medicine, but not know himself? Critias' answer, on the one hand, must involve the idea that the knowledge possessed by the sagacious, *sophron* man is directly relevant to his own benefit, though he does not make this point explicit. Socrates' answer, on the other hand, may include the realization that his knowing self is incomplete—a self-knowledge we have already seen him enact in the prologue.

While Critias does not explain himself, it is not difficult to infer his thought from what he has said. The contrastive phrase, "knowledge of itself and the other sciences" is the guide. Contrary to Tuckey's supposition, Critias does not introduce this merely out of a sophistic love of antithesis.[17] Rather, he seems to have gotten hold of the idea of a ruling art or science—whether from the Sophists or from Socrates—and has interpreted it his own way. He thinks of *sophrosune* as a master or ruling science.[18] The art of architecture, for example, involves the knowledge of itself and other knowledges: the architect must understand the arts of carpentry, masonry, glass work, structural engineering, plumbing, electrical wiring, financial and personnel management, and so on, as well as architecture itself. The idea of "self-knowledge" Critias has in mind would appear to be something like this, but on a comprehensive scale: a "governing science" ultimately directed to self-benefit and including all of the other sciences, productive and nonproductive, under its purview and rule. It would be nonproductive, but this does not mean it would be purely theoretical. We have already seen Critias attempt to distinguish making and doing in his defense of the understanding of *sophrosune* as "doing one's own" (163b f.), and though his account there was unsuccessful, we might suppose that this distinction is relevant here also. On that assumption, Critias would be affirming the existence of a *science of rule*, possessed by superior men, issuing not in physical products but in actions or in commands to subordinate artists, aimed at the benefit of the ruler-knowers. Such men would "know themselves" both in the sense that they would know how to benefit themselves, and in the sense that they would presume to recognize the difference between themselves (the knowers) and others (the nonknowers). To say that "this is what Critias has in mind" is not to say that he is fully cognizant of his own mind, of course. Otherwise he would realize that his notion of self-knowledge must be oriented by an understanding of self-benefit, as will become clear in the final segment of the inquiry. Critias does not yet realize this, however, presumably because he assumes that whatever the self-certain *sophrones* want is good for them—because he does not consider, to employ the language of the *Gorgias*, that they might not will what they want (cf. 466bd8–e2).

SOPHROSUNE AND THE
CLAIM TO MORAL KNOWLEDGE

The relation drawn here between knowledge as wisdom and virtue as superiority is both familiar and central to the representation of Socratic dialectic in the early Platonic dialogues, where it is a feature of the sophistic claim to knowledge made by many of Socrates' interlocutors. Euthyphro, for example, draws the same relation in the dialogue named after him, when he says that if he did not know the divine things, he would not be superior to the majority of men (4e–5a). Nicias also apparently believes that his claim to virtue rests on his claim to possess a science of courage (*Laches* 200a). And much the same is true of Thrasymachus, Ion, Hippias, Euthydemus, and others, all of whom also rest their self-image on the claim to knowledge and virtue. Plato attributes the same attitude to the foremost Sophists, Protagoras and Gorgias, each of whom, in his depiction of them, makes claim to a kind of "science [*techne*] of rule." Critias is like other interlocutors insofar as his claim to possessing *sophrosune* in the sense of a knowledge of the other knowledges and itself implies two different claims: the first is to possess a superior form of knowledge; the second, deriving from the first, is to be a superior kind of person. Knowledge in the sense of sophistic wisdom implies virtue in the sense of human superiority. It is a claim to self-knowledge as well as to moral knowledge.

In questioning sophistic claims to knowledge in the Platonic dialogues, Socratic dialectic also takes aim at the implicit claim to superiority. But the expectation in some of the dialogues, anyway, is that Socrates is perfectly within his rights in questioning his interlocutor's claims. Nicias, for example, fully expects Socrates to question his claims, and to question his way of life through the questioning of his claims to knowledge (cf. *Laches* 187e–188c). This is not Critias' attitude, however. He shares with Ion, Euthyphro, Nicias, and others the belief that he, by possessing the knowledge he possesses, is virtuous and superior; but by his irritation and anger he shows that he rejects completely Socrates' right to test his claim to knowledge. Again and again, we have seen him insist that Socrates simply agree with, not question him. In the case of Critias, the claim to a knowledge that knows itself is equivalent to a refusal to acknowledge the possibility that he does not know—that he is not superior. Critias' conception of the "ruler's self-knowledge" is, on the epistemological level, nothing more or less than a dogmatic assertion of authority. It is, in other words, a form of epistemic pride. But it is evident that this kind of attitude is a cognitive vice, not a virtue, for how could anyone who held it genuinely question his own beliefs? How could he ever discover his own ignorance? How could he come to know, explicitly and thoroughly, the reasons underlying his claim to knowledge? How could he relate openly and self-critically to himself qua knower? The contrast between the self-assertive dogmatism or *epistemic absolutism*, such as Critias has expressed, and the dialogic openness or *epistemic self-criticism*, with which Socrates began the section, could not be greater.[19] The articulation of this distinction in the words and deeds of Critias and Socrates respectively is the chief vehicle in the *Charmides* for setting the parameters of how the phrase "knowledge of knowledge" is to be understood, such that it can appear both as a vice and as a virtue.

It must also be recognized that Critias might have acquired his model of self-knowledge or self-wisdom as the "knowledge of itself and other knowledges" from Socrates himself. (Thus, as I mentioned earlier, Critias might be thought to have taken *both* of his definitions from Socrates.[20]) For the notion that virtue is knowledge is characteristic of Socrates in the early dialogues, where he nonetheless distinguishes the kind of truth he seeks—moral knowledge—from the kind of truth sought by the other disciplines, be they practical arts or theoretical sciences. It is clear in the *Apology*, for example, that Socrates recognizes that there is technical knowledge and there is moral knowledge, and that moral knowledge is different from, and more important than, the technical (21a–23b, 28b–30b).[21] In the *Euthydemus* Socrates moots the idea of an "art of rule" that stands as a kind of second-order science to the other, first-order sciences, directing and ruling over them.[22] In the *Gorgias* Socrates suggests that he alone possesses the true art of arts, the statecraft and soulcraft of making men virtuous and happy (521a f.). Socrates will pick up on this model of the relation of *sophrosune* to the other sciences later in the dialogue, in his description of the ideal society, which Critias will embrace as if it were his own (171d1–172a6, 173a7–d7). And it was the model of a knowledge standing apart from and somehow above the other sciences that Socrates seemed to advance in the prologue to the *Charmides*, when he claimed, if playfully, to know what was most important to human happiness (the health of the *psyche*) and to be a psychic physician, that is, to possess the ability to diagnose and perhaps even to induce psychic health, *sophrosune*.

The *Charmides* might provide therefore, at least in some manner, Plato's depiction of Socrates' own self-examination, albeit one reflected through the distorting mirror provided by Critias. For one aspect of Socrates' conception of virtue might be captured by the phrase, "the knowledge of itself and of the other knowledges." This would be the aspect in accordance with which Socrates (1) recognizes the distinction between moral and technical knowledge; (2) affirms the primacy of the former over the latter (corresponding to the primacy of the rational soul over the body and all external goods); (3) believes himself to know what is good for human souls (*sophrosune*; not doing harm; the examined life); and possibly (4) believes that he knows how to bring about what is good in himself and others. Such moral knowledge would be implicit in his notion of "care for the welfare of the soul" as suggested in the prologue and in the principles that substantively define his moral philosophy, the enactment of which would constitute moral health. It would not be altogether strange for Critias to associate his own notion of self-certain, kingly men with a Socratic ideal of moral knowledge. The fact that Critias might have heard of an ideal self-knowledge and "science" of the good from Socrates would also help to explain why he seems surprised and annoyed that Socrates is unwilling to agree with him here and now. The fact that Critias might have heard of such an ideal from Socrates does not imply, however, that Socrates ever claimed to *possess* the ideal in question—at least not in the manner supposed by Critias. And it does not imply that what Socrates might mean by such an ideal would be the same as what Critias means. For the last thing we would suppose Socrates would insist on is that his beliefs should merely be agreed to and not questioned. The task of the dialogue might then be to expose the flaws in the "Socratic" image of virtue as *falsely* represented by Critias, while displaying, for the "quiet" reader, an alternative, genuinely philosophical ideal that is not susceptible to the same criticisms. In fact, the ideal of self-knowledge Critias offers will be thoroughly examined in the course of the dialogue, and it will be refuted in the uncritical form in which Critias has presented it. The ideal Socrates displays will be not be refuted, however, and the dialogue will suggest how it might be justified.

SOCRATIC *SOPHROSUNE* AND SELF-KNOWLEDGE (166c6–e3)

Socrates takes the charge of eristic, which Critias has hurled against him seriously and responds as follows:

> What a thing you are doing! I said, by believing, even if I do refute you, that I am refuting for the sake of anything other than that for the sake of which I would also search through myself as to what I am saying, fearing that unawares I might ever suppose that I know something when I don't know. So I do assert that this is what I also am doing now: investigating

the argument most of all for the sake of myself, but perhaps also for my other companions. Or don't you suppose that it is a common good (*koinon agathon*) for almost all human beings that each thing that exists (*hekaston ton onton*) should become clearly apparent just as it is? (166c6–e3.)

Socrates' self-declaration here articulates, in the clearest manner possible, his own self-understanding of his moral-dialectic practice—his own practical self-knowledge.[23] This self-understanding involves several components, each of which is attested in other early dialogues as well:

1. His *disavowal of (absolute) moral knowledge*, which we also noted at the beginning of this segment of the inquiry; this disavowal is the best known of all his cognitive attitudes, and is the chief element in his account of his own manner of wisdom in the autobiography of his mission at *Apology* 21a–23b.
2. His equally characteristic *avowal of rational inquiry* (*zetesis*) as the means by which one can determine whether oneself or another possesses moral knowledge; this avowal is also a characteristic feature of his practice, as he recognizes both in the course of examining others in other early dialogues, for example, *Euthyphro* 9e, and as is reflected in the "turn to the *logoi*" described in his autobiography in the *Phaedo* 96a–99e. This avowal includes his identification with the values of such inquiry. He is not practising eristic; he is seeking truth, not victory—and he is seeking it not in isolation, but with others, in the context of a common linguistic practice.
3. His *avowal of epistemic fear*, here left incompletely explained, concerning the evil of not knowing that he does not know, in a situation in which he thought he knew.[24] The fear of thinking you know, but not knowing, concerning matters of moral importance, and thus of being out of harmony with oneself and of doing what is wrong and in conflict with the will of the gods, is the greatest evil, according to the ethical philosophy Socrates articulates in the *Apology* 29b–30b, *Crito* 46b–49e, and *Gorgias* 466b–482c, which corresponds to the order of human welfare as he discussed it in the prologue.
4. His *avowal of eudaimonic purpose* to his dialectic, the self-benefit he believes he may attain in the present inquiry, with its final goal of "revealing each of the beings" and grasping truth. The recognition that the goal of inquiry is the good of truth, and

the attendant ability to do what is virtuous and beneficial, is also a characteristic feature of Socrates' self-understanding in other dialogues, for example, *Gorgias* 486e–488b, though his emphasis in this passage is not on the value of knowledge as a guide to conduct, but strictly on the value of revelation or truth itself, as opposed to error and self-deception.

5. His *avowal of social purpose* to his dialectic, namely the concomitant goal of benefiting those others who may share in the "common good" of revelation and truth. This principle is also a feature of Socrates' approach to dialectic in other early dialogues, but nowhere else is it quite so clearly enunciated. Note that Socrates does not disjoin self-examination, as beneficial to oneself, and other-examination as beneficial to them; the examinations he conducts of others apparently contributes to the same result as examining himself.[25] Of course, sharing in such a common good, even as a shared goal, provides the basis for friendship (cf. *Lysis* 223a; also Socrates' appeal to the god of friendship at *Gorgias* 500b). Note, too, there is a hint—but only a hint—of indignation in Socrates' remarks, reflecting his self-restraint of temper here in contrast to Critias' just previous outburst against Charmides. Unlike Critias, Socrates knows his role in the community of rational dilaogue, which is neither to dominate nor to be dominated, but to participate as a free and equal partner.[26]

If we step back from the philosophical outlook represented by this set of ideals for a moment, there would appear to be two larger contexts in which it may be set. The first is the broader context of theories of knowledge and inquiry. In this regard, the Socratic-dialectical approach is very different from the dominant approaches to knowledge in the modern philosophical tradition. On the one hand, it is clearly oriented to the norm of truth. In this regard it differs from both subjectivist and relativist coherentist conceptions of knowledge and truth (such as are developed by Rorty and Davidson among contemporary philosophers).[27] On the other hand, it is a self-consciously communal-linguistic form of inquiry. It is neither individualistic and mentalistic—as in the Cartesian tradition—nor is it foundationalist—as in the empiricist tradition. It shifts the locus of reason and truth from the individual mind to the interaction of dialogue, but it does this in such a way as not to fall prey to subjectivism or relativism. This distinctively Socratic approach to knowledge has been called "objectivist-participant" in an important new study by Christopher Gill.[28] It is objectivist, insofar as it supposes that the objective truth can be found; it is participant, in that such discovery is thought to depend on the right kind of participation in the right kind of communal epistemic practice.[29] It is an activity in which self-knowledge can be attained—but only through a specific kind of critical linguistic practice that both valorizes and seeks to create a rational community.

A second context in which this Socratic philosophical outlook or ideal of active self-knowledge can be set is the context of moral theory, specifically the theory of the virtues.[30] In fact, it identifies the realm in which a theory of moral virtue and a normative theory of knowledge intersect: a theory of dialogic rationality or enlightenment (albeit human, not divine), and the relevance of such open-minded rationality to moral practice. Again it is crucial to see this cognitive perspective emerge within a dramatic context—to see how it bears on human lives and their actions. Attending to the epistemic seriousness and responsibility that Socrates brings to the inquiry, and contrasting it to the attitudes of his interlocutors (which is not to deny Charmides a moment of intellectual virtue at 160e), we are made to see connections among cognition, integrity, virtue, selfhood, and interpersonal relations that we would otherwise not consider. The possibility that self-knowing in the Socratic sense involves moral commitment and achievement begins to seem not only plausible, but necessary. The thought emerges that the complex set of qualities that are summarized by the definition of *sophrosune* as the practiced ability to know what one knows and does not know in the matters under discussion— in the Socratic quest to determine how we ought to live and what constitutes genuine happiness—might really be virtue.

It is clear that Socrates' involvement in the dialogue is characterized by an attitude that is uniquely attendant to his own and others' possible epistemic limitations, and that he possesses a very high level of self-consciousness in his practice as a dialectical inquirer. He knows what he does not know. But he also knows— and seems to enjoy the knowledge—that he and his friend in dialogue are in pursuit of that very good, the truth they need. His testimony reveals the value dimension he attributes to that inquiry, and its potential for creating bonds with others. It also reveals the reason why he might conceive of dialectic as a way of confirming, or changing, his own identity, since it involves a division of the self into (1) the present unsparing investigator of opinions (one's own or others), (2) the past speaker and holder of those opinions, and (3) the future person who will go on to act and live by the opinions that appear, as a result of inquiry, to be best. (I will discuss the relation of dialectic to the self in the next chapter.) And it suggests why he might believe dialectic participation offers the same opportunity to others, as they engage with him in a common quest for the good. Why would anyone not wish to share in that community?

Thus understood, Socratic self-knowledge involves the orientation of the person to the process of rational inquiry, to the moral participant-community established with others through such inquiry, and to the harmony established within oneself, when one submits ones' moral thought to the potentially disorienting test of reason, and through that process discovers the reasons for provisionally confirming or disconfirming what one thought one knew. Through its practice, the person becomes ever-more bonded to the norm of reason and more confident of the moral beliefs she has tested—hence ever-more *principled* in her knowledge of who she is and what she stands for— but at the same time ever-less dogmatic concerning even those "products" (those beliefs)—hence ever-more *open* to reorienting herself to the truth she discovers concerning herself, her companions, and her moral world.[31] This is, in fact, the cognitive attitude associated with the classic ideal of rationality. It includes, as we shall see, elements not only of logical consistency, but also of autonomy, objectivity, reflexivity, and morality. But as we have already seen, it is not *this* ideal of self-knowledge that Critias has in mind.

Nonetheless, Critias quickly agrees that it is a common good for each of the beings to be revealed, and Socrates goes on from there to calm, if momentarily, Critias' social fears. For he asks him to "let go" of, whether it is Critias or Socrates who is being refuted, and merely focus on the *logos* and determine what way it turns out under examination. This shift away from the personalization of the argument—a technique Socrates also employs successfully with other interlocutors at crucial moments—succeeds in its task of keeping the volatile Critias involved in the conversation.[32] It is as though Critias has been lifted, if only for a moment, above his subjective concern for distinction, so as to participate in a nobler thing, the objective enterprise of critical science. Plato even leaves it to him to speak in a nobler fashion: "You seem to me to speak with due measure (*metria legein*)."

THE IDEAL OF SELF-KNOWLEDGE (166e4–9)

Socrates is now ready to draw together what they have learned. From Critias he extracts a clear and simple definition of *sophrosune*, whatever it may be that Critias intends by this phrase: it is the "knowledge both of itself and of the other knowledges" (166e5–6). But Socrates is not content with this statement. He offers yet another question, whether such a knowledge is also of nonknowledge, that is, of ignorance (*kai anepistemosunes episteme an eie*, 166e7), if it is also of knowledge? Critias agrees: it is also the "knowledge of knowledge and of nonknowledge" (166e7–9).

Thus there are two notions of self-knowledge implied in the discussion between Critias and Socrates, which are reflected in the expressions put forward at the end of the section. (1) The first, the "knowledge of itself and the other knowledges," is associated in word and deed with Critias. Its most prominent feature is the aspect of rule, apparently based on sheer self-assertion. (2) The other ideal is distinguished by the additional phrase, "the knowledge of knowledge and of nonknowledge." This is the ideal associated in word and in deed with Socrates. Its most prominent feature is the knowledge of ignorance.

Both of these ideals of self-knowledge have objects. The Critian ideal has as its objects artisans and their knowledges (arts, sciences), presumably after the manner of an architectonic ruling science, and the knowledge of itself, in the sense of the self-recognition of the knower of himself *as* knower and, in light of that, as superior. As represented by Critias, this kind of self-knowledge amounts to nothing more than the assertion of self-certainty, and it does not wish to even permit, much less require, critical examination of the grounds of its own claim to knowledge. It takes for granted that its willful action is in accordance with its own self-interest.

The second ideal of self-knowledge is represented by Socrates. Its immediate object is the moral belief it has taken under investigation, together with the determination that that belief, on critical examination, constitutes a piece of moral knowledge or of ignorance. But its structure is more complex. For this kind of self-knowledge presupposes an orientation to oneself in which one's rational being and the good of such a being is primary: it presupposes self- and other-relations mediated by the values of reason, not emotions of self-assertion or appetite. And it further presupposes a self-relation that recognizes it is possible to be out of touch with one's own true values, mistaken concerning what one supposes oneself to know of moral truth, caught in self-delusion. (We will develop this point further, especially in relation to Critias, in chapter 5.) The orienting goal of such self-knowledge is one's own welfare, which, however, this ideal of self-knowledge, unlike the Critian ideal, does not presume itself to know.

The Critian ideal of *sophrosune* was developed in three stages. (1) The first step involved blurring the distinction between *gnosis* (acquaintance or recognition) and *episteme* (knowledge or science). In fact, to be a knower was not conceived of by Critias epistemically, as a function of how you possessed knowledge, but politically, as a position of authority, knowers being those who regard themselves and are recognized by others as knowers. Socrates did not object to the reconceptualization of self-knowledge as epistemic, but he clearly also does not conceive of it in the same manner as Critias. His reason for not objecting to this reconceptualization is clear: it is only through the process of self-examination that one discovers the limitations of traditional virtue, and reconceives of virtue in relation to reason. (2) This step was followed by Critias's denial that self-knowledge was a productive art, another point to which Socrates did not object, and to which he would not object, if he accepts the distinction between technical knowledge—which issues in products—and moral knowledge—which issues in actions and is oriented to the person's overall well-being. The second step involved conflating the distinction between knowledge of the self and a knowledge's knowledge of itself. This was again a function of Critias' understanding of this science, for the self was conceived as a "knower-master" who possessed the correct art of rule.[33] But in Critias' case, this art has no content—it is the mere self-assertion of the would-be ruler, the would-be wise man. In Socrates' case, however, the self would appear to be conceived as the rational self, the self qua knower and seeker of moral knowledge. (3) The second step was followed by denying that self-knowledge took an object other than itself (and other knowledges) as its object. Again Socrates did not object, though he added a further, crucial element, before he and Critias joined as a team to formulate the final definition.

Both Socrates and Critias are thus made to agree that *sophrosune* is a kind of science, but it is neither a productive-technical nor a theoretic-objective science.[34] But Critias's conception of self-knowledge certainly does not coincide with that of Socrates. For the action of the dialogue has revealed that Critias's criterion of knowledge is nothing more than self-assertion, on the one hand, and social recognition, on the other. It was when he did not receive this from Socrates, who insisted on submitting his claim to criticism, that Critias became angry and accused Socrates of eristic.

This accusation was perfectly understandable. There can be no difference between eristic and dialectic for Critias, since for him moral knowledge reduces to self-assertion, and is not bounded by truth or reason.

THE DEFINITION OF *SOPHROSUNE* (167a1–8)

The final step in the articulation of the new ideal of *sophrosune* forged in the *Charmides* was made by Socrates, when he pointed out a feature that had been absent, as Critias defined it. This was the knowledge of ignorance. It is also this feature that Socrates now emphasizes, in his descriptive summary and definition of what *ho sophron* and *sophrosune* is:

> Then only the moderate person will himself both recognize himself and be able to examine both what he happens to know and what he does not; in the same way it will be possible for him to investigate others in regard to what someone knows and supposes, if he does know, and what he himself supposes he knows but does not know. No one else will be able to. And this is what being moderate, and moderation, and oneself recognizing oneself [*to sophronein te kai sophrosune kai ho heauton auton gignoskein*] are: knowing both what one knows and what one does not know. (167a1–7)

We are now able to begin to understand what this definition means in relation to the *Charmides*.

The definition as stated is ambiguous in two respects.[35] (1) First, it is not clear if the moderate person on this account distinguishes between what he knows about technical or mathematical matters and what he knows about living a good life; if he makes the kind of distinctions Socrates makes at *Apology* 21a–23b and in the prologue when Socrates contrasted the knowledge relevant to the good of the soul to other, radically less valuable knowledge. (2) Second, it is not clear if the *sophron* person realizes, as a result of his investigations, what Socrates claims to realize, namely that no one simply possesses moral knowledge and wisdom of the kind his fellow citizens make claim to. Thus it is also not clear whether the person is concerned, as a result of this insight, to continue his quest for moral knowledge and wisdom. This twofold ambiguity in the meaning of the definition will naturally contribute to the ambiguity of its examination as the inquiry continues—particularly since Critias does not seem to be aware of the relevant Socratic distinctions. Socrates will exploit the ambiguity concerning the object of self-knowledge in such a way as to leave it unclear if it has any substantive content at all. He will be able to do this because Critias does not realize his own ignorance concerning human good—an ignorance he will demonstrate both in speech and action. Socrates will then clarify matters, by revealing that this is, indeed, the object of self-knowledge. But by then things will seem so confused that it is not clear how they might reunite the two.

The definition of *sophrosune* that Socrates and Critias formulate at the midpoint in the inquiry, then, is ambigious, and these ambiguities will affect the entire remaining discussion. But despite this fact, it is also evident that the definition refers to Socrates, and specifically to his self-description in the *Apology*.[36] Critias may be confused as to what the definition really means, but Plato clearly intends the reader to relate the definition and the following discussion to Socrates, even more than to whatever Critias may make of it. Indeed, by shifting the emphasis of the description of *sophrosune* from the "knowledge of itself and the other sciences" to the "knowledge of knowledge and nonknowledge," Plato is clearly indicating that it is the *Socratic* ideal of rationality and self-knowledge that is really intended by this definition—again, whether Critias appreciates that ideal or not (and we have good reason to believe already that he does not). Thus the final definition of *sophrosune* in the *Charmides* would appear to be a virtue that has been articulated, by word and by deed, by Socrates: an ideal that (1) emphasizes the relation of the rational examination of moral beliefs to the possession of self-knowledge; (2) emphasizes the examination of what others claim to know, no less than to what one claims to know oneself; (3) lays even greater emphasis on the discovery of what oneself and others do not know than what one may know; and (4) knows as a consequence of these examinations what is known and what is not known. It is an ideal that identifies the self who is known with the rational or cognitive self, the self who is not only the particular, individual possessor but who even more strives to be the universal, dialectical investigator of her own and others' moral beliefs, and who therefore holds to orienting values such as truth in the practice of her virtue. It is the dynamic Socratic ideal of cognitive moderation that is put forth here as the human virtue of *sophrosune*.

But if this is correct, then what relation does this definition have to the other ideal that has been put forward in this part of the dialogue, the Critian ideal of sophistic self-superiority?

Another way of asking the same question, as regards the further development of the inquiry, is: What understanding does Critias have of the Socratic ideal? For he agrees to it as if there were no difference between it and his own ideal. But if he does not appreciate the difference, how will Socrates be able to examine and refute the definition he has just offered? Will Socrates not actually be examining *Critias'* understanding of the definition, rather than his own? In other words, will he not be refuting a *sophistic* conception of self-knowledge, rather than a Socratic, philosophical conception? Or is there a Socratic or philosophical sense to Critias' ideal of a knowledge of the knowledges and of itself, and if so, is it also refuted?

The answers to these questions must wait until we move deeper into the dialogue. Socrates will be testing Critias further, to determine the implications of his understanding of moderation and self-knowledge. As we might imagine, they are different from those we have inferred from Socrates' practice in the dialogue thus far, and they will be refuted. But again this does not mean that the understanding of *sophrosune* displayed and articulated by Socrates is also refuted. In the next chapter, I want to draw from the *Charmides* the relation developed in it between moderation and the elenchus, and show how that characterization relates to the discussion of several important topics in Socratic philosophy. This will allow us to understand better the definition that Socrates has given at 167a1–7.

FOUR

THE SOCRATIC
IDEAL OF RATIONALITY

*Philosophy means philosophizing. It is not truth but the
search for truth, a constantly baffled but passionately
and stubbornly renewed pursuit of understanding.
Socrates declared himself the lover, the wooer, the pur-
suer of truth, not the bridegroom in complacent possession. So the philosopher remains today.*
                                        —*Brand Blanshard*

In this chapter I will draw together some of the larger themes
considered in the *Charmides*, including dialectic, virtue and
the soul, and relate them to Socrates' self-description in the
prologue and to their representation in other Platonic dialogues.
Socrates appears to believe that virtue or moral health (*sophrosune*)
comes about in human beings through "beautiful speeches," and
while we are not yet certain whether these speeches can be identified with his practice of dialectic, the definition he and Critias have
formulated at the midpoint in the dialogue strongly suggests this is
the case. But why should the cognitive virtue of "knowing what
you know and do not know" imply moral virtue, as the argument
would appear to require? And what is the relation between such
cognitive moderation and the concept of the soul, which Socrates
made so much of in the prologue?

These questions concerning the role of dialectic in the
Charmides relate to two important questions about Socratic philosophy as a whole. The first involves the possibility that the
dialectic may have positive, as well as negative results. Socrates
clearly asserts as much in the *Gorgias*, for example, and the implication seems to be the same in the *Apology*, that his life of elenc-

tic examination has given rise to the distinctive moral values and principles that structure his outlook and life. But the dialectic appears to function in a purely negative fashion in the early dialogues prior to the *Gorgias*, and even there it is not obvious how the logic of examination-and-refutation might lead to positive results. I believe that this problem was solved, at least in one respect, by Gregory Vlastos in his classic essay, "The Socratic Elenchus." But there is another aspect to this question that I will address here.

A second question adumbrated in the *Charmides* bearing on the interpretation of Socratic philosophy as a whole concerns the relation between dialectic and the concept of the soul. Plato would seem to develop in the middle dialogues, beginning with the *Phaedo*, a metaphysical conception of the soul that treats it as sharply separate (or separable) from the body, and in that dialogue he also suggests that philosophical inquiry is relevant to the process of "purification" or "detachment" (*katharsis*) by which the philosopher prepares for death. As we have seen, the prologue to the *Charmides* also suggests if not a separation, at any rate a hegemonic relation of soul to body, such that the welfare of the whole person is seen to be entirely dependent on the one and not the other. As we shall see, the inquiry segment of the *Charmides* will go much further in articulating the idea of soul, displaying its complexity and examining its relation to the life of reason—though the idea of soul expressed in the *Charmides* does not treat it as a separate entity from the body.

"VIRTUE IS KNOWLEDGE" IN HISTORICAL CONTEXT

The place to begin the discussion of these matters is with the extraordinary role that the concept of knowledge as expertise had in late fifth-century Athens. Thanks to the efforts of scholars such as Michael O'Brien, Lowell Edmunds, G. B. Kerferd, and Jan Moline, we are now able to appreciate the extent to which Socrates' appeal to the conception of virtue as knowledge was grounded in the historical context. O'Brien, in his pioneering work, *The Socratic Paradoxes and the Greek Mind*, showed that Socrates' intellectualism was hardly a new development, and had rather to be understood in relation to Greek intellectualism as a whole and to the Sophistic Movement in particular.[1] Edmunds has shown how the categories of *gnome, techne,* and *sophia* dominate the political world of Periclean Athens in Thucydides' *History*.[2] Kerferd has drawn the connections between Pericles and the Sophists centered around Protagoras, and Moline has further extended our appreciation of these connections in his work on Plato's conception of knowledge.[3]

The upshot of these studies has been to cast an entirely new light on the relation of Socratic intellectualism to Greek thought. This background should then be coupled with the further insight that it is chiefly Socrates to whom the Athenians owed the notion of a nontechnical concept of wisdom—a notion of wisdom in which not technical mastery and control, but the knowledge of ignorance has the decisive role.[4] This is not to say that there are not skeptical moments in the writings of the prominent Sophists; but the theme of moral self-examination and epistemic self-criticism was moved to center stage by Socrates, not his Sophist counterparts.[5] His pivotal role in Greek intellectual history was not that of the "theorist" who drove it in the direction of intellectualism (the role Nietzsche attributed to him), but rather that of the "philosophical therapist" who called its *uncritical* brand of intellectualism into question.[6] The slogan "Virtue is knowledge" was not, on this view, originally Socratic at all: it was an originally Athenian, originally sophistic notion. It is the notion that we find represented in the dialogues not only by major figures such as Protagoras and Gorgias, but also by so many of Socrates' interlocutors, as we noted in the last chapter (Euthyphro, Nicias, Critias, Euthydemus, Polus, etc.); and it is also the view we find reflected in the Socratic portrait of Athenian society offered at *Apology* 21a–23b, which is the image of a society in which many of the citizens believed themselves to be "wise" (i.e., have the equivalent of technical self-certainty and expertise) in moral and political things, no less than in genuinely technical subjects. That is the picture of a society in which Sophistry, in the sense of the claim to rational dominion over its object, be it nature or a field of human endeavor, is the prevailing ethos of mind and the presumed ground for the assertion of human excellence. Thus Socrates' self-description in the prologue to the *Charmides* is a perfect image of his role in Athenian intellectual life as a whole. Socrates, rather than being the chief proponent of unbounded rationalism in Athenian life, was in fact its chief physician. In deflating the sophistic ideal of moral/political expertise, he also deflated the sophistic claim to virtue, that is, superiority, and the associated claim to rule. The elenchus was the surgical knife, the "drug and incantations" (*to te pharmakon kai tas epoidas*, 157b1–2) by which he sought to purge the Athenians of their fever of wisdom, and bring them to a state of cognitive moderation—the knowledge of what they knew (the *technai*) and what they did not know (the knowledge of good, *phronesis* or moral and political wisdom)—and thus to philosophy.

THE SOCRATIC ELENCHUS

To appreciate the therapeutic nature of Socratic dialectic in relation to the individual, we need to take a close look at its manner of operation. The "standard form" of the definitional elenchus is familiar:

1. The interlocutor asserts a definition of a virtue, *d*.
2. Socrates secures agreement to further premises, *q* and *r*.
3. Socrates then argues, and the interlocutor agrees, that *q* and *r* entail *not-d*.
4. Socrates claims that *not-d* has been proven true, *d* false.[7]

This description of the elenchus makes it appear to operate in a manner essentially similar to any other refutative argument, directed toward a single object, the truth of the propositions under consideration, the conception of the world represented in the *logoi*. In this respect, dialectic is an essentially impersonal process, and the focus of inquiry is strictly on the logical consistency of the interlocutor's statements.

But the elenchus is also a highly personal experience, as a result of four additional factors: (1) First, the fact that the virtue under consideration is central to the value system of the interlocutor, to his practical understanding of life.[8] (2) Second, the fact that dialectic requires that the interlocutor *say what he believes*. (This is a point that Brickhouse and Smith, Seeskin, and Vlastos, as well as other scholars have emphasized.[9]) (3) Then, too, the fact that the examination and resulting refutation take place in public, where the interlocutor's self-image and reputation, as well as self-understanding, are at stake. (4) Finally, and perhaps most important, the fact mentioned earlier (cf. chapter 3), that the interlocutor typically believes he *knows* the truth about the ideal under discussion and about the good, that is, he possesses practical wisdom. He may not acknowledge this claim initially—indeed, he may not be fully aware of it—but it emerges in the course of the inquiry. Because of these factors, the interlocutor's words become vehicles for his self-expression and self-determination, no less than his self-understanding and conception of the world—that is, they become vehicles of self-knowledge.

Thus the practice of Socratic dialectic is directed both to the *logos*, the account of the matter, and to the speaker, his self-image and way of life, and these two aspects of the inquiry are not neatly separable: the subject matter of Socrates' questions reflects the central value in his interlocutor's self-understanding, while that self-understanding itself determines, at least to some extent, the meaning of the conceptions examined in the inquiry. This would seem to be why the interlocutor typically agrees that his definition of the virtue in question (*d*)—rather than the premises underlying Socrates' argument (*q, r*)—is refuted: somehow this central item in his self-understanding has been overturned; not comprehending how this could be possible, he infers that *he* has been refuted; since his understanding of this virtue is central to his self-knowledge, he accepts that *it* has been refuted.[10]

It is the self-expressive, self-revealing, and potentially self-reformative nature of the elenchus, the fact that it involves the interlocutor's desires and emotions as well as his beliefs in the dialectical situation, which makes it such a powerful tool for moral inquiry. The elenchus, in calling forth from the speaker his most profound moral beliefs, also calls forth his life and values in a way he may never have experienced before. As Nicias puts it in a well-known passage:

> Anyone who is close to Socrates and enters into conversation with him is liable to be drawn into an argument, and whatever subject he may start, he will be continually carried round and round by him, until at last he finds that he has to give an account both of his past and present life . . . (*Laches* 187e–188a).

Such speech has the potential to engage the whole person—to put the interlocutor's very identity at risk.

The *Charmides* turns out to be a more important guide to understanding this process than is generally recognized in the scholarly literature on Socratic philosophy, which has largely focused on the presentation of the elenchus in the *Gorgias*.[11] In the *Gorgias*, where the concern is to distinguish philosophy and sophistic rhetoric, the focus is on the formal structure of the elenchus, its function in revealing inconsistent beliefs. Socrates speaks in the *Gorgias* of his own concern for self-harmony, that he would prefer to "have the majority of mankind should disagree and oppose me, rather than that I, being one, should be out of tune with and contradict myself" (482c). Thus when he refutes his interlocutor, as with Polus or Callicles, he implies that the interlocutor is self-discordant, someone disconnected from himself. The elenchus is the means by which he might come back into self-harmony, namely the rational self-harmony of affirming a consistent set of moral principles which he already, that is, which his "true self" believes in (such as the principle that it is better to suffer than to do injustice).[12] The question as to why Socrates believes that his interlocutor must agree with these principles, and therefore must assume that his views have been refuted if they are shown to be in contradiction with them, has been thoroughly discussed in the scholarly literature in recent years; and as I mentioned above, I believe this problem has been solved at least in part by Vlastos.[13] It involves Socrates' projection of universal agreement with the moral principles he has come to in the course of his inquiries and experience. But there are other aspects of the elenchus that Plato scholars have not discussed as thoroughly, particularly the relation of the Socratic ideal of rational self-harmony to a diagnostic moral psychology.

In the *Charmides*—in contrast to the *Gorgias*—the dramatic setting and the content of the dialogue focus attention to the psychotherapeutic rather than the logical structure of the elenchus, and thus to the question of the nature of the "diseases" for which the elenchus might be the cure. One of the more important contributions of the *Charmides* to the understanding of Socratic philosophy in general consists in the fact that it provides answers to this important question—answers in the persons of Socrates' two main interlocutors: (1) *Charmides represents the psychic illness of moral thoughtlessness and heteronomy*, of "weakness of thought" and its attendant sense of inferiority. The dialogue shows us through drama and argument how this disease might be cured by personal involvement in the dialectic process of Socratic self-examination and reflection; shows us how personal identity might be transformed through the practice and developing habit of critical reason; shows how autonomy is related to cognitive no less than moral life. (2) The other chief interlocutor of the dialogue, *Critias, represents the opposite moral and cognitive disease, sophistry*, with its twin incapacity (and characterological disinclination) to recognize the limits of one's own wisdom, together with the arrogance of superiority (*hubris*) following on that inability/unwillingness. Morever,

Critias will prove no less lacking the practice and habit of critical reason than his ward, despite the fact that he, unlike Charmides, *seems* to be a morally autonomous agent. (This is a feature of his moral psychology the *Charmides* does not have the theoretical tools to explain, though it does display the fact.) Together, Charmides and Critias represent the two chief and opposite types of deficient or vicious relationship to one's own rationality and self-knowledge. It is this deficiency that the Socratic dialectic is intended to address and "cure" in an intellectual therapy with moral significance for the patient.[14]

There is both a positive and negative aspect to the operation of the Socratic elenchus. Of the two, the negative aspect is more obvious: the interlocutor claims wisdom, is refuted, and should be cured at the same stroke of his self-deception of wisdom and self-conceit of virtue. The process itself and the resultant state of cognitive moderation are described in the *Sophist*:

> They cross-examine a man's words, when he thinks that he is saying something and is really saying nothing; and easily convict him of inconsistencies in his opinions; these they then collect by the dialectic process, and placing them side by side, show that they contradict one another about the same things, in relation to the same things, and in the same respect. Those who see this become angry with themselves, and grow gentle toward others, and thus are freed from high and mighty opinions of themselves (*hautous megalon kai skleron doxon*), in a way which is most amusing to the hearer and produces the most lasting good effect on the person who is the subject of the operation . . . the purifier of the soul is conscious that his patient will receive no benefit from the application of knowledge until he is refuted, and from refutation is brought to modesty, and thus purges him and makes him *think that he knows only what he knows and no more*.[15] (230a–d, my italics)

This latter condition is the "best and most moderate (*sophronesteron*) state of the soul," according to the young Theaetetus. This process—this experience—should release the interlocutor's latent human desire for genuine knowledge and wisdom. But this description, which seems to characterize so accurately the operation of Socratic dialectic, poses a problem that has seldom been recognized in the scholarly literature on the dialogues.

THE ELENCHUS AND THE
SOCRATIC IDEAL OF RATIONALITY

The problem with the description in the *Sophist*, which sets out the claim of the elenchus to constitute a form of moral therapy, is that it practically never works that way in the Socratic dialogues. The interlocutors are refuted, again and again—but they hardly ever admit and learn from it! This might be called the chief paradox of the representation of negative dialectic in the dialogues, the fact that in theory it should work perfectly, but in Plato's own representation of it in practice, it almost never does. What is the meaning of this contradiction?

I would like to suggest that it is only after we appreciate the apparent failure of the elenchus to do the educational work Plato would appear to expect of it that we are led to see its real method of operation. I believe four points should be emphasized:

Dialectic and autonomy. As we have seen above, the interlocutors are personally attached to certain moral values and under the right guidance these values can be rationally articulated and thereby brought out "into the common world of reason" (Robinson) and subjected to critical examination. This self-disclosive aspect of the Socratic dialectic has only recently begun to be more fully appreciated in the accounts of his method.[16] With regard to it we realize that the key definition for Charmides himself is the second, in which the young man does not merely express what his society expects him to say, but he is led to articulate his own self-understanding in the virtue and his own implicit claim to possess it, which is why Socrates both directly and in his narrative praises Charmides for his articulation of it (160e2, 6). Only after his self-understanding has been exposed and Socrates has refuted it, is Charmides put in the position where he has to decide whether he will continue down the path of critical thought—even if it means overthrowing the ideal at the center of his own self-understanding—or retreat from that path. That is to say, the Socratic dialectic challenges him not only to acquire the correct moral opinions, but to *question himself* and *think for himself* and develop his own moral rationality. Thus Socrates' inquiry with Charmides displays the relation of the elenchus—and of the ideal of rationality associated with it—to the formation of personal autonomy.[17] If the interlocutor chooses to think for himself, he begins to adopt a new relation to his beliefs and to his life insofar as it is guided by those beliefs. In this relation, he is no longer simply guided by conventional norms or authorities, but he also does not simply assert himself against them; instead, he begins to take moral responsibility for them, begins to hold his received beliefs and values up to a norm of "universal reason." This is why, when Charmides elects to retreat from self-expression and puts forward Critias' definition for criticism, it represents not merely an intellectual, but also a moral failure: the failure to develop *himself* as a morally thoughtful and questioning person (which was why Socrates called him a "foul wretch"). Charmides chose the seemingly safe but cowardly option of examining his uncle's definition over the seemingly dangerous but potentially far more rewarding possibility of attempting to think on his own. He thereby chose to abandon the opportunity he had been given to remake his own values and to appropriate the practice of critical thinking as his own, as part of who he was to be. He chose *not* to identify with his rational self, but with a lesser self-identity, which took its guidance from his uncle, the future tyrant.

Dialectic, objectivity, and virtue. This way of understanding the pedagogical structure of the elenchus brings out the fact that it is not only a cognitive, but also an emotional and potentially value-inducing process. Socrates' inquiry with the self-assertive Critias will prove to be particularly revealing of this second aspect of the elenchus, the relation of dialectic to the ideal of rationality and to the formation—or refusal of the formation—of the normative attitude of objectivity. In fact, as Kenneth Seeskin has shown in considerable detail, the structure of elenctic inquiry ideally involves a process of reciprocal interplay between anticipatory acts of several types of moral virtue and the genuine personal engagement in cognitive inquiry.[18] Because of the necessity of self-exposure, the elenchus can test the willingness of the interlocutor to endure the fear of embarrassment and ignorance, that is, it can test his *moral courage and constancy* in the dialectical quest for the good; because of the possibility of self-contradiction, it can require intellectual *moderation*, in the sense of humility before the truth, to admit that one was mistaken or that one's reasons fall short; because such inquiry is interpersonal, one may relate to the other in an attitude of competition and jealousy, as a rival for the selfish good of victory, or in an attitude of *fairness and cooperation*, as partners in the quest for the common good of truth, and it is possible in this process to care for, or to be indifferent to, the other's well-being, not only one's own. One of the first scholars to develop this line of reflection on the relation of the elenchus to moral virtue was Myles Burnyeat:

> In other words, Socratic education can only be successful with someone like Theaetetus, who is aware of and can accept his need for it; that much self-knowledge is an indispensible motivating condition, for always the greatest obstacle to intellectual and moral progress with Socrates is people's unwillingness to confront their own ignorance.[19]

If these challenges are met, the interlocutor is involved in a process that results in the formation not only of new opinions, but of new values—the values of critical reason, the principles of the rational self.

Dialectic and community. There is another aspect of Socratic dialectic displayed in the *Charmides* that I believe should be highlighted. This is the sense in which it involves, in addition to the values of autonomy and objectivity, the element of community. The social dimension of Socratic dialectic has seldom been discussed by Plato scholars, but it is obvious from the drama of the *Charmides* that this is all-important to the pedagogical aspect of the conversation. Will Charmides break loose from the domineering influence of his "father" and guardian Critias—an influence both moral and intellectual—and enter into the influence of Socrates and his way of reflective concern? Or will he hold back from giving himself over to the community of moral thinkers, the community established in the dialectical practice? Socrates' obvious willingness to engage in dialogue with Critias—the mockery at 161b seems intended to force his entry into the conversation—may well be a function not only of the fact that the definition they have taken under consideration derives from Critias and that Socrates wishes to continue the investigation of the idea of *sophrosune*, but also of Socrates' recognition that whatever influence he may have on Charmides can only come about through the refutation and hence diminishment of the authority of Critias. Had Socrates been more successful in that regard, he might have performed a political service to his city. Unfortunately, the ending of the dialogue suggests that Charmides remains firmly under the influence of his uncle, despite Socrates' efforts and Charmides' own superficial attraction to him.

Notwithstanding the fact that Charmides, like so many others, finally rejects him, it is clear that what is at stake in conversation with Socrates is not only the topic of this particular exchange, but the opportunity for other conversations and indeed perhaps for the whole rich social relationship of his educational-dialogical circle. The call to commit oneself—one's thought and ultimately one's life, as Nicias suggests—to the test of the elenchus is also a call to involve oneself in the third aspect of the dialectic, the involvement it presupposes of *membership in rational community* with Socrates. Appreciation of the value of autonomy should not obscure the fact that what Socrates offers is not only thought, but friendship, not only discourse, but shared values and a shared life. One does not engage in the practice of Socratic dialectic as a solitary individual, but as one person among others, all equals in the epistemic community.[20] Furthermore, however aversive most of his interlocutors may be to Socrates' power to expose their ignorance—at possible cost of "face"—they are also generally attracted to the prospect of sustained community with him. It is not just his ideas that make him interesting; it is the fact that he embodies those ideas/values, and that the interlocutor, through rational intercourse with him, may make those ideas/values his own, as he participates with Socrates in the open-ended, but rule-guided and virtue-demanding deliberative assembly the dialectic forms. The failure of so many of Socrates' partners to persist in the elenchus is a turning away not only from exercising their own reason, but also from the opportunity Socrates offers them to join with him in a community of people committed to reason. Of course, many appear not to appreciate what they are giving up, but a few seem to realize that they are abandoning something of vital importance (e.g., Alcibiades). It must have been puzzling to the young Plato that anyone would choose against, rather than for, membership in the Socratic community. (I will take up this aspect of the dialectic again in chapter 7, in considering the themes of utopia and dystopia in the last segment of the *Charmides*.)

Dialectic, Akrasia, *and Choice.* This last point brings us back to the fact that it *is* possible to reject Socratic rationality, and that this possibility is dramatized so often in the dialogues as to constitute one of their most characteristic features. Charmides rejects the further pursuit of self-knowledge at 161b4–6. Critias will reject it even more obviously at 169c3–d1. Laches and Nicias reject it at the end of their dialogue. Euthyphro to all appearances runs away from it at the end of his. Meno and Anytus turn away from self-examination in the *Meno*. A wide assortment of sophist-types fail to acknowledge the elenchus they have suffered in many other dialogues. The most dramatic account of the rejection of elenctic self-insight is given by Alcibiades in the *Symposium*:

> He compels me to agree that, being deficient as I am, *I neglect myself*, when I involve myself in the affairs of Athens. . . . So I flee from him as if I were a slave running away from his master; but then when I see him again I think of those admissions, and I am cast into shame. (216a–c, my italics)

Contrary to the Socratic paradox that "no one willingly does wrong," the dialogues show people akratically rejecting moral knowledge again and again. This is a crucial fact about the relation of drama and argument in those dialogues—and one that, I have suggested, has tended to be overlooked in the scholarly literature.[21]

The fact that Socrates' interlocutors consistently reject the opportunity for moral insight and personal growth he makes available to them indicates a decisive reason why he cannot be said to possess a *techne* of moral education, and why he insists that virtue cannot be taught. Ideally Socrates should lead the student into a deeper understanding of his own moral beliefs, to the recognition that they are inconsistent and that he "does not really know what he is talking about." Ideally this process should prick his inflated self-evaluation and lead him to a deeper commitment to rationality, out of the state of inconsistency and/or heteronomous dependence on moral authorities into the attitude of mind in which he examines his actions in the light of universal reason and in which the policy of testing what he believes himself to know becomes a chief vehicle of his self-evaluation. But this call to self-investment in reason can be and typically is rejected by Socrates' interlocutors. The development of the moral habit of dialectical reason implies overcoming habits of self-inferiority and achieving the willingness, through intellectual courage, to question authority figures and think for oneself in matters of personal values (this is where Charmides fails); it also implies overcoming, through intellectual humility, habits of self-assertion, in the sense of the unwillingness to submit one's values to rational criticism (this is where Critias will fail); and it involves a commitment of self-election in the community of rational inquiry, with its ideals of truth, fairness, and mutuality (both fail in this respect). When his interlocutors reject reason, they reject also the moral principles that orient and underlie the commitment of the citizen in the dialectical community. Their motives for rejecting Socratic rationality may be found, at least in part, in their resistance to those principles.

The elenchus cannot compel the choice of self-knowledge on behalf of the interlocutor. Socrates can use logic, charm, even social pressure, but he cannot force his "patient" to prefer the good of truth to his desire for safety and comfort, or for superiority and honor. It is one of the chief contentions of this study that the *Charmides* teaches that this preference, this choice, depends on the interlocutor himself, and that this volitional dimension of self-knowledge cannot be eliminated, but is inherent in the process of the elenctic inquiry. For this reason, if for no other, Socrates cannot "teach" virtue, in the sense of produce in a consistent and predictable manner the right values in his students; the process of learning through the elenchus—the process of rational self-development, the process of appropriating the values and principles of critical reason—is not a matter of correct instruction, but of rational elicitation that must be responded to by personal choice.

DIALECTIC, RATIONALITY, AND VIRTUE

The picture I have drawn of the elenchus has implications for the interpretation both of the relation of Socratic dialectic and virtue, on the one hand, and for the categorization of Platonic psychology, on the other. With regard to the relation of dialectic inqury to virtue, it suggests why the dialectic may be held to have not only negative, but also positive results. Focusing primarily on Socrates' self-description in the *Apology* and the representation of dialectic in the *Gorgias*, many scholars—including Thomas Brickhouse and Nicholas Smith, Alphonso Gomez-Lobo, and Kenneth Seeskin, in addition to Vlastos—have argued that this must be the case: that Socrates clearly has arrived, through his lifetime of inquiry, at a core of fundamental moral beliefs that he is now convinced are both consistent and irrefutable.[22] These are the beliefs that have stood the test of many examinations. They are no mere beliefs, but reasoned, "proven" beliefs—beliefs concerning which Socrates can "give an account," beliefs the contradiction of which he believes he can show to be ridiculous. The analysis offered here of the *Charmides* adds a different kind of empirical component to that understanding of Socratic rationality, by enabling us to appreciate how Socrates might have come to his principles through participation in the practice of dialectic; how that practice might have led him from within its dynamic, participant form to the values he lives by; and why, despite his conviction that the beliefs he has come to are irrefutable, he must still disavow any claim to certainty regarding them. For on this view, *Socrates' ethics would emerge out of and reflect the practice of rational inquiry itself,* the values of moral-philosophical discourse. His ethics may then be understood as the substantive embodiment of the formal principles of such discourse and mutual involvement: the primacy of the good of truth over superiority or honor or safety or physical desire; the commitment of the rational inquirer to values of moral courage, intellectual humility, and dialectical fairness; the willingness to suffer "punishment" (refutation), if such punishment/refutation is warranted, rather than do it to another, if it is not; the realization of personal interest and the common good; and the imperative of applying one's findings to the conduct of life.[23] Socratic ethics, on this view, is the idealized extension of the norms required by and created in the very practice of dialectic.

The value-creative dimension of dialectic makes it something other than mere mental gymnastics aimed at throwing the opponent, despite its outward appearance. It is true that there is an external isomorphism between dialectic and eristic, in the sense that the process of Socratic elenchus aims at criticizing and overthrowing the *logos* put to the test.[24] This partly explains why Critias, not appreciating the moral principles that guide dialectic, thinks Socrates is merely trying to refute him. Dialectic, no less than eristic, has the logical form of a refutative argument, aimed at the interlocutor's statements. But the inner nature of dialectic is entirely different than that of eristic. Its goal, its guiding principle, is not the good of acquiring victory for oneself; it is the community-creating good of truth, of the "revelation of each thing that exists" (166d5–6).[25] But what is this revelation? What all does it entail?

As we may now appreciate, the phrase clearly has a double meaning.[26] For the "revelation of each thing that exists" in a Socratic dialogue does not only refer to the goal of making evident things as they are in the world—of expressing/uncovering the truth in propositional terms (truth in words). It also refers to the revelation of selves—of exposing/uncovering the speakers and their innermost values, even if they are in a state of confusion—and of bringing them to the life of reason (truth in souls). Charmides is not prepared for such truth, and will fearfully withdraw from it; Critias will angrily reject it. But the interlocutor who would persist in the process of dialectic comes to a revelation of himself, his beliefs and values, not only to an understanding of the objects of those beliefs, and thus it takes him to a point of moral decision: Will he persist in and submit to the process of rational inquiry, a process that requires and indeed takes the form of a new kind of self-determination? Or will he withdraw from and refuse such self-formation and self-knowledge, in anger or fear?

In other words, the elenchus potentially involves the interlocutor in a kind of rite of passage, a confrontation with a self whose irrational attachments of appetite and ego are exposed and must be overcome for the interlocutor to progress in and through the cathartic element in the inquiry. The true elenchus is no mere philosophical conversation, but a "going down" of the whole self—which is why so many reject it, but also why it can lead to a genuine "rebirth" of the *psyche* and of self-knowledge at the other end of the zetetic tunnel. It is the potential rebirth of the interlocutor's selfhood in the values of universal reason that makes it not merely an investigative, but a "medical" or therapeutic and even a kind of religious practice. For if the interlocutor is virtuous and persists in the dialectic process, he will find himself taken out of his "accidental and irrational arbitrariness" and revealed in the light of reason, and he will also begin to find and remake the very structure of his self-identity in the values of that rational process, as he identifies more completely with his cognitive self. He will find that the pursuit of knowledge has involved him in the values and virtues of cognitive life and in the participant community of that life.

The practice of dialectic should form, in the life of the Socratically *sophron* individual, an intellectual conscience, and this quality of thoughtfulness about her life should make it significantly different from that of a person who does not engage in critical thought.[27] There is an amusing characterization of this difference in the (possibly spurious) *Hippias Major*, where Socrates, having failed utterly to lead Hippias to recognize his own self-contradiction and conceit of wisdom, proclaims ironically that he, unlike Hippias, cannot rest easy with eloquent and beautiful speeches about beauty and virtue, because he, unlike Hippias, is held to account for his beliefs by a man who is always cross-examining him:

> He is a very close relative of mine and lives in the same house, and when I go home and he hears me give utterance to these opinions he asks me whether I am not ashamed of my audac-

> ity in talking about a beautiful way of life, when questioning
> makes it evident that I do not even know the meaning of the
> word "beauty." (304d)

In other words, Socrates has come to live in the dimension of rational self-examination, but Hippias' "inner house" is empty—there is nobody home. The dialogue displays not only Hippias' inability to define the beautiful; it also displays his deeply engrained unwillingness to reflect upon the meaning of that failure for his moral self-assessment and epistemic self-confidence.[28] But the dialogue displays the contrary, very beautiful quality in Socrates—whatever his critical friend may say.

This analysis of Socratic dialectic has important implications for understanding how knowledge is depicted in the early Platonic dialogues. It points up the fact that Plato's concern in these works (and not only in these works) is not only with the object of knowledge, but with what is involved in becoming and being a *knowing subject*—what kinds of moral/intellectual virtues must be appropriated and made part of the personal value system for philosophical self-knowledge, regarded as a personal and yet nonetheless curiously impartial achievement, to be realized. It helps us to see why the distinctive virtue of Socratic rationality does not lie merely in its realization of logical consistency, but in its embodiment of personal commitment to the norm of reason: "So we must examine the question of whether we ought to do this or not; for I am not only now but always the kind of *person* who follows nothing but the reasoning (*logos*) which seems to me best" (*Crito* 46b, my italics). It is this performative principle that connects the will to reason and determines that emotion shall be subordinate to deliberate guidance. It is this that is the guiding principle of a rational self, one critically self-conscious of the fact that the good she values may not be what she *should* value—so that if she determines it is not what she should value, she must act otherwise, because for her to *be* a self—to enjoy self-harmony—is to be committed to reason, to be a rational self.[29]

This interpretation of the way in which Socratic dialectic may yield positive results also accords neatly with the description of *sophrosune* we found at 167a1–7. The state of mind corresponding to such practice originates out of the critical awareness of the values governing dialectic, including the primacy of truth, the necessity of the virtues, and in general the appreciation of oneself as a *psyche*, a rational being. But it also originates out of the active disposition to submit one's own values to the community of dialogic inquiry, and to do this as a matter of principled habit—the chosen habit of the examined life.[30] It is a volitional, no less than a cognitive state; an intentional policy, rather than a mere psychological or naturalistic disposition. The former, cognitive aspect of this trait is conspicuously missing in Charmides, who is unwilling or unable to think for himself and to take rational responsibility for his own values; the latter, volitional aspect is not only conspicuously absent in Critias, but he displays its very opposite. For Critias is characterized by an attitude of mind that is deeply aversive to knowing its own cognitive limits and morally blind to the common good of reason and truth.

It is obvious that the Socratic ideal of rationality—of the "knowledge of knowledge and nonknowledge" as thus described— is not the would-be Critian science of rulership and unbridled self-certainty. If I am correct, however, Plato believed, and had reason to believe, that persistent involvement in Socratic dialectic might have profound consequences for the moral and rational formation of its practitioner. Out of the practice of dialectic might arise a quality of moral reflection and even moral commitment that would be both liberating and binding, freeing the interlocutor from the accidental and irrational arbitrariness of the values in which he had been raised—which would have taken the form of a particular contingent heteronomy—and directing him toward the values of universal reason implicit in the practice of inquiry. In that process, the person might choose to identify with those first-order desires that were consistent with the rational self, and reform his own self-understanding through a new process of self-determination. This is not to say that Plato believed, when he wrote the *Charmides*, that dialectic was the cure for all evils. It is evident that the dialectical therapy depends on the willingness of the patient to endure and persist in it—the patient must want to be cured and in some anticipatory manner must already be cured, in order to progress, and we may assume that experience of the limitations of other ways of living would play an important role in the protreptic to dialectic commitment. The life of the mind is a matter of choice and cognitive endurance, no less than rational insight, and the attraction to such choice and effort must arise from interpersonal, as well as intellectual involvements.[31] Moreover, it is evident from the scene involving Socrates and Charmides in the prologue that the commitment to truth must be applied in one's life as a whole, not only in those contexts in which it might be expected. This, too, calls for moral and cognitive practices of attention that extend beyond the confines of dialectic alone. But does seem clear from the *Charmides* that Plato believed, during the period of the early dialogues, that Socratic dialectic was instrinsically, causally related to the formation of a central human virtue, the virtue of Socratic *sophrosune*, introduced in quasi-mythological fashion in the prologue and then articulated, if somewhat ambiguously, at 167a1–7. On this view, the humanly virtuous person is morally centered in the principles embedded in dialectical inquiry. I am not arguing that Plato thought this virtue represented the totality of *arete*, but I am arguing that he thought, and had reason to think, that it was its distinctive and special form.

SOCRATIC RATIONALITY AND PLATONIC PSYCHOLOGY

The account I have given of Socratic dialectic has important implications for Platonic psychology. On the one hand, it is evident, by his representation of dialectic in the dialogues and in the *Charmides* in particular, that Plato did not conceive of moral knowledge in the Socratic sense as a purely cognitive achievement, but rather as a habit of choice no less than of reason. The state of mind indicated by the Socratic notion of moderation and self-knowledge, which in the *Apology* is called human wisdom, implies a moral, not merely intellectual practice, a value-formative, not simply concept-formative process, a volitional, not merely cognitive state. The fact that interlocutors so often choose to reject the development of their own rationality constitutes an anticipation, within the psychology of the dialectic, of the division between the rational and irrational parts of the soul, and of a dynamic model that regards the soul itself as a field of possible conflict. It is possible to choose moral knowledge, but also possible to reject it in favor of ego or appetite; and this fact—the fact of dialectical *akrasia*—requires a more complex conceptualization of human choice and decision-making than its reduction to simple intellectualism.

To interpret the understanding of the dialectic process as I have represented it here, we need to import two frameworks for the conceptualization of Plato's psychology. The first is the framework of the tripartite soul, as it is first explicitly developed in the *Republic*. On this model, the human being is motivationally and cognitively divided into three systemic components: (1) the rational or logical faculty (*to logistikon*); (2) the emotional/assertive faculty (*to thumoeides*), and (3) the appetitive faculty (*to epithumetikon*). The emotional faculty is particularly related to those emotions bearing on the well-being of the whole person, for example, shame and pride, aggression and fear. The appetitive faculty is oriented to the desires of the body, the impulse for pleasure and the aversion to pain. While this division of the self into three factors is not articulated in the argument of the *Charmides*, it is represented dramatically, in the persons of Socrates (reason), Critias (associated by Socrates with pride or ambition, *philotimia*, at 162c1–4, 169c6–d1), and Charmides (represented as the seductive object of appetitive sexual desire at 155c5–e2 and as a willful young beloved at 156a1–3).[32] In book IV of the *Republic*, when Socrates introduces this model, he suggests that the developing self always follows the guidance of the rational element, which there consists in a heteronomous authority (the laws of the just city). But in the later books of the *Republic* he acknowledges that it is possible for the emotional and appetitive elements in the self to overthrow the rule of law, and indeed that something like this is common in the worldly cities. What the *Charmides* has already shown us, in its depiction of Charmides' and Socrates' very different kinds of involvement in dialectical inquiry, and what it will show us clearly again in a later depiction of Critias' refusal of self-knowledge, is a pattern in which the self is conceived not merely in static terms, but in a model of dynamic self-relation, self-understanding, and self-determination. The elenchus is the dramatic theater in which Socrates' interlocutor is forced to make a choice concerning his own identity, to choose what kind of self he wants to be.

In addition to the above tripartite articulation, a second framework is needed to represent the complex psychology of the *Charmides*. This framework places the tripartite division within a larger pattern, concerned with the category of humanness as such. This framework involves four conceptions of the human being: (1) The first concept is *mind* (*psyche*), the totality of cognitive, emotive, and active potentiality and tendency subjectively encompassing the body as its vehicle. (2) The second is human being or *person* (*anthropos*), the objective social and legal entity in the world, whose identity is realized in the story of his life on the stage of the city and whose possibilities are shaped by the roles and expectations assigned to him by others. As is suggested in the dichotomy of these two categories in the prologue (156d8–157a3), from this point of view *psyche* does not contain, but is itself contained within the whole, albeit as its essential part. (3) A third category is the *self*, which corresponds to the Greek *autos* ("I") and may also translate as *psyche*. This is the notion of the human being specific to the dimension of self-reflection and self-determination.[33] This is the category of self-relation, of a practical-evaluative origin determining which impulses to follow and which beliefs to accept, who it is to be. (4) But it does not imply identification with the true self, the *rational self* and the values corresponding to it.

In the Platonic dialogues, *psyche* in the sense of self is the category of rational life relating distinctively to the possibility of autonomy and the formation of personal values. It is the "I" who is subjectively and objectively active, intentional and in the world, but who also—unlike mind and person—is necessarily self-relational, creatively present to herself in and through her acts and narrative of experience. It is the self who is the agent and subject of second-order intentions, the self who says "yes" or "no" to acts of thought and desire, and who confirms or denies to them the warrant of responsible valuation.[34] Thus in the prologue Socrates was in danger of losing neither his mind, nor his person, but his chosen self—his rational self, the valuational identity he knew and wished to be; but as he persevered in the *logos*, and Charmides accepted him in that action, he was "rekindled to life," that is, reintegrated with his chosen identity. Similarly, in the course of their elenctic conversations with Socrates, Charmides and Critias are given the opportunity to reveal their selves and to determine the values that will morally shape those selves in the future. As we have seen, this is a distinctive power of Socratic dialectic, to open the possibility of self-reflection and new self-direction, above all to allow the interlocutor to refashion his self-understanding and very identity through the values of rational discourse. The rational person on the Socratic model is not merely committed to attaining her ends and preferences, but to holding those ends and preferences up to rational consideration, and to revising them in the light of compelling reasons. When the I is reformed through the mediation of universal reason, the result is Socratic *sophrosune*—the commitment to critical rationality and philosophy—which from the point of view of the *Charmides* is the human analogue of wisdom and virtue. When the self is determined through other values, such as the preference of honor or victory over truth, or the preference for safety and reliance on the rational authority of another, the result is still a product of self-determination, still a self. But it is then also, in Plato's eyes, a diminished, superficial being—a being for whom self-deception and willful ignorance or moral submissiveness blur the openness of vision to truth and inhibit participation in the deliberative community of mutual concern that rational people can enjoy. It is a self that, when confronted by the power of Socratic dialectic, proves to be out of harmony with its deeper self, proves to be unstable, inconstant, self-alienated.

Thus understood, the self is not alone. She exists essentially in relation to others, through the practice of dialogue, and she knows herself—or may come to know herself—in and through such dialogue. That even conventional self-knowledge is social is evident both in the case of Charmides, whose self-image has been formed by his uncle/guardian Critias and the many suitors who have inflated his view of himself, and in the case of Critias, who appears so driven to find confirmation of his own sense of superiority from the others present and especially from Socrates. And it is true of Socratic, rational self-knowledge also. His mode of self-knowledge is not monological. His identity is formed and reformed in the space of his conversations, in his pursuit of goodness and wisdom in the communal practice of dialogue. But for Socrates, the relation to others is not merely one in which his self-image is mirrored or denied; it is rather one in which the potentially autonomous mutual relation to reason and truth is the crucial element. He hopes that his partner will enjoy the same relation to the good of truth and the community of inquiry as he does, and he acts in such a way as to test and deepen that mutual involvement.[35]

The category of selfhood introduces a dynamic, self- and other-relational element to the idea of human being. This element is not captured by the category of mind, or person, or reason. But the self, in one respect both artist and ongoing product of her own choices and actions, is an inclusive category of human reality—if it is not separated from the categories of reason and the other, partner in the quest for the good. The *Charmides* shows that a self can be stunted in its relation to one's own and others' rationality. Thus both Charmides and Critias fail to attain an enlightened self-relation due to their rejections of the light in which such self-relation is attained, the light of universal reason and the community-forming good of truth. Charmides' selfhood is bound up in a relation of heterarchy; he exists, but he is still morally contained within his guardian's domineering will, the will of a future tyrant. Critias's selfhood is not dependent in the same manner; but his self/other relations are mediated entirely by the struggle for recognition, rather than by reason, friendship, and truth. Consequently, his mode of being in the world—like that of Hippias and anyone who does not engage in critical self-reflection—is two-dimensional. There is Critias and there are the others, separate selves in competition (the evil belongs to them, the good is "his own"). When they acknowledge his superiority and reflect back to him the self he wishes to see, all is superficially well, but when they do not, he is displaced, dislocated, and he can do nothing more than reassert his identity, seeking to impose it by rhetoric, insistence, or force (by *mere* "poetry").

Socrates' mode of being, by way of contrast to Critias and most all of his interlocutors, is genuinely three-dimensional, for his relation to himself and to other selves is mediated by the common relation they all have to universal reason and the good of truth. In his life, but not in the lives of Critias (or the others), there is "somebody home," an inner voice of reason that he engages in the dialogue of moral thought, and this dialogue has implications not only for how Socrates views himself, but also how he views others. Critias either is what he takes himself to be, or he is not, and his relation to the other is purely instrumental: the other will or will not affirm his self-conception, his good, his pride. But Socrates' mode of being is more complex, for he must, in dialectical quest with the other, rationally examine and redetermine what he takes himself to be, while aiming at a good he believes will complete them both. "Are we to examine this position also, to see if it is sound?" Socrates asks Euthyphro, who would be only too happy to accept it on his own authority. "Or shall we let it through, and thus accept our own and other's statement, and agree to an assertion simply when somebody says that a thing is so? Must we not *examine* what the speaker says?" (*Euthyphro* 9e, my italics). Socrates is sincere when he implies that he is committed to examining his own no less than Euthyphro's statements, for he projects for his interlocutor, no less than for himself, the same objective concern: they are to be partners and friends in the quest for truth. The irony lies not in Socrates' unwillingness that his partner fulfill this role, but in his realization, based on what he already knows of him, that he will almost certainly fail to do so (cf. *Euthyphro* 3b–c, 5a–b). Nonetheless, Socrates attributes to Euthyphro, Charmides, Critias, Meno, Nicias, Polymarchus, Lysis, and Menexenus and all the others the same valuational self-relation he attributes to himself: the other is also, on his view, a (potentially) three-dimensional being, existing in a free but teleological relation to his own rationality and well-being. Socratic dialectical rationality may seem coercive to the interlocutor who is the subject of refutation, but in truth it embodies democratic, political values, insofar as it involves its practitioners in the ideals of self- and other-respect, ideals of fairness and friendship.[36]

I have argued in this chapter that the *Charmides* provides an especially valuable perspective on the multidimensionality of Socratic dialectic and on Socrates' place in ancient Greek cultural life. Far from being a mere "despotic logician" (Nietzsche), Socrates is better understood as the logotherapist of the two chief illnesses of the Athenian mind—the psychic diseases of moral heteronomy and thoughtlessness, on the one hand, and of Sophistry and self-conceit, on the other. The elenchus was the medicine by which Socrates sought to lead his interlocutors into the world of moral autonomy, social responsibility, and critical reason, but this cure could not function without the willing cooperation of the dialectical partner—a cooperation and commitment virtually none of his interlocutors in the aporetic dialogues will offer (the chief exception, of course, is Theaetetus). If the interpretation I have offered is correct, we can understand why the early Plato might have embraced, but insisted on a reinterpretation of the notion that "Virtue is knowledge," and also why he would have agreed that virtue cannot be "taught," at least not by means of mere instruction. The definition of *sophrosune* and the ideal of rationality to which the first part of the dialectic in the *Charmides* ascends, and which has Plato's Socrates as its perfect representative, does not presuppose a simple intellectualism; moral knowledge, on the model it suggests, is an achievement of dialectical practice, and this practice requires courage, humility before the truth, and a sense of solidarity with the other participants. The *sophron* individual described by Socrates and Critias is morally centered in the social practice of critical reason.

The account of Socratic rationality offered here also has important implications for the conceptualization of Platonic psychology. The characteristic, but widely ignored fact of dialectical *akrasia* in the dialogues requires a more complex way of conceiving the human being than is generally found in the scholarly literature on Plato's early psychology. Neither the category of mind nor the category of person nor that of reason will suffice. It is also necessary to import the category of the self, with its reflexive dimensions of self-articulation, self-examination and self-determination. In the next segment of the dialogue, Socrates will discuss the metaphysical implications of this concept, as he presses Critias to be clearer about his notion of a knowledge that knows itself and the other knowledges. Socrates will argue that it is not obvious that such a thing is even possible, much less beneficial. These arguments drive Critias to the point where he could acknowledge his perplexity and make a new start in the inquiry and in his life. As I have already indicated, however, he chooses not to do so. Self-knowledge is something that can be accepted, or pushed away, and this decision has moral implications. But how is it possible for a human being to prefer not to know himself?

FIVE

⊶◇⊷

METAPHYSICS

The great service of Socrates to humanity was in suggesting to Plato certain doctrines as to the nature of the soul and ideas—doctrines which in spite of their impracticality have served for over two thousand years to raise men above the groveling, clawing existence in which so much of our life is sunk.

—Morris Cohen

Having arrived, with Critias, at a definition of *sophrosune*, Socrates turns in the second part of their inquiry to examine it. This examination comprises three phases, though he describes it as two: (1) the investigation of the possibility of knowing what one knows and does not know, discussed from 167a8–169d2; and (2) the further investigation, if such self-knowledge is possible, of what benefit there would be in possessing it. This latter question is examined in two phases or sections, (a) the first concerning whether it is really only possible to know *that* you know or do not know, and what benefit that would bring, discussed from 169d3–172c3; (b) the second concerning whether, even if you can know *what* you know and do not know, such an ability is truly beneficial, discussed from 172c4–175b4. At the end of the second discussion, Socrates concludes that they have not been able to discover what *sophrosune* is.

As I suggested earlier, the dialogue reaches a peak with the definition at 167a1–7, and the rest is a descent.[1] The basic insight of the *Charmides* is that Socratic wisdom is at its core neither a technical-productive nor theoretical-objective form of knowledge, but a form of self-knowledge, a volitional habit of rationality that both sustains and helps create moral autonomy and community. But the examination Socrates conducts in the second part of the inquiry is fascinating and perplexing. It considers the ideal of a "knowledge of knowledge" in relation to its metaphysical, epistemological, and ethical implications. In each of these respects, the argument, as Socrates later will point out, will prove their idea wanting. It will appear that no clear account can be given of the metaphysical implications of the notion; that the ideal is epistemologically confused; and that it is at any rate morally irrelevant, in the absence, or presence, of moral knowledge. So the discussion ends in *aporia*.

I will argue that this conclusion is misleading, and that Plato intends for the reader to find a positive message in the dialogue. This message is largely conveyed by the drama of the work, and in the way in which that drama is intended to contextualize and reflect back on the argument. Rather than demonstrating the metaphysical impossibility of self-knowledge, the *Charmides* reveals its metaphysical implications; rather than proving that the knowledge of what you know and do not know is impossible, the dialogue suggests a epistemological model that makes it conceivable; rather than rejecting the relevance of what you know and do not know for moral guidance, the dialogue shows how the lack of such self-knowledge exposes one to morally disastrous consequences, and how the ideal of inquiry may offer a model for human relationships in general.

These suggestions fly in the face of the overt arguments. Why would Plato choose such an indirect way to represent his positions? How could one determine whether or not these conclusions were justified?

There are two keys, I shall argue, formal and substantive, to understanding the second part of Socrates' inquiry with Critias in the *Charmides*. The first, formal key is the hermeneutic principle I have emphasized throughout, the necessity of relating the argument to the dramatic context. The reader is meant to discover that the dialogue relates itself to itself, speech to action, in a manner analogous to what Socrates is calling into question. Every Platonic dialogue is made in this way, made to become self-reflective through the responsive efforts of the reader, who must complete the text by using its deeds (*erga*) as a check on what is set forth in its speeches (*logoi*). The process of reader-response then reopens the text; it raises doubts concerning apparent conclusions, and suggests alternative possibilities.[2] This literary quality is most clearly present in the early, especially aporetic dialogues, where, despite the surface arguments that trade on ambiguity, the dialogues often suggest a positive teaching. Socrates, speaking for Plato, pedagogically withdraws from such affirmation—but he leaves it open to the reader to discover it and subtly points them toward it.

The second, substantive key to the interpretation of the *Charmides* concerns the distinction established earlier between the two different ideals of self-knowledge in the work, the conceptions which reflect the views of the two interlocutors, Critias and Socrates, respectively. Dramatically, Socrates is testing Critias' understanding of *sophrosune*, and he will find it grievously wanting. Critias and his sophistic notion of *sophrosune* as self-certain rule will be refuted. But as we saw in the last chapter, the *logos* also exhibits a different ideal of *sophrosune*, the Socratic ideal of morally reflective rationality. This conception will not be refuted. Indeed, the *Charmides* will suggest that this ideal is essential to human moral and political well-being.

By depersonalizing the inquiry at 166c7–e2, Socrates was able to calm his volatile interlocutor, avoid the charge of eristic, and secure Critias' agreement to an account of *sophrosune* reflecting Socrates' own, dialectical conception of self-knowledge, rather than the Critian ideal of a self-certain art of rule. Socrates is content to begin the second phase of the inquiry with Critias (the third phase of the inquiry as a whole) in the same manner: they are now investigating together; he and Critias are a team. But he abandons this neutral perspective in a moment, and makes the dialectic personal again, driving Critias to a conclusion that confronts him with his own perplexity. At that point Critias will reveal in deed both what he cannot comprehend in speech and why he cannot comprehend it. The interplay of speech and deed, *logos* and *ergon*, is the key to the interpretation of the next section of the dialogue (167a8–169d2), but most commentators, having failed to see this point, have also failed to understand it.[3]

Socrates begins by suggesting that they investigate as if from the beginning, and seek to determine whether *sophrosune* as they have defined it (1) is possible; and next, if it is possible, (2) if it is beneficial to them. But Socrates immediately shifts to Critias' conception of the idea, saying that if what he, Critias, was just now saying were true, then there would be *one* knowledge, a knowledge of itself and of other knowledges and also in particular a knowledge of non-knowledge as well; but he, Socrates, is perplexed by the strangeness of what they are saying, and he thinks it will seem impossible to Critias, if he investigates it in other things (167a8–c7).

What is Socrates' problem in this passage? Does it have to do with the idea of a "knowledge of what one knows and does not know"? Or does it have to do with the attempt to unify the knowledge of itself and other knowledges with the knowledge of knowledge and nonknowledge? As we have seen and will see more fully later on, these two notions, insofar as they are associated with Critias and Socrates respectively, are incompatible. Or is the problem on the personal level, having to do with *Critias'* inability to relate these two aspects of the ideal of *sophrosune*, or with Critias' inability to make sense of it in comparison to other things?

Socrates sets out to develop his argument in several stages:

1. First he surveys a series of mental acts and ostensibly shows that none of these fit the model of knowledge of itself and of other knowledges and also of nonknowledge (167c8–168b1).
2. Then he introduces the discussion of quantitative relations, and shows that like mental acts, these too do not appear to allow for the possibility of something that is related to itself and to others in such a way as to have the same power to itself as it has to others (168b2–d3).
3. Summarizing the entire argument, he concludes that it raises an ontological puzzle, namely that whereas in some things it is clearly impossible that something should have its own power with regard to itself, in other things some might not believe it, but others would; so in any case "some great man" is needed who could make this distinction and explain it all clearly, and thus also explain how the knowledge that he and Critias call *sophrosune* (a knowledge that does possess a self-relational power) is possible (168d3–169a7).
4. He ends by stating that *he*, Socrates, cannot trust himself to affirm one way or another whether there is a knowledge of knowledge, and besides even if it were he would still not be willing to accept that it was moderation before investigating if it were beneficial. So he calls on Critias, son of Callaeschrus ("the Beautiful-Ugly"), to demonstrate that it is possible and beneficial, and Critias must respond.[4] It is at this point that Critias's claim to knowledge and virtue comes to a crisis (169a7–d1).

I will try to show in this chapter that the crisis Critias is made to face reflects again the important thesis we have already seen at work in the dialogue, namely that self-knowledge is a function of moral choice, as well as rational insight. The reader will misunderstand the arguments leading up to it, however, unless she also realizes what I have emphasized concerning the reader-response structure of the dialogue, namely, the fact that the *Charmides* relates reflectively and critically to itself, speech to action, in a manner analogous to what Socrates is calling into question. Socrates, speaking for Plato, pedagogically withdraws from affirming the reality of self-knowledge—but he leaves it open for us both to discover it and to reflect on its wide-ranging metaphysical and psychological implications.

SELF-RELATION AND MENTAL ACTS (167c8–168b1)

The first part of Socrates' argument is deceptively simple. He surveys nine separate mental or psychic acts, and throughout seems to show that these do not conform to the pattern of a mental act that is an act of itself and other mental acts, and of nonacts. Thus:

1. There is not in Critias' opinion a seeing (*opsis*, 167c8) that is a seeing of itself and of the other seeings, and of nonseeing.
2. There does not seem to be a hearing (*akoen*, 167d4) that hears no sound, but hears itself and the other hearings and nonhearings.
3. In sum, there is not in his opinion a kind of perception (*aesthesis*, 167d8) of perceptions and of itself that perceives nothing of what the other perceptions perceive.
4. There also is not in his opinion a kind of desire (*epithumia*, 167e1) that is a desire of no pleasure but is of itself and the other desires.
5. Nor is there a wish (*boulesis*, 167e4) that wishes nothing good, but wishes itself and the other wishes.
6. And he would not assert there is a kind of love (*eros*, 167e8) that happens to be a love of nothing beautiful, but is of itself and the other loves.
7. Critias has never noticed a kind of fear (*phobon tina*, 167e10) that fears itself and the other fears, but does not fear the terrible things.
8. Nor an opinion (*doxan*, 168a3) that is of opinions and of itself, but opines nothing of what the others opine.
9. And yet they assert there is a kind of knowledge (*epistemen*, 168a6) that is of nothing learned, but is of itself and the other knowledges.

Socrates does not think they should yet affirm "strongly" (*diis-churizometha*, cf. 153b9, 160c2) that this does not exist, but wants to investigate it further.

This list of mental acts is interesting in several respects, including the specification of objects in the case of desire (pleasure), wish (good), and love (beauty), but the key to making sense of it is the fact that it breaks up into three groups of three.[5] The first group is concerned with perception, the second with desire, while the third is a mixture of cognition and emotion. Of the three, the first group is immediately puzzling as evidence for Socrates' perplexity, if only because it suggests the phenomenon of self-consciousness, the fact that perception (if not sensation) involves the awareness that we perceive. Thus the faculty of perception, whether of sight or hearing, does seem to be of itself in some respect, even if it is not of a color or a sound.[6] The connection among the second group is not brought out as clearly, but an important contrast is made in the early dialogues between desire (*epithumia*), as a simple act of mind, and wish or rational desire (*boulesis*).[7] The category of *boulesis*, with its relation to the good, pertains to the rational life, and to the Socratic principles that the rational agent seeks to attain her own perceived good, and more fundamentally her own real good (cf. esp. *Gorgias* 466d–468e).[8] Again Socrates' example might seem to suggest that a mental act can somehow be of itself, in the sense that rational choice involves an evaluative relation to itself and to other acts or nonacts. But in the case of the third group, there is no obvious connection to be made at all. Thus it does seem strange, offhand, that there might be a knowledge that was of itself and other knowledges and nonknowledges. Some mental acts would appear to support the possibility, others to deny it.

The meaning of Socrates' examples changes entirely, however, as soon as they are dramatically contextualized, for the three groupings correspond perspicuously to three events that have occurred already in the dialogue:

1. Socrates alone, as we noted earlier, was aware not only of his own feelings in viewing Charmides when the young man entered the gymnasium, but also of the others' viewings of him, and of the absence of any nonviewing of him:

   He appeared wondrous to me in both stature and beauty, and indeed, at least in my opinion, all the others were in love with him, so confused and excited had they become as he

> came in. . . . Nor was this wondrous on the part of us men;
> but turning my attention to the boys, I noticed that none of
> them, not even the littlest, looked anywhere else, but all
> were contemplating him as if he were a statue. (154b10–c8)

Unlike the others, however, whose sight was purely directed to
the perceptual object before them, Socrates, as we know from the
subsequent conversation with Chairophon, brought a moral perspective on the scene, and thus he did not attend solely to the
boy's body, but was able to remain emotionally self-attentive in
that situation, knowledgeable not only of what he was knowing
(the beauty of form he was seeing) and of what the others were
knowing (the beauty of form they were seeing), but also of what
he was not knowing (the beauty of soul he was not seeing). It
might seem no less impossible to the reader than it does to
Critias that there could be a perception of itself and of other perceptions and of nonperception, if we did not notice that precisely
such a perception has already occurred—if the events of the dialogue had not *demonstrated* the reality of what the arguments
called into question. But Critias, perhaps because he has not
experienced such self-perception, has no answer to Socrates.

2. The second group of mental acts stands in an even more obvious
   relation to a crucial event in the dialogue, Socrates' act of self-
   control after he had inadvertently seen inside Charmides' cloak.
   We recall:

> I saw inside his cloak. I was inflamed, I was no longer in
> control of myself, and I held Cydias to be the wisest in
> erotic matters, who, speaking about a beautiful boy, advised
> someone that "a fawn coming opposite a lion should
> beware lest he be taken as a portion of meat." I myself
> seemed to myself to have been caught by such a creature.
> Nevertheless, when he asked me if I had knowledge of the
> drug for the head, with difficulty I somehow answered that
> I had knowledge of it. (155d3–e3)

I discussed this event in detail in the first chapter, and I refer the
reader back to that discussion. The decisive fact is that Socrates
here appears to be threatened, if momentarily, by desire (*epithumia*), but he does not allow himself to act on that desire, and in
fact he implies that so long as he is possessed by it, he is not himself. What may be regarded as Socrates' second act of self-restraint
at the beginning of the dialogue again displays a vivid example of

someone whose second-order desire (his will or rational choice) exercises control over his first-order desires, and in this instance prevents himself from acting on a first-order desire, so as to make it into a nondesire.[9] It is a desire of itself (of wisdom and his epistemic self) and of other desires (impulses he choses to act on) and of nondesires (impulses he choses not to act on, as not belonging to him). Again the action of the dialogue makes apparent to us what the argument cannot: that a self-relational structure of desire—the structure of rational desire—*is* possible. But again Critias, perhaps because he has not experienced the self-restraint belonging to such desire, has no answer to the argument.

3. Finally, the third group of mental acts also points very clearly back to something Socrates did earlier (which was also discussed at some length in that context):

> "What a thing you are doing!" I said, "by believing, even if I do refute you, that I am refuting for the sake of anything other than that for the sake of which I would also search through myself as to what I say, *fearing that unawares I might ever suppose that I know something when I don't know.* So I do assert that this is what I am also doing now: investigating the argument most of all for the sake of myself, but perhaps also for my other companions. Or don't you suppose that it is a common good for almost all human beings that each thing that exists should become clearly apparent just as it is?" (166c7–d6, my italics)

Critias—though supposedly a student of Socrates—has failed ever to notice the kind of fear Socrates has, which is not a fear of things that are known to be terrible, but of *not fearing* out of ignorance of what is truly fearful; nor does Critias have an opinion, after the manner of his supposed teacher, concerning the status of his own opinions—namely, that they might be nothing more than opinions—because, again unlike his "teacher," he does not fear that. Critias merely holds his opinions and does not suppose that he is confusing them with knowledge. But in truth Critias does have an opinion about his opinions (his thoughts), he just does not know it: the opinion he holds regarding his opinions is, as we learned in chapter 3, one of epistemic dogmatism ("all of my opinions are knowledge"). This is the very opinion Socrates will never hold, out of his moral fear that he is not fearful of the very thing he should be fearful of.

The fearful relation Socrates holds to his own and others' moral opinions ("these opinions may not be knowledge") is a kind of self- and other-knowledge, indeed the principle of his dialectical practice, though it is not the knowledge of a mathematical or technical object (like the kinds and relations of numbers, or how to build private and public buildings). This self-critical relation would also provide the basis for knowledge of one's moral principles (of their commanding, but dialectical status), in comparison to the other knowledges (the *technai*). These conclusions are not evident from the argument, but they emerge if the argument is completed by the drama of the dialogue—which it is the reader's job to carry out.

SELF-RELATION AND
QUANTITATIVE RELATIONS (168b2–d3)

The second phase in Socrates' discussion of the possibility of self-knowledge, dealing with quantitative relations, also bears critical reflection.[10] Socrates points out that in the case of quantitative relations, such as the relation "greater than," that which has the power to be greater is greater than something, and that in relation to which it has this power must be something lesser. Therefore there cannot be anything concerning which this relation can be applied to itself:

> So if we should discover something greater that is greater than the greater things and than itself, but is not greater than any of the things that the other things are greater than, then surely it would altogether be in the situation that if it was greater than itself it would also be less than itself, wouldn't it? (168b10–c2)

"Most necessarily," Critias answers. Socrates gives a similar argument as regards the numerical quantitative relation "the double of": if there were a kind of double that was of itself and of others, it would have to be the double of itself, but then also be half of itself, which is absurd. And the same reasoning applies to what is more than itself having to be less than itself, if things stood in relationship to themselves in this manner, and what was heavier would also have to be lighter, and what was older, younger. Socrates draws from this the following ontological conclusion: Then "whatever has its own power (*dunamis*) in relation to itself will also have that being (*ousia*) with regard to which it has the power" (168d1–3). The problem is that whatever stands in such a self-relation seems not to possess a firm identity, since it seems to be both the thing that is still in potency and the thing in which the potency is realized (the being or essence, *ousia*). But how can the same thing exist both in potency and in realization?

Before examining this priniciple further and relating it to the concept of the self, I want to note that there is something perplexing about this argument. It appears to be straightforward and evidently true: whereas the kind of self-relation Socrates has in mind may be possible in the case of the mental or soul-relations just discussed, here in the case of quantitative relations it seems to be truly impossible. At any rate, it is easy to show that an x which was greater than itself or the double ($2x$) of itself would also have to be less than itself or one half of itself ($1/2x$) and that this is logically absurd. What is intriguing, however—and certainly relevant to the question of prolepsis in this dialogue—is whether Socrates might be alluding here to the concept of a Form and to relations among the Forms.[11] Notice the phrasing: a "something greater" (e.g., the Great?) that is of/greater than the greater things (which participate in it) and of/than itself (the self-relation of the Form); a "kind of double" (e.g., the Two?) that is of the other doubles (the participation of all twos in the Form) and of itself (the self-relation of the Form). But while these relations are absurd on the level of things, the later Plato does not think they are absurd on the level of the Forms. For on the level of the Form, Greatness and Smallness have their powers of exceeding and being exceeded by only in relation to themselves, but the things that are ontically greater and smaller have their powers in relation to one another because of their ontological methexis relation to the Great and the Small.[12] As regards the Two, it does not correspond to the mathematical double of logistic, but to a far more comprehensive domain, inclusive even of Forms.[13]

The ontological conclusions that Socrates seems to want to draw here against the possibility of anything existing in relation to itself will clearly have to be abandoned, if Plato is later to affirm the self-relation of the Forms. A metaphysics that denies the possibility of self-relation is a metaphysics of beings that conform to purely quantitative relations. Plato's rejection of such a metaphysics is anticipated in the *Charmides*, by his implicit affirmation of self-relational beings. Neither rational selves nor Ideas conform to a world composed simply of objects and their relations.

APPERCEPTIVE SEEING AND HEARING (168d3–e2)

Having arrived at his general ontological principle, Socrates now attempts to apply it to the mental acts of hearing and seeing once again. Hearing, Socrates insists, must be of a sound, and therefore if it is going to hear itself, it must have a sound of its own. "Most necessarily," Critias says. And the same with that which sees itself, it too must have a color, and Critias again agrees. He continues:

> So you see (*horas*), Critias, that of the things we have gone through, some of them appear altogether impossible to us, while we vigorously distrust that the others would ever have their own power with regard to themselves. (168e3–5)

But what Socrates has said in the latter part of this sentence is qualified by what he let slip at the beginning: "So you *see*, Critias . . ." This is not the first time Socrates has used a word for sight in this manner. He did so also in characterizing his puzzle: "See (*ide*) what a strange thing we are attempting to say . . ." (167c4), and he will use it again at the end of the section, when he says that "When Critias heard this and saw (*idon*) me in perplexity, then . . ." (169c3).

Thus this whole part of the inquiry with Critias is framed and marked at its center with the metaphorical usage of what it means to "see," characterized by the usage corresponding to apperception.[14] What Socrates actually means therefore is something like this: "So you *realize*, Critias, if you understand what I am saying, what you should realize: seeing and hearing are no mere acts of sensation directed to sound and color, but are involved in acts of mind directed toward the meaning and truth of one's own and others' arguments and toward the moral knowledge of one's own and others' souls." If Critias cared about these things, he would be thinking himself about them, he would have a "sound of his own" concerning them. But then he would appreciate that he was himself, in the act of caring and understanding, applying his own rational power with regard to itself, trying to be sure that he understood what he understood in the doubling act of mind that is self-critical understanding.[15] Moreover, even if he does not understand he might still achieve this kind of reflexivity, if he were to take a critical perspective on what he has said and, listening critically to the sound he has made, were to realize that he is "saying nothing." The discovery that you do not know would also confirm the possibility of self-relational being. But here again, and decisively in just a moment, Critias seems incapable of affirming the possibility of self-relational cognitive being, for the simple reason that he is not willing to experience it.

THE FUTURE OF THE ARGUMENT (168e3–169a7)

Now let us return to Socrates' ontological principle and see what he makes of it in relation to the distinction he has introduced between those kinds of things that cannot exist in self-relation, and those beings that might be able to. Having noted such self-relation is impossible with respect to sizes and quantities (168e5–7), he notes that in relation to hearing and seeing (acts of mind), and also in relation to a "motion moving itself" and "a heat kindling" and all such things, while some may distrust its possibility, others might not, so that a "great man" (Plato?) is needed to draw this distinction:

> Whether none of the things that are has itself by nature its own power with regard to itself, or whether some have it and others don't; and again, if there are some things that themselves have it with regard to themselves, whether among them is a knowledge that we assert is *sophrosune*. (169a3–7)

This idea will seem incredible to some, Socrates admits, but perhaps not so to others.

The passage from 168e3–169a7 is pregnant with significance for Plato's future metaphysics and epistemology.[16] Let me just make four observations:

1. First, Socrates characterizes the attitude one initially takes to such a possibility as that of trust or mistrust. Trust (*pistis*) is one of the terms used in relation to the Divided Line in the *Republic*.[17] There it is the second level of cognitive being, the level associated with perception and unexamined experience, with "appearances" in the sense that includes not only perceptual observations but commonsense beliefs or what generally are taken to be facts. Socrates' assignment of this crucial distinction to the realm of trust indicates that he believes that here again there is a fundamental division to be drawn among people

between those who can and those who cannot appreciate a principle (compare *Crito* 49d). Some people are going to be epistemically closed to the metaphysical distinction in question, but "certain others" are going to be open to it, and the basis for this open- or closed-mindedness is experiential. This point will soon be confirmed dramatically.

2. Second, Plato has made it evident that the logic of objective, mathematical relations will not provide a metaphysics that can account for self-relational being. The mathematical notion of identity is one-dimensional; it does not and cannot conceptually reflect beings whose identities are complex and self-relational. The "doubled" reality of cognitive life—a doubled reality Socrates may now be extending to nature in the forms of self-moving motion and self-kindling heat—does not fit the categorial frame of quantitative relations. This point is relevant to the Line also, for its highest level, we recall, is not that of mathematical thought, but of a kind of thinking that continually recurs to problem of reflexivity, for example, of things and their shadows, even at the level of intellect.[18]

3. Third, Plato has also made it clear that this distinction is fundamental to the metaphysics of the *Charmides*, in which the realm of being apparently is divided into (1) a world of things or entities adequately characterized by the mathematical logic of objective relations and closely associated with the realm of ordinary sense-perception; and (2) another kind of being, which is somehow self-effective in its nature and which does not fit into the categorization of the first kind of being. This second realm, of self-relational existence, is closely associated with reflective thought, on the one hand, and with self-motion, on the other—it is the realm of being associated by Socrates in his discussion of the worldview of the Thracian physicians with the realm of *psyche* and the relation of human being to the Whole (156d6–e6).

Let me add here another point that may be of great significance for understanding Plato's psychology in the later, especially middle dialogues: he clearly recognizes here in the *Charmides* that the category of soul cannot be reified, but that its conceptualization is deeply at odds with the world of "trust," at least as that world is generally experienced (or at least as it is experienced by everyone who cannot appreciate the possibility of a hearing that listens to its own sounds, or a motion that moves—or refrains from moving—itself). T. M. Robinson, in his authoritative *Plato's Psychology*, notes that the *Charmides* "suggests a fruitful and sophisticated approach to the problem of soul and body," but he goes on to claim that Plato failed to appreciate its implications or rejected them, in favor of a radically dualistic theory.[19] I suggest this alternative: the *Charmides* shows that Plato understood early on, but in a proleptic, anticipatory manner, the metaphysical, epistemological, and linguistic problems involved in the articulation of this philosophical problem; and he did not abandon this insight, but we should try to read the later dialogues, even the *Phaedo*, in the light of his discoveries here. Then the metaphysics and psychology of the later works will never be confused with any form of Cartesian dualism, and it will be understood that Plato's metaphysics and psychology of the soul is at least as difficult to comprehend, and perhaps for similar reasons, as his theory of the Forms.

4. Finally, Socrates' addition of a "self-moving motion" and of a "heat that kindles itself" reminds us of the fact that he had earlier characterized his own act of rational self-restraint, his act of *sophrosune* with respect to his impulse of *epithumia* toward Charmides, as one in which he, Socrates, was "rekindled to life" (156d2–3). We saw that in that context this meant he had reunited himself emotionally and cognitively with the person, Socrates, who lived in the life of the mind, the life of rational inquiry in community with other souls who shared or might share in the same good. We saw there that it was in virtue of his second-order desire, his self-motion in not moving one way, but in moving in another, that he was able to reintegrate with his own rational identity and love of wisdom—and with his deeper erotic relation, through the concern for wisdom, to others. Thus the words "a heat that kindles itself" have a basis in the action of the dialogue, and the reader is once again put in a position to complete or go beyond the mere argument by referring the one to the other, and to be the means by which the dialogue becomes itself self-relational, so as to confirm the evidence of Socrates' narrative: rational, self-relational being exists. But note that both in relation to the reality associated with this new phrase and in relation to acts of apperception, the critical evidence for the reality of self-relational being is provided by moral and cognitive acts of moderation. In other words, the experiential ground for recognition of the self-relational reality of *psyche* is found in dialectical insight and self-restraint in the interests of the good.

It is through such acts of sophrosune, *oriented by the love of wisdom, that the "doubled metaphysical world" of the* Charmides *comes into view.* Indeed, it is through virtue that metaphysics itself becomes relevant, because prior to such acts the world is naturally assumed to conform to the quantitative logic of objective, perceptual relations and there is no possibility of changing one's intentional relation to the world. Thus the metaphysics of the *Charmides* is a "metaphysics of moderation" or "metaphysics of virtue" for the simple reason that the crucial self-relation of human being lies in the discovery of its potentiality for such virtue and rational self-fulfillment.[20]

The interpretation I have offered of this part of the *Charmides* has important consequences for our view of Plato's work as a whole. For one thing, it is apparent that Plato was conscious from a relatively early point in his career of the epistemological and language-philosophical problems associated with the categorization of human being, and of the very different framework of thought it seemed to call for in contrast to the positivist framework of perception and objective, mathematical relations. For another, it would seem he was also aware early on of a close relationship between ethics, metaphysics, and epistemology. Insights concerning metaphysical possibility are shown to rest on intellectual experiences that have a moral, self-formative dimension, and morality is shown, correspondingly, to be in part a function of intellectual effort. There is a mutual dependency, reciprocity, and complexity to the cognitive, moral, and psychological world of the *Charmides* that goes beyond what we would expect in any ancient philosopher, even Plato, and certainly beyond what we would expect in an early dialogue.[21]

SOCRATES' WITNESS (169a8–d1)

Having seen all this, we are now able to understand the implications of the last step in this part of the dialogue. For the whole structure of the argument clearly depends, if my interpretation is correct, on the principle that the virtue of self-knowledge is a function of choice as well as rational insight, and that successful elenctic inquiry operates through insights that correlate with such choices and refer to the experiences they invoke. Again, the overall characterization of the Socratic elenchus is determined by the fact that it is not merely addressed to the interlocutor's words, to "propositions" (*logoi*), but to his beliefs, to the quality of his thought, and indeed to his whole life (see chapter 4). This personal aspect of the elenchus is so primary, that Socrates believes that if he can catch hold of his interlocutor's convictions, then even in the face of contradiction by a thousand witnesses, he may refute him and in refuting, catch him up in the life of *paideia* that he lives in himself:

> If I cannot produce in you yourself a single witness in agree-
> ment with my views, I consider that I have accomplished
> nothing worth speaking of in the matter under debate; and the
> same, I think, is true for you also, if I, one solitary witness, do
> not testify for you and if you do not leave all these others out
> of account. (*Gorgias* 472b)

Mutual self-criticism and epistemic integrity, not other-directed persuasion and common opinion, comprise the courtroom for Socratic truth.

So here, with Critias, Socrates will attempt to produce such a witness. He begins by confessing that he does not "trust himself" to be able to draw the metaphysical distinctions in question, and that he therefore also cannot "strongly" affirm whether it is possi-ble for there to be a "knowledge of knowledge" (this phrase being neutral between the Socratic and Critian concepts of self-knowl-edge); and he cannot, if it is possible, accept that it is *sophrosune*, until he has investigated whether such a thing would be beneficial or not. (Critias, in a mistake shared with many commentators, apparently does not realize that Socrates has not ruled out the pos-sibility that he might, after such investigation, come to the con-clusion that it was possible, and was beneficial; he has only ruled out the notion that he should "trust himself" to form an opinion about this matter *without* such investigation—that is, in the man-ner that Critias apparently has done.[22]) Having characterized his own cognitive attitude toward the possibility in this ambiguous manner, Socrates then turns the full, personal power of the elenchus on Critias, demanding that since *he*, Critias, affirms that *sophrosune* is a knowledge of knowledge and particularly of non-knowledge (recall this was Socrates' emphasis, not that of Critias!), it should be possible for him to demonstrate what Socrates was say-ing. Will Critias demonstrate that the kind of self-relational being involved in the knowledge of knowledge or most particularly in the knowledge of nonknowledge is indeed possible?

He will not:

> When Critias heard this and saw me in perplexity, then, just as those who see people yawning right across from them have the same happen to them, so he too in my opinion was compelled by my perplexity and was caught by perplexity himself. Now since he is well-reputed on every occasion, he was ashamed before those present, and he was neither willing to concede to me that he was unable to draw the distinctions I called upon him to make, nor did he say anything plain, concealing his perplexity. (169c3–d1)

The narrative is potentially misleading, for it is evident that Critias was not "caught by perplexity" in the full sense of the phrase.[23] Critias' perplexity was not like that of someone who sneezes of his own accord, but like that of someone whose sneeze is derived: he experienced an imitation-perplexity, not a real one. Critias was perplexed enough to realize that he did not know how to deal with the problems Socrates had raised; but he had not appreciated those problems, because he was never really interested in the truth concerning them, only in how he would appear before the others in terms of his ability to remain on top of the discussion, to seem knowledgeable and wise. But this is not yet the crucial point.

The crucial fact in Socrates' narrative is that Critias in this situation is set before his own ignorance, and he refuses to acknowledge it. He is given the opportunity to prove the reality of self-relational being, to demonstrate "in particular" the possibility of *sophrosune* after the Socratic model—the possibility of knowing that you do not know—but *he turns away from this opportunity*, choosing not to appropriate this insight into his own thought or to reveal it to the others (including his ward). In the manner I discussed in chapter 4, Critias prefers holding on to his claim to knowledge and superiority, rather than chose truth and self-knowledge; he prefers his emotional to his rational self. Critias' act presents us with the "negative" or shadow side of self-relational human being: the possibility of willful self-deception, of choosing a self who is blind to itself, of self-ignorance, self-shaped blindness to one's true beliefs, values, and abilities.

Thus Critias, even more than Charmides, is the figure in the dialogue who is intended to display for the reader the vicious or corrupting counterpart to the dynamic element in the life of moderation and self-knowledge. For just as the choice of the good of truth over the impulse of pleasure can confirm Socrates in the rational being who possesses self-knowledge and self-identity (156d2–3: "little by little . . . I was rekindled to life"), so the choice of pride and self-image over truth manifested in his denial of ignorance can confirm Critias in a self who does not conform to who he really is, in a self-image that is blind to who he really is. Again, if what Plato will later insist is true, no one can say directly to themselves: "I prefer my self-image to the actual truth about me"; no one can admit openly that they are telling themselves a "lie in their souls."[24] And yet such self-deceptive self-relation is possible, as Critias' act of dialectical *akrasia* illustrates and the tripartite theory of the soul will later help to explain.

The paradox—the "illogic"—of self-deception lies in the fact that the self-deceiver must somehow both know *and* not know what he is doing.[25] How can this be possible? In fact, Socrates' narrative provides the key to understanding the phenomenon: the self-deceiver, in refusing to accept what he realizes is true, and in choosing to deny his own beliefs in order to defend a cherished public image of himself, must "tell the lie in the soul," and this will not only make it more difficult for others to see him as he is, it also begins a process of intellectual self-alienation whereby the words he speaks and the beliefs he ostensibly holds are no longer expressive of a genuine relationship to reality and to reason, no longer what he actually knows to be true.[26] Plato's dramatic insight into the paradox of self-deception, which relies on this contrast between what the interlocutor is *made to realize* about himself and what he is *willing to accept* as true, is comparable to the analysis offered recently by L. Jonathan Cohen—though I think it is important to note that Plato is perhaps more conscious even than Cohen of the socially alienating consequences of dialogic self-deception.[27] Having been at least potentially a member of a shared rational community, Critias has violated the law of truthful self-expression and thereby exiled himself from that community. Lying to himself as he lies to others, he has begun to live a mask, and may become ever more desperate to secure confirmation of that mask, by whatever means available. The choice of self-deception in the act of dialectical *akrasia* is made against moral and intellectual honesty, against the rational self, on behalf of lesser values and a lesser self, which comes to be identified with the pleasures it seeks and the image it asserts—and thereby becomes ever less disposed, or even able, to examine and evaluate its goals. If this account is correct, self-knowledge depends to a significant degree on how careful a person is in relating her words and beliefs—the life of her mind—to her deeds and experiences—the life of her person. Both Critias and Charmides bear witness to the fact that human beings can live shadow-lives, lives of self-deception in which one says one's lines as an actor and not as a rational agent in the world.[28] Critias' mode of acting out his lines is more complicated than Charmides' was, perhaps, but it is every bit as self-deceptive. Nor, we may suppose, did he become any less self-blind and self-deceptive, as he grew in political power.

In dramatic contrast to his interlocutor, Socrates has reaffirmed his self-knowledge as one who does not "trust himself" to know, but who must first "investigate" (*exetaxein*) before he asserts himself on moral matters, that is, as one "who knows what he knows and does not know." Whereas Critias rejected the opportunity he was given to acknowledge his own ignorance, and chose instead to maintain the self-image of one who was wise and virtuous (superior). With this refusal we were able to gain insight into the paradoxical Socratic claim that evil is involuntary. The elenchus shows that this is not simply the case, that instead both choice and insight (or the lack thereof) are involved in the process of moral self-formation. However, it is possible through such acts to become self-blind. In that state, despite his seeming rationality, a person such as Critias "does not know what he is doing," for he has cut himself off from self-knowledge and is driven by motives he cannot fathom.

This manner of characterizing the difference between Socrates and Critias also shows how *sophrosune* is beneficial and its counterpart harmful: Socrates, but not Critias, appears to take a free and rational relation to his own life, and reflective rationality of the kind he exemplifies and enjoys appears to be at least a necessary, if not sufficient condition of happiness.[29] However, despite the dramatic evidence offered in the *Charmides* that *sophrosune* is beneficial, the argument in its last segment will only partially support this conclusion. The reason for the failure of the argument would appear to lie in the confused starting-point of inquiry. As we have seen already and shall see further in this and the next chapter, the Socratic virtue of moderation and self-knowledge is beneficial to its practioner. It is the Critian ideal of self-certainty and rule that is less evidently beneficial to the person who claims to possess it, or to the city with such people as its rulers. Ignorant of their epistemic limits, they will be disinclined to respect the rights of others, and in the end may seek to install a tyranny so as to govern by force and not persuasion. The driven, immoderate character of their claims to knowledge and virtue would then impact not only their own lives, but on all those who fall under their sway. Unrestrained by wariness of their own natures or by respect for others in a community oriented to the common good of truth, they might command the obedience and admiration of a violent few who had also chosen to live for their passions and deny their own ignorance. Thus the cauldron within might create a cauldron without, if, as Plato insists in the *Republic*, the quality of the *polis* is inevitably determined by the quality of its leading citizens.[30]

⊰◈⊱

SIX

KNOWLEDGE OF KNOWLEDGE

*Socrates was unpopular, in spite of the fact that he used
no technical language, for his ignorance, if it is to be
thoroughly grasped and retained, is more strenuous to
carry out than all of Hegel's philosophy put together.*
—*Søren Kierkegaard*

The inquiry concerning moderation and self-knowledge
might have ended with Critias refusing to acknowledge his
own ignorance, but Socrates chooses to carry it forward,
and, on the supposition that self-knowledge is possible (which has
been confirmed in the action, if not the speech of the dialogue), he
now inquircs how, if one were to possess a knowledge of knowledge, it would enable one to know what one knew. For it seems that
such a knowledge would enable one to know *that* one knew or that
one did not know, but not *what* it was that one knew or did not
know. This part of the conversation—which continues the discussion of the possibility of self-knowledge, but now on an epistemological, rather than metaphysical level—leads into consideration of
the benefit of such knowledge.

As Thomas West notes, this section of the *Charmides* "is very
abstract . . . and difficult."[1] Some of the problem goes back to the
difficulty of determining what Socrates means by a "knowledge of
knowledge." Does it refer to Socratic dialectic (this seemed confirmed by the apparent reference to the Socrates of *Apology*
21a–23b)? to a superordinate art of government (this seemed to be
the idea behind the phrase "knowledge of itself and the other
knowledges")? to epistemology (this was the view of such eminent
Platonists as A. E. Taylor and Gerasimos Santas)? to self-consciousness (this is suggested by the list of mental acts at 167c4–168a8)? If

the reader has no way to ground the reference of that concept, the argument seems hopelessly obscure.[2] The argument also offers difficulties, with many puzzling features, including variations in the terminology used for the concept of self-knowledge under discussion, the relation between the two different arguments (at 169d2–70e3 and 170e3–171c10), and the surprising distinction Socrates draws at the end of the section, that while *sophrosune* as they have characterized it might not be of great benefit, it might still be of some benefit if one could combine it with other things one had learned.

Two things do seem clear about the section as a whole. The first is that insofar as the knowledge of knowledge is conceived of as having no subject matter, it must also prove not to yield knowledge of anything in particular, and therefore not be beneficial. This criticism is clearly relevant to Critias' conception of *sophrosune*, which as we have seen is characterized by sheer self-certainty, and which also involves, as we will see exploited in this section, a very simple model of knowledge. But is it revelant to the Socratic conception of *sophrosune*? I will argue that this part of the *Charmides* is constructed in such a way as to indicate that it does not apply to the Socratic ideal.

There is another aspect of the argument on which interpreters agree, and which is also relevant to the interpretation of Socratic philosophy as a whole.[3] Socrates argues in this overall segment that the "knowledge of knowledge" cannot test the validity of claims to a given technical knowledge. If the knowledge of knowledge is to be identified with Socratic dialectic, and dialectic is taken to concern itself with moral values, this would both define one limit of its powers and in the process exhibit a reasoned awareness of that limit, that is, a self-knowledge. Such self-knowledge conforms to his self-description at *Apology* 21a–23b. It also stands in marked contrast to Gorgias' attitude toward rhetoric, and in general to the sophistic conviction that the power of their art is unlimited (cf. especially *Gorgias* 456a–c; also *Ion* 540d–542b, *Hippias Minor* 363e–364a, *Euthydemus* 273c–274a, *Sophist* 232e–234e). Socrates' reasoned awareness of the limits of his practice indicate, together with the consciousness of moral and social purpose affirmed at 166c7–d6, crucial respects in which philosophy differs from sophistry.

The correct interpretation of this part of the dialogue, I suggest, depends on the reader importing again the distinction between the two conceptions of self-knowledge we found at work earlier in the inquiry with Critias leading up to the definition at 167a1–7. As Plato makes clear in later dialogues, the distinguishing mark of genuine dialectic consists in the ability to make such distinctions—for example, between the "good" and "bad" madness in the *Phaedrus*, between the philosopher and the sophist in the *Sophist* and *Statesman*. I believe that Plato intends to represent a similar basic distinction here in the *Charmides*. Socrates and Critias have and exemplify very different conceptions of *sophrosune*—a true, Socratic concept of moral self-knowledge and a counterfeit, Critian one—and Plato makes use of both as he weaves a complicated pattern of *logos* and *ergon* in the text, allowing the reader to discover the difference between the one and the other.

The section divides into three or four parts: (1) the first argument, which concludes that *sophrosune* can only know that one knows or does not know, not what it knows or does not know (169d2–170e3); (2) a second argument, which concludes that someone with *sophrosune* would not be able to tell the difference between someone who actually possessed knowledge of something (such as a doctor) and a mere pretender, who claimed to possess the knowledge but did not (170e3–171c10); and (3) the application of these findings to the question of the possible benefit of *sophrosune*. The third part may then be divided into (a) the argument that the benefit is certainly not the "grand benefit" that if we possessed it we and all those who were ruled by us would live a perfectly scientific, errorless, and happy life (171d1–172a9); and (b) the conclusion that the benefit possibly is the more modest benefit of learning more easily, having a clearer understanding of what we have learned, and being more able to examine others concerning what we have learned (172b1–c3).

I shall argue that these parts are meant to be understood in relation to the two different conceptions of *sophrosune*, and are further meant to suggest two different epistemological models, which correspond to those conceptions.[4] The first argument and the discussion of the "grand benefit" of the knowledge of knowledge in the third section pertains specifically to the Critian, sophistic conception. It corresponds to a simple epistemological model, whereby knowledge is taken as direct perception or recognition of its object. The knower of health knows the healthful. The knower of knowledge knows the knowledgeable. There is no effort here to further characterize the object of knowledge. Socrates shows that on this model it is impossible to know what one knows and does not know. The most one could know is *that* one knows, not *what* it was, but this characterization is utterly empty. This conclusion shows in almost comic fashion how bankrupt Critias' understanding is.

The second argument and the fourth section, in which the "lesser benefit" of self-knowledge is discussed, have a very different purpose in the dialogue. Contrary to appearances, they do not merely continue the same critique of the knowledge of knowledge, but are intended to evoke the Socratic conception of *sophrosune* in the mind of the reader. They do not address this ideal directly, but they provide the reader with the materials for envisioning a more complex epistemological model and for relating that model to the Socratic concern for moral health. The epistemological model evoked in this part of the dialogue is not one of direct perception or recognition of its object, but rather one in which the act of knowing is mediated by a testing process that focuses on the *reasons* the knowledge-claimant has for holding or rejecting the judgment or performing or refraining from the action. This model of knowledge is introduced specifically in relation to the art of medicine, but it seems chiefly intended to cause the reader to reflect on its relevance to Socrates' original claim to possess a therapy of moral health and to the Socratic ideal of dialectical wisdom (moderation). Having evoked this alternative model of the knowledge of knowledge, Socrates goes on to suggest some of the benefits of dialectic to those who have discovered what it is.

THE FIRST ARGUMENT (169d2–170e3)

Socrates develops the first argument in eight steps:

1. Knowledge of knowledge implies the ability to identify that some *x* is or is not knowledge.
2. Knowledge of knowledge and nonknowledge of the healthful and knowledge of knowledge and nonknowledge of the just are not the same.
3. Someone who only has knowledge of knowledge, but does not have in addition knowledge of the healthful and the just, would recognize that he or others know *something* and that he or they are knowers.
4. But he would not know by this knowledge that which (what) he knows.[5]
5. For one knows what one knows by means of the determinate knowledges, for example, the healthful by doctoring, harmon-

ics by music, house building by architecture, not by means of *sophrosune.*

6. Thus if *sophrosune* is a knowledge only of knowledges, he cannot know by it that he knows the healthful, or that he knows house building.

7. Then he who was ignorant of this (e.g., the healthful, or house building) will not know what he knows, but only *that* he knows.

8. And therefore *sophrosune* [thus conceived] is not knowing both what one knows and what one does not know, but only that one knows and that one does not know.

Socrates then makes two further points, which lead into the next argument:

9. Nor would such a person be able to examine others claiming to possess knowledge, whether they had what they claim to have knowledge of; he could only know that he did or did not have knowledge, not what it was of.

10. Therefore he would neither be able to test between those who pretended to be doctors but were not and those who really were, nor any others claiming knowledge, whether they had what they claimed or not.

The argument seems straightforward. It offers a simplistic model of knowledge by direct perception or intuition, and proves that if someone possessed a knowledge that could only determine whether someone knew or did not know something (a "knowledge of knowledge"), he could not know by such a knowledge *what* the person knew. But just prior to and in the course of offering this argument, Socrates also says several very puzzling things that must also be considered, if we are to fully appreciate this segment of the text.

1. Socrates prefaces the discussion with an ambiguous remark to the effect that he, Socrates, characteristically does not understand how knowing what one knows and knowing what someone does not know are the same (169e4–170a4). This statement, interpreted self-referentially, would suggest that in Socrates' own view the crucial distinction is not between knowledge that one knows and knowledge of what one knows—as the rest of the argument indicates—but rather between knowledge of what one

knows as opposed to what one does not know. The latter distinction would bring out again the specific difference in the Socratic ideal of moral self-knowledge, namely that the person with the habit of critical reason ("moderation-science") never claimed to know absolutely what he believed to be true, that is, never "trusted himself" (or another) to know, prior to investigation of his reasons. But this was also, as we saw, the specific point on which Socrates may be contrasted to Critias, who believed himself to know what he knew without concerning himself with what he might not know. Is Socrates trying to tell us that the argument as a whole is really about the difference between someone like himself, for whom the key to *sophrosune* has to do with concern regarding the knowledge of ignorance, as opposed to someone like Critias, for whom it has to do with self-certainty and claiming the knowledge of knowledge vis-à-vis others?

2. Still more puzzling: After asking Critias if the knowledge of knowledge can distinguish anything more than that of two things one is and the other is not a knowledge, Socrates asks him if the knowledge and nonknowledge of the healthful and the knowledge and nonknowledge of the just are the same, with the result that there would be three different knowledges: (1) doctoring, that is, knowledge of the healthful; (2) politics, knowledge of the just; and (3) *sophrosune*, the knowledge of knowledge. Socrates' question implies that politics is a technical science in the same sense that medicine is. Most commentators—including Tuckey and Hyland—fail to notice what a remarkable thing this is for Socrates to say. What is its relevance to the argument at hand?

3. Socrates then makes an absolute separation between knowledge of a subject matter and knowledge of what constitutes knowledge in relation to a subject matter, as if one could only know x = knowledge or x is not knowledge, or that x = healthful or x = diseaseful, but not that one knew x = healthful or diseaseful. This point will be made explicit in the beginning of the next argument, where he makes the startling claim that a doctor knows nothing of medicine (170e5–7). But such a separation of the knowledge of the subject matter from the knowledge of the particular science is clearly artificial.[6] To know, for example, that eating light meat is healthful, is a true proposition of medical knowledge, but it qualifies as medical knowledge in light of the *reasons* the knowing subject can offer for it, not merely in virtue

of the fact that it is true.[7] The doctor knows *x*, and he knows *why* *x* is the case: he knows that he knows *x* (what he knows), his reasons constituting the difference between knowledge and mere correct opinion. (Similarly, he knows what to do, and he knows why to do it.) Why does Critias agree to this impersonal, non self-reflexive manner of conceiving the relation of knowledge to itself and to its object?

4. Socrates shifts between different ways of characterizing the knowledge belonging to *sophrosune*—as the knowledge of knowledge (*epistemes*) at 170a6, as the knowledge of the knowledges (*epistemon*) at 170c6, and again as the knowledge of what you know and what you do not know (*eidenai ha te oiden kai ha me oiden*) at 170d2–3.[8] If these differences do not represent errors in the transmission of the text—and we have no good reason to suppose that they do—why does Plato have Socrates characterize self-knowledge in these different ways?

Assuming that these puzzles must be accounted for, I suggest that the first argument is aimed specifically at Critias' conception of *sophrosune*. This interpretation explains the argument and the above-mentioned facts in the following manner:

1. First, there is no room in Critias' conception for the knowledge of nonknowledge, since there is no role for the critical and open-minded *testing* of one's own claim to knowledge. Rather, it is presented as something one simply knows, as if by direct inspection. For Critias, the knowledge of knowledge would appear to be nothing more than the experience of self-certainty, his claim of wisdom and the right to rule and the recognition of this same attitude in others. He does not conceive of it as mediated by examination and reasons. The argument fits his conception of self-knowledge precisely.

2. Critias' lack of knowledge of what he does not know is demonstrated dramatically by his failure to question Socrates' introduction of politics as if it were one among the other *technai*, over which *sophrosune* as a supreme and self-knowing science would have command. This point needs discussion, since it may seem to be Socrates' own position.[9] On my reading, Socrates introduces it elenctically, to test whether Critias can sustain the insight introduced earlier concerning the differences among the technical-productive (e.g., medicine), theoretical-objective (e.g., geometry), and moral–self-relational sciences (e.g., political sci-

ence), the distinction Critias had insisted on at 165c4–167a7 and Socrates had accepted. And the representation of politics as a *techne* does not reflect the definition of *sophrosune* as Socrates shaped at 167a1–7 (which seemed to refer specifically to *Apology* 21a–23b). For the theme of moral knowledge and nonknowledge (including knowledge of justice) is precisely what must be addressed by the "moderation-science" of moral dialectic on the Socratic model. This is the predominant view represented by Socrates in the early dialogues. In contrast to the Sophists, it is Socrates who does not regard politics as an established science, does not think of it uncritically as one among the many *technai*.[10] To the extent that the definition of *sophrosune* at 167a1–7 is Socrates' own, he must believe that there is a fundamental difference between politics—conceived as the self-critical knowledge and nonknowledge of the just—and the arts of medicine, music, and architecture—conceived as technical-productive or theoretical-objective knowledges of physical health, musical harmony, and house building, respectively. For then he believes that such moral and political knowledge as we may actually possess must remain dynamically open to refutation in a way in which technical expertise is not. And it is evident that this is the case, despite his elenctic use here of the notion of a *techne* of justice. Rather than represent Socrates' own position, then, the example is intended to reveal the weakness in Critias' understanding of *sophrosune*.

3. Critias' inability to confute Socrates' absolute, artificial distinction between the knowledge of knowledge (or *that* one knows) and the other knowledges (which are of *what* one knows) derives from the fact that Critias conceives of knowledge on the model of direct perceptual or social recognition, rather than rational understanding. For Critias, the knowledge which is "of itself and of the other knowledges" is really just of oneself (as a "knower" and hence as superior). This is completely different from the knowledges associated with the *technai*, since it has neither content, for example, moral claims, nor reasons to back them up. And Critias does not appreciate the epistemically self-reflective nature of medicine and the other arts, which is consistent with his representation in the dialogue as a mere poet and decadent aristocrat.

4. Thus the distinctions in terminology are deliberate on Plato's part: the first (*episteme tes epistemes*, at 170a6) picks out the feature associated with Critian self-certainty, the claim to knowledge of knowledge which, however, ignores the fearful,

self-critical element, the knowledge of ignorance (which Socrates drops in most of the next part of the argument); the second (*episteme ton epistemon*, at 170c6) picks out another element especially associated with the Critian model, which centers on its hegemony over the other knowledges; and the third, which employs Socratic terms (*eidenai ha te oiden kai me oiden*, 170d 2–3) would conclude that *this* understanding of what it is to be *sophron* and possess *sophrosune* would not bring about Socratic understanding of what one knows and does not know.

The first argument ends with Socrates' remarks to the effect that then it also seems that the *sophron* person would not be able to examine whether another claiming to have knowledge has or does not have knowledge of what he claims, but could only recognize *that* he had knowledge. If the reading I have offered here is correct, this is exactly the state Critias is in: he claims or asserts for himself the status of knower—he is one who "knows that he knows." But in truth Critias is incapable of critically examining his own or another's claim to knowledge, because he is morally undisposed to and unpracticed in the "moderation-science" of dialectic. It is this lack of the habit of critical thought that has also rendered him ignorant of and blind to his own moral beliefs. The reader is meant to see in Critias someone who is unable to investigate others as to what they know and do not know, someone who does *not* know "what he himself supposes he knows, but does not know."

THE SECOND ARGUMENT (170e3–171c10)

In the second argument, Socrates focuses on the art of medicine, questioning whether the man with "moderation-science" could judge that a man who pretended to medical knowledge had what he claimed to have. It goes like this:

1. If the *sophron* person "or anyone else" is to know who is a doctor and who is not, he will not converse with him about medicine. For the doctor knows only about health and illness, not knowledge; but medicine is a knowledge, and therefore the doctor knows nothing about medicine.
2. So if one wishes to know what kind of knowledge the doctor has, he must examine him concerning the objects of his knowledge, that is, the healthful and diseaseful.

3. This will involve examining whether what is said regarding these objects is said truly or what is done regarding them is done correctly.
4. But no one without knowledge of medicine, and certainly not the *sophron* person, could do this—unless he was a doctor in addition to being *sophron*.
5. Therefore *sophrosune* will not be able to judge between a genuine doctor and one who does not have but only pretends or supposes to know medicine.

Socrates then adds:

6. But like other artists the *sophron* person can judge between the one who has or only pretends or supposes himself to have *sophrosune*.

This argument is even more puzzling than the first. For one thing—as Malcolm Schofield notes, on the way to suggesting that the text be emended to eliminate some of its puzzling features—Socrates would appear to have already shown at 169d2–170e3 that knowledge of what one knows is impossible.[11] So we must ask why he develops this argument at all, what its purpose is in the dialogue. The answer Schofield suggests is that the first argument argues generally for the thesis that *sophrosune* cannot render knowledge of what someone does or does not know, whereas the second is meant to draw out the specific implication that *sophrosune* cannot judge between a real and fraudulent claimant to medicine.[12] But if this is his aim, why does Socrates leave room at the end of this argument for the possibility of *combining* the knowledge of knowledge with another knowledge, such that one could know what one knew and did not know? This was what the first argument implied was not possible. Now he says is possible, and offers it as the reason for the modest benefit he ascribes to *sophrosune* at 172b1–c3.

Certainly, it is part of Plato's intention in this section of the dialogue to show that dialectic cannot test claims to technical knowledge, but is restricted to claims to moral knowledge (though even on this point, the argument seems overblown).[13] And certainly also, if the reading I have offered of the first argument is correct, it is his intention to expose the inadequacies of Critias' conception of self-knowledge and of the epistemology underlying that conception. But the fact that he has Socrates conclude—contrary to the initial impression suggested by the argument—that the knowledge of what one or another knows or does not know is somehow both possible and potentially beneficial requires us to review our understanding of its overall meaning in relation to the dialogue.

The place to begin is again to focus on the features of Socrates' discourse that do not conform to its overt meaning. I will try to show that these features can be best accounted for if we interpret them as invoking the conceptions of moderation and knowledge associated with the Socratic rather than the Critian ideal. Let me first point out the anomalies, then summarize my interpretation.

The puzzling features of the argument include the following:

1. The focus of this argument, unlike the first, is on the ability to test someone who claims to have the specific art of medicine, but may not have it.
2. Socrates' account of the relation of the doctor to his own art is very strange, specifically his claim that the doctor has no knowledge of medicine, only of the healthful and the diseaseful. But this, as we noted above, is absurd, importing to the model of knowledge a strictly transitive relation of knower to object, without any element of self-relation, whereby the knower knows why he knows.
3. Socrates now speaks of medicine as the knowledge of the healthful *and* the diseaseful, whereas earlier he had only spoken of the knowledges with regard to their respective "positive" objects, for example, health, justice, harmony, and well-formed buildings.
4. Another curious point is that he speaks here of the *need* to try to grasp that of which the doctor has knowledge, and of the *wish* to investigate doctoring correctly. There was no emphasis in the first argument on the needs or wishes of the investigator, and no emphasis (until the transition to this argument) on investigation at all, but only on what the person with the knowledge of knowledge(s) could know of his or another's knowledge. Why does Socrates now import the matter of practical concern?
5. Socrates defines the criteria to be used in the investigation of one who claims knowledge of doctoring, namely whether he speaks truly (*alethe legetai*, 171b8) and acts correctly (*orthos prattetai*, 171b9). This goes beyond the indications of the first argument, which implied that that one determined another's claim to knowledge by direct perception or recognition—without a process of examination.
6. The point mentioned earlier, that this argument does not exclude (as the first apparently had done) the possibility of the

combination of the knowledge of knowledge together with medicine, with the implication that someone might know both "the
healthful and diseaseful" and "knowledge and non-knowledge."
Here Socrates implies that it *is* possible to know both the subject
matter of a science and whether the knowledge-claimant's
speeches and actions in relation to that subject matter are scientific.

7. Finally, having ruled out the possibility that someone with
sophrosune alone could judge between the genuine doctor and
the fraud, Socrates adds that someone with it could judge someone who claimed to possess the same knowledge as himself,
"just like any other artist" (171c8–9). This is again a surprising
remark, since his whole point until now seemed to be that someone with only the knowledge of knowledge could not know anything of what the other claimed to know, except that he knew an
indeterminate "something" or that he did not know anything.
But now it seems he can determine if the other has the *sophron-*
knowledge, even if he cannot determine if the other has knowledge of a specific technical field.

Assuming again that these details must be accounted for, I
suggest that the second argument is intended to invoke the possibility of knowing what you know and do not know on the pattern
of the Socratic ideal. Consider the following:

1. Focusing attention solely on the medical art clearly has self-referential import, since it was a medical art that Socrates, on
Critias' suggestion, had pretended to possess toward the young
Charmides.[14] The specificity of this argument directs our attention, in particular, to the question whether Socrates' claim to
have "learned" (*emathon*, 156d4; cf. also *didaskon*, 157b1) the
Thracian art of psychic medicine was legitimate.

2. But then the fact that the self-relational nature of the arts is mis-
represented here (due to Critias' ignorance) is also significant. As
Socrates suggested in the prologue by means of the Thracian criticism of Athenian medicine, and as the argument will make
clear in the next segment of the dialogue, there is a way in which
the arts do not reflect on themselves: namely, they do not reflect
on the relation of their truths to the whole or on the governing
value of the goods they seek to attain. It is apparent, however,
that the arts know not only about their subject matter, but about
their science as well, insofar as the artist is able to give clear,

explanatory reasons as to *why* he says what he says (e.g., that light meat is healthy) and does what he does (e.g., gives his patient a dose of cod liver oil).[15] If the examination of a supposedly "knowledgeable" practice focuses inevitably on the reasons he gives for his beliefs and actions, then a dialectical practice presumably would do the same with respect to the things it took under its purview.

3. This point is also relevant to the mention of the negative object of medicine, disease, which had been left out in the first argument. On the Critian model of self-knowledge, the focus was on knowing that/what is known and only secondarily on knowing that/what is not known; but on the Socratic model, the first concern is the negative object, since to think you know what you do not know (or to think that someone else knows what he does not know) is not merely not to be healthy but to be *unhealthy*: there is no neutral state, and the process by which disease is removed is the same process by which health begins to be restored. Moreover, from the Socratic point of view the discovery of what you do not know is crucial to moral health, because it provides the motivation to engage in the pursuit of knowledge, not mere opinion. Not the conviction that you lack some sort of knowledge, but the realization that you lack moral knowledge, is the decisive experience associated with the elenchus and with Socratic dialectical moderation.

4. This fact underlies the element of self-concern motivating the investigation of the claim to *sophrosune* (or any other virtue), the "moral fear" we found at 166d1–2 to accompany the inquisitive attitude of Socratic self-understanding. The Socratic therapy becomes relevant to someone who has come, through a process of self-critical inquiry, to *lack* the self-certainty of his own virtue, and who wishes, therefore, to investigate whether the person who claims to be able to help him really can. On the analogy to medicine, the Socratically moderate person is like the physician who fears he might be ill and not know the cure, and therefore must test his own, as well as others' knowledge of health and disease, his own and others' ability to benefit him.[16] There is no internal motivation to test one's own or others' claim to knowledge for the Critian ideal of self-certainty, but there is for someone with Socratic moderation, since it suspends certainty with respect to its own truth-claims.

5. The discussion of the two criteria of knowledge, truth of speech and correctness of action, brings out the fact that in testing a

claimant to practical knowledge one is concerned not only with what he says about the subject matter, but also with what he does, and with both in relation to a good to be obtained. This is irrelevant to Critias' notion of self-knowledge, which separated self-knowledge from any normative standard, and did not involve a relation to a future good. It is not irrelevant, however, to the Socratic notion of self-knowledge, which is concerned to test both what someone said and the application of their beliefs to their lives (as Nicias emphasizes at *Laches* 187e–188b; cf. also the discussion in chapter 4).

6. The suggestion that one might be able to combine medical knowledge with the knowledge that is able to investigate claims to knowledge emerges therefore as a primary suggestion of this argument. But this model applies only to the Socratic conception of self-knowledge. *Sophrosune* would be that self-critical dialogic science, applied by the person who was concerned with whether what he thought he had learned of moral health and illness was true.

7. If such a combination is possible, then it *is* possible to test what you or another have claimed to learn, and this suggests that it should also be possible for the Socratic dialectician to investigate and judge his own or the claims of anyone else to possess virtue, by evaluating the reasons offered for moral beliefs and actions and testing claimants for logical and practical consistency. This is what it would mean to evaluate someone's claim to moderation-science, which Socrates now asserts *can* be done, "as is the case with other artists."

The interpretation I have offered here of 170e3–171c10 may seem to pay undue attention to its puzzling details, rather than the surface of the argument. I certainly do not wish to ignore that surface. As I mentioned earlier, it is evidently part of the intention of this segment of the dialogue to define limits to the scope of Socratic dialectic; it is shown here to be inadequate to test for technical expertise. But these puzzling details and their relevance to the larger framework of the dialogue must also be accounted for. And the value of this kind of reader-responsive approach to their interpretation is apparent, I submit, when the argument is placed in the overall dramatic context—in the context of the struggle between Socrates and Critias and their respective conceptions of *sophrosune*, and the context of the role of Socratic philosophy and moral therapy in the dialogue as a whole. Then the first argument is seen clearly as a refutation of Critias, of his ideal of self-certainty without rational justification, and of the simple epistemological model that underlies that ideal. The continuation of the discussion into the second argument offers the reader an opportunity to do what Critias cannot: to realize that *the knowledge of what you know and do not know is possible on a different, self-relational model of knowledge*—on a model that sees it as a self-critical enterprise driven by concern for the truth of its own moral findings. This interpretation also accounts for why Socrates will now go on to suggest that there might indeed be a benefit to the "knowledge of knowledge and non-knowledge," despite the fact that the argument does not seem to have prepared us for this possibility.

For the strangest thing about Socrates' argument at 169d2–172c4 is his conclusion that even if *sophrosune* thus conceived does not offer the "great" benefits he thought it might, it nonetheless does offer other, "smaller" benefits to anyone who has learned something![17] These benefits depend on the possibility, suggested in Socrates' second but not in his first argument, of combining the knowledge of what you know and do not know with the knowledge that you do or do not know it—of clarifying or deepening your understanding of the subject matter by your knowledge of what science and nonscience is concerning that subject matter. This possibility must be accounted for. But it cannot be accounted for on Critias' autocratic model of *sophrosune*. How could someone who knew only *that* he did or did not possess some completely undetermined knowledge more easily learn *what* he was learning? Such knowledge could not possibly contribute to any insight into the subject matter. Nor would it be at all relevant to knowing "more clearly" what he learns, unless he realizes more clearly what he is coming to know, not merely that he knows something. Socrates' conclusion makes no sense, if we regard him as referring to the same conception of the knowledge of knowledge throughout the argument at 169c2–172c4.

Tuckey recognized this problem, and suggested that Plato meant the reader to import here something like "the ability to think clearly," or possibly some form of mathematical knowledge that might provide the basis for all *epistemai* (though he admits there is no textual evidence to support the latter possibility).[18] What Tuckey does not consider is the relation of this discussion to the definition at 167a1–7 and to Socrates' dialectical practice in the dialogue. The crucial concept in the passage presenting the definition, as in this discussion, is that of examination (*exetasis*). Some do it well, others "weakly and poorly" (172b7–8; *asthenesteron*, "weakly," is cognate with *astheneia*, the term used for Charmides' weakness of the head). But the idea of examination surely refers to the Socratic practice of dialectical questioning, which treats beliefs as opinions to be tested for justification, not merely, *pace* Tuckey, to an ability to think clearly. Nor is it the case that the knowledge of knowledge performs its function only in relation to specialized knowledge, as Tuckey also claims.[19] We recall the puzzling fact that the *sophron* individual might test others as to their claim to possess the self-knowledge, "just like other artists." This is what Socrates does, examining others to determine whether what he believes he has learned concerning human well-being is true. What he may also learn, if he examines them "beautifully," is that they do not possess the knowledge they make claim to. This would be the very kind of benefit he was hoping for in the first place, albeit one that applied only to nontechnical practical wisdom.

I conclude that the possibility of the combination of a substantive knowledge with the knowledge of knowledge (and nonknowledge) can be accounted for on the Socratic conception of *sophrosune*, without appealing to either notion Tuckey imports to the discussion. This possibility does not consist in technical knowledge of a subject matter, but in the dynamic, voluntary habit of critical reflection with respect to moral values. This habit is self-referential in its concern to determine whether the practitioner himself, or his possible teacher, has good reason to believe that he or the other is speaking truly and acting correctly. It presents a type of knowledge exemplifying the complex, self-relational model of knowledge adumbrated by Socrates in the second part of the overall argument we have surveyed. It carries the benefits that accrue from bringing its practitioner to investigate quietly, again and again, whether or not he knows what he claims to know; it is motivated by the self-concern awakened when one discovers that one might not know what is truly good (cf. 173a3–5). Socrates' elenchus, which seems to refute the very possibility of a knowledge of what it knew or did not know and therefore would seem to be of no possible benefit, great or small, is not conclusive after all. It refutes decisively the Critian ideal of such a knowledge, but it also alludes to Socrates' own conception of *sophrosune*, which is not susceptible to these criticisms and may still be of real benefit to its practitioner.

THE POSSIBLE BENEFITS OF *SOPHROSUNE* (171d1–172c4)

This section divides into two parts, the first considering the "greater" (*megalosti*, 171d5) benefits of *sophrosune*, which it now seems must be dismissed, the second with the apparently "lesser" benefits, which Socrates does not rule out. He begins by summarizing the benefits he thought they might have—the possibility of a "science of sciences" that would enable us and all those with it to conduct their lives without error, as well as those under our rule (including Charmides, who is still under the rule of his guardian). Those with it would not attempt things they did not have knowledge of, but would find those who did and hand it over to them; and they would let those whom they ruled do what they knew to do correctly, but not other things. Therefore such a science would have political implications as well: a household managed economically this way would be managed beautifully, as would be a city governed politically this way, and everything else *sophrosune* would rule. It is a fascinating discourse, if only because Socrates is here beginning to delineate the model of a rationally governed society, something that in the next segment of the dialogue he will identify as his "dream" (*onar*, 173a7), and which seems remarkably prescient of the ideal society in the *Republic*, where in theory the rulers may have such superordinate powers. I will reserve discussion of the utopian aspects of his idea for the next chapter. Socrates concludes his account of these "greater" benefits by arguing that with error (*hamartias*) removed and correctness (*orthotetos*) leading the way, those so situated would necessarily act beautifully and well, and those who do well are happy. This is what they were saying, but did Critias not now see that no such knowledge has appeared? "I see," Critias answers (171d1–172a9).[20]

At this point it would seem that the discussion must stop. Socrates has listed the benefits that presumably would accrue from the knowledge of what one knows and does not know, but Critias has not seen it appear, and of course it did not appear, at least not in such a form. The discussion does not stop, however, for Socrates surprisingly goes on to consider the benefits of the knowledge they have now "discovered" *sophrosune* to be—having knowledge of knowledge and nonknowledge—and it turns out that this *is* beneficial, if not so much as the other might have been. For he who has it (1) can learn more easily; (2) will be clearer about what he has learned; and (3) will be more able to examine others concerning whatever he has learned, while those without it will do so in a weaker, poorer manner. But it seems that they are looking at something "greater" and requiring it to be "greater than it is" (172c2).

I have argued that this second part of Socrates' evaluation of the benefit of *sophrosune* is best understood if we relate it to his own dialectical ideal of intellectual moderation and self-knowledge.[21] This interpretation situates the argument in the dramatic context of the contrast between Socrates and Critias, and explains the series of puzzling clues that Plato seems to have left for the reader to find and apply to the text. Certainly, it makes no sense to assert a benefit for the knowledge of knowledge and nonknowledge on the basis of the arguments Socrates provided in 169d2–171a10. The knowledge that one knows cannot help one learn what one knows, unless there is some connection between the two, which is precisely what Socrates denied. Nor is there reason to suppose that this knowledge would make him better able to examine others, if it consists merely in the ability to see that they do or do not have knowledge, unless it also consists in the ability to test whether they have the specific knowledge they claim to have. This possibility was ruled out on the original, Critian understanding of the knowledge of knowledge and nonknowledge, but now it seems to have found its way back into the discussion. This part of the discussion appears, therefore, to adumbrate the benefits of dialectic for someone who believes that he has learned something in the area of moral values, by a process that included discovering the reasons why he thought he knew what he knew, and why he thought another knew, or did not know, what they thought they knew. Socrates, because he examines and tests his convictions, *knows* what he knows in the sense that his beliefs are "held firm and fastened . . . with reasons of steel and adamant" (*Gorgias* 509a).[22] This is the "lesser" benefit of dialectic, together with what he does not mention here, but which has been vividly displayed throughout by the negative example of Critias, namely the benefit of not thinking he knows what he knows when he does not know it. This is not the kind of "great" benefit that Critias had hoped for from self-knowledge. It is not the kind of *sophrosune* guaranteeing one absolute knowledge and superiority and justifying absolute rule over others. But it would be a significant human benefit, nonetheless.

Socrates' discussion of the "lesser" benefits of *sophrosune* would appear to suggest, contrary to what Critias has seen, that "we" may have discovered (*heuriskomen*, 172b1–2) a form of the knowledge of knowledge and nonknowledge that is beneficial by way of making us clearer about what we believe we know and what we and others do not know. Indeed, it is with regard to this second aspect that such a "moderation-science" might be most beneficial, by bringing us to realize that we had an overinflated conception of our own or other's knowledge and virtue. For the chief conclusion of this part of the inquiry is that "we," that is, Socrates together with Critias (and the reader), have been contemplating something greater than the principle of critical moral reason, and that in contemplating *sophrosune* in that manner we were conceiving of it as "greater than it is." This possibility of conceiving of something as greater than it is—ruled out, we recall, in relation to merely mathematical relations at 168b2–d3—is the crucial dramatic event of this section of the dialogue. Recall that in conceiving of *sophrosune* as greater than it is, Critias also conceived of *himself* as greater than he was, though Socrates did not fall into that delusion. The drama of the *Charmides* shows that the overinflation of moral ideas and the overinflation of one's self-concept is not only a possibility, but a fact of moral life. A sober-minded appreciation of limits, however, brought about through a lifetime of serious, critical examination of beliefs, teaches that "less is more," that is, less of what seems great but is fraudulent. Appreciation of the benefits of *sophrosune* also deepens as one discovers what it cannot provide and what a false conception of it leads many to expect or project on their own and others' lives. Whether it is the sophistry of a self-styled religious prophet (Euthyphro), a would-be "military scientist" (Nicias), or a would-be aristocratic "*sophron*-king" (Critias), Socratic dialectic reveals again and again not only the benefit of being willing to take a critical perspective on what you believe, but also the harm of thinking it is unnecessary, because you possess something more than merely human, fallible knowledge.

SEVEN

UTOPIA, DYSTOPIA,
AND KNOWLEDGE OF THE GOOD

Some conception of the good for man is required. But whence is such a conception to be drawn? It is in looking for a conception of the good which will enable us to order other goods, for a conception of the good which will enable us to extend our understanding of the purpose and content of the virtues, for a conception of the good which will enable us to understand the place of integrity and constancy in life, that we initially define the kind of life which is a quest for the good. . . . A quest is always an education both as to the character of that which is sought and in self-knowledge.

—*Alasdair MacIntyre*

There are two major developments in the last part of the *Charmides.* Toward the end of the discussion of the epistemology of self-knowledge, Socrates envisages a city that in many respects seems to anticipate the utopian society of the *Republic.* It is a city guided by *sophrosune,* the knowledge of knowledge, the virtue that appears to guarantee both individual and civic happiness. But Socrates then argues that even if the self-knowledge they had been contemplating were possible and one were able to know what one knew and what one did not know, it still would not be of any benefit. For he leads Critias to conclude that what is missing from such self-knowledge—and what would be lacking in the *sophron* rulers of such a city—is knowledge of good and evil. But absent *this* knowledge, *sophrosune* does no good; whereas with such knowledge, it is not needed. It seems their definition was mistaken.

The introduction of Socrates' vision of an ideal society is relevant not only to the question of the relation of the *Charmides* to the *Republic*, but also to the question of Socrates' relation to the Thirty. As I suggested in chapter 1, one of the matters foremost in the minds of Plato's ancient readers would have been the extent to which Socrates might have contributed to the political immoderation of his followers, and the *Charmides* would be a very important text in that regard. Certainly, Socrates' well-known, antidemocratic belief that rule in the ideal society is not based on consent but on knowledge was one of the sources of the conviction that he had been a corrupting factor in the education of Charmides and Critias in particular. So it will be relevant to determine how Socrates' treatment of this ideal functions in the dialogue, and to assess it in relation to that charge.

It is also important to assess the final argument, which has taken on special significance in Plato scholarship since the publication of Terence Irwin's *Plato's Moral Theory*. Drawing in part on the *Charmides*, Irwin argues that Socrates accepts what he calls the "technical conception of virtue," that is, the view that "virtue simply is craft-knowledge."[1] Now, it is evident that Socrates, in leading Critias to acknowledge that his conception of self-knowledge is entirely separate from knowledge of good and evil, brings out an essential failure in Critias' understanding of *sophrosune*. But I will argue that this argument is not intended to refute the Socratic notion of *sophrosune*. In fact, as we have seen throughout, the basic insight of the *Charmides* is that virtue, at least in the form in which it is present in this dialogue, takes the form of nontechnical knowledge—the form of self-knowledge, oriented to dialectical practice. To make this reading stick, I must show how Irwin's account goes astray.

UTOPIA, DYSTOPIA, AND SELF-KNOWLEDGE

The introduction by Socrates of a *sophron* city is yet another one of the puzzling features of this stylistically earlier, but thematically ambiguous dialogue. What is its chief purpose? Is it intended, as Tuckey suggests, to adumbrate the idea fully developed in the *Republic*—albeit with *sophrosune* replaced by *dikaiosune*—of a utopian society ruled by men (and women) with certain knowledge of the good, who would be able to ensure "universal happiness"?[2] Or does it have another purpose? Robert Elliott, in his fine study of the literature of utopia, writes:

> If the word ["utopia"] is to be redeemed, it will have to be by someone who has followed utopia into the abyss which yawns behind the Grand Inquisitor's vision, and who then has clambered out on the other side.[3]

Many of Plato's critics, noting the totalitarian aspect of the *Republic*, have charged that he failed in just this respect: he never descended into the abyss—never plumbed the depths of human corruptability— and as a result never fully liberated his own utopian vision of a Grand Inquisitorial, authoritarian-idealistic element. I cannot comment here on the relevance of this criticism to the *Republic*.[4] But I believe the *Charmides*, if viewed in conjunction with Plato's autobiographical remarks concerning the Thirty recorded in the *Seventh Letter*, offers evidence that Plato *did* descend into and ascend out of that abyss. Seen in this light, the rejection of the utopian ideal city in the *Charmides* is not merely a function of what Socrates will reveal next, namely, Critias' failure to realize that *sophron* leaders must possess moral wisdom. Rather, it also seems intended to convey the connection between Critias' manifest lack of *sophrosune* in the Socratic sense of not knowing what he knows and does not know, and the dystopic political implications of this ideal, when reflected through such immoderation.[5] In fact the chief purpose of the utopian ideal in the *Charmides*, I suggest, is not to adumbrate the society of the *Republic*, but to expose the corrupt meaning of that ideal as interpreted by Critias. The drama of the *Charmides* takes us into the part of the human *psyche* to which Elliott claims one must descend, if one is to emerge to a liberating utopian vision.

I will discuss the theme of utopia and dystopia in the *Charmides* in two steps. First, I will compare the radically individualistic city introduced at 161d1 f. to the knowledge-community characterized by Socrates at 171d1 f. This comparison will bring out several features of the second city that seem to anticipate the utopian ideal later realized in the *Republic*. Then I will examine the further characterization of the second city in Socrates' discussion with Critias at 173a7 f., and assess the relevance of these passages to Socratic politics and education.

The "do one's own" society at 161d1 f. is very unlike the *sophron* city at 171d1 f.:

The egocratic city	The *sophron* city
Each person "produces and does" everything for himself, whether he knows the art relevant to it or not.	Each person does only those things about which he has knowledge, and there is a division of labor.
Each person is concerned only for himself.	At least some care for the well-being of others.
There is no division of rulers and ruled.	Divided into rulers and ruled.
Ruled by a law (*nomos*).	Ruled by men (and wisdom).
The focus is on the care of the body.	The focus is on knowledge and action in accordance with it.
No distinction between making and doing.	A basic distinction between the knowledge belonging to rule and other forms of knowledge.
Property is an absolute possession, and people may not even touch the things of others.	The assumption of goodwill, and private property is not held as an absolute.
No mention of the knowledge of ignorance.	The ability to distinguish what oneself and others do and do not know is the crucial factor of life.
No distinction of *oikos* and *polis*.	Both *oikos* and *polis* are mentioned.
Socrates concludes that this city would be "poorly managed."	Socrates claims that a *sophron*-led household would be "beautifully" managed, and a *sophron*-led polity would be "beautifully" governed.

The first, purely private city is an anti-erotic dystopia of isolated, selfish individuals who apparently devote all of their efforts to cover and care for their naked bodies, so much so that they never even touch one another, much less engage in conversation oriented to truth and happiness. It is a society in which there is no distinction between making and doing, or between knowledge and ignorance, and in which no one strives to distinguish these out of concern for their own and others' welfare. It is a city without love or beauty or moral wisdom. But the second city includes many elements that look forward to the *Republic*: the presumption of mutual goodwill (at least among the rulers); the division not merely in terms of *technai*, but in terms of rulers and ruled, with the authority of the leaders apparently resting on their excellence; the notion that happiness is a function of "doing well" (*eu prattein*) and the identification of well-doing with action in accordance with knowledge; the quality of beauty as well as goodness; the assignment of work by merit. There is even the thought that people in such a society might live through life "without error." But the depiction is different in one crucial respect from the *Republic* ideal: this discussion is framed, at beginning and end, by Socrates' emphasis on the good of knowing what you know and what you do not know. Whereas in the *Republic* the emphasis is on the rulers' knowledge of the highest and the other sciences, in the first description of this idea in the *Charmides* the emphasis is no less on the rulers' knowledge of ignorance, *including their own*.

The significance of this difference becomes evident when we attend to two subtle changes from the initial characterization of Socrates' *sophron* city at 171d1 f. and its further characterization in discussion with Critias at 173a7 f. Socrates hints at the first of these changes when he asks whether, even granting that one possessed knowledge of what one knew and did not know, it would still be of any "profit" (*onesei*, 172d2) to us. This is the same term that was used at 164b9, and again it has the connotation of narrow self-interest. As Socrates goes on to describe the "dream" society from 173a7 to the end of the discussion at 175a8, the concern for others quietly goes unmentioned. The perspective of concern Socrates had adopted at 171d1 f. was that of the leader who regarded himself as responsible for the well-being of others, at least all of those in his own household, perhaps all of those in his city.[6] The perspective Socrates now adopts—the perspective natural to Critias—is one that does not concern itself with others, but only with one's own body, safety, and possessions, that is, with prudence in a narrowly defined sense of the term (compare the sense intended by Critias at 163c7).

The second striking change has to do with the characterization of *sophrosune* itself. The point that Socrates emphasizes in framing his description of the *sophron* city and their leaders at 171d1 f.—the emphasis on the knowledge of ignorance, no less than the knowledge of knowledge—is replaced by another emphasis in the discussion from 173a7 onward. On the one hand, Socrates underscores the ruling function of *sophrosune*—that it would "rule us," and "rule over" (*epistatousan*, 173c5) the other sciences. This shift in emphasis accords well with Critias' image of a "knowledge of the knowledges" and of himself as a "master" in command of the other, lesser knowers (cf. chapter 3). On the other hand, Socrates now begins to bring out the extraordinary scope of knowledge as found within this city. He does this by introducing an art of divination, the possessor of which would, he suggests, know everything that is to be, has been, and is now, and would "be ignorant of nothing." Critias does not object to this fantastic idea; it is the other side of his own ideal.

For if we return to what Critias showed himself at 164c5–166e9 to mean by *sophrosune*, we recall that he had in mind a "knowledge of itself and the other knowledges," that is, a kind of "self-certain science" that might be possessed by rulers, and we further recall that the defining characteristic of his own attitude was one of "epistemic absolutism" (cf. chapter 3). Socrates has now also made a division between the rulers and the ruled, and associated the rulers with the possession of a supreme *sophron* science. But this science, if it is understood as Critias understands it, does not have a self-critical moral function. Critias, believing himself to possess *sophrosune*, envisions himself as a technocratic ruler, disposing with perfect errorless power over what he seeks to bring about in all that is "his own" (whether his household or city), ruler over all and drawing all the appropriate subordinate sciences into his purposes. This is a very heady prospect, just the kind of fantasy a future tyrant would entertain.

The ideal of a scientific society is transformed in the "more beautiful" *polis* of the *Republic* into a vision of true social justice, and of course *that* ideal has been an inspiration to philosophers interested in self-government ever since. But it also seems possible that the tyrannical distortion of the Socratic ideal of government was an animating factor behind the Thirty, and that this historical fact is at work in the drama of the *Charmides* also. We do know that Plato, in describing the revolution, reports that he had himself nurtured the belief that "they [the Thirty] would lead the city from an unjust life, as it were, to a just way and 'manage it,' as they put it . . ." (*Seventh Letter*, 324d). The term for "management" (*oikeisthai*) suggests an art of administration, of authoritarian rule by men who believed themselves empowered to establish "justice" by force.[7] There is an ideological element to their attitude that may have been partly inspired by the Socratic "dream" of wise rule: a strangely decadent, quasi-fascistic synthesis of aristocratic/Laconophilic and epistemic/sophistic presumption. But as Socrates indicates, this dream— the meaning of which would appear to be just as ambiguous as the terms used for *sophrosune*—may well deceive (173a7–8).[8]

In the *Charmides* we see Socrates trying to lead two future tyrants, especially Critias, to recognize their lack of the kind of self-certain wisdom that such a political ideal presupposes; we see him fail utterly in this effort (again, especially with Critias); we see why he fails, and how that failure is relevant to his own insistence that he did not teach virtue; and we see that it is particularly someone such as Critias who is most attracted to such an ideal of government. Rather than serving to introduce the authoritarian ideal of a scientific society run by political "experts" in a positive, utopian sense, the *Charmides* appears instead to be intended to show up the negative, *dystopian* significance of this ideal, for the simple reason that it is developed in this dialogue as the sophistic fantasy of a future tyrant. Thomas West:

> [Critias] very much likes Socrates' vision of a technocratic utopia managed by knowers of knowledge who make sure everything is done by experts. . . . It seems that Critias suffers from the tyrannical temptation that occurs precisely when one sees no limit to one's own knowledge.[9]

But if the pseudo-utopian ideal of a society governed by wise strongmen is repudiated in the *Charmides*, what is offered instead as a model of *sophron* government?

It is at this point, it seems to me, that the Socratic practice of dialectic, on the one hand, and the Socratic ideal of moderation, cognitive openness, and rationality associated with it, on the other, may be seen to have political, as well as moral significance. Of course if one is simply guided by the well-known criticisms that Socrates makes of majority rule, he may appear to be nothing more than a relentless critic of democracy. But it is also possible to judge democracy's friends by whether or not they oppose its enemies, and dialectic as Socrates employs it is critical of the enemies of democracy.[10] In particular, the *Charmides* depicts the philosopher in dialogue with a man who became one of most famous spokesmen for the Laconophilic element within Athenian politics, and then the greatest enemy and traitor to Athenian democracy—a man who was also Socrates' known companion, and perhaps a known admirer of a utopian ideal of government based on wisdom, an ideal that may have been associated with Socrates. To create a dialogue in which Socrates decisively refutes this man and the ideal of scientific government as he defends it on the grounds that it does not include the knowledge of good and evil constitutes in itself a powerful critique of the historical authoritarian alternative to democracy.

Moreover, the process of dialectic Socrates tries to draw Critias into within the dialogue suggests a very different model of government than authoritarian rule. We recall that Socrates had urged him to participate in their mutual deliberation and inquiry, on the grounds that the discovery of the truth about moral ideals is "a common good" (166d4–5). Is not the model suggested by such inquiry—the model of mutual deliberation in pursuit of the common good—the best alternative in a world without perfectly self-certain wisdom to authoritarian rule? Is not dialectic itself an idealized analogue of democratic decision procedures, albeit one in which deliberation is guided by reason, not mere self-seeking, one that is dialectical and not merely eristic?[11] The true Socratic art of government might then be conceived in this manner: not as one operating coercively in the interests of a foreknown, preestablished good, but one operating persuasively, seeking consent in a common deliberative and rational pursuit of the yet-to-be-established good; not as one presupposing the epistemic and moral/political inferiority of the ruled, but one in which every interlocutor has the equal right to participate and refute and establish, and in which the ruled no less than the rulers are called on to think for themselves and take on the responsibility of self-rule, personal and collective; not as one presuming that political life reduces to a mere contest for power among conflicting preestablished desires or interest groups, but one holding out the possibility of self-change and of a collectively rational society—a society that really does fulfill the Periclean vision in the Funeral Oration of a city in which "instead of looking on reasoning as an impediment to action, we think of it an indispensable preliminary to any wise action at all" (Thucydides, *History* II.40). The ideal of such government would be a truly *sophron* society, modeled on the Socratic dialectical community that we find in the *Charmides*. It would be a deliberative democracy, not an authoritarian government of self-certain knowers, for the simple reason that no such knowers have been found to exist.[12]

The *Charmides* depicts two men, Socrates and Critias, each of whom represents a specific ideal of moderation and self-knowledge, virtue and wisdom. Somehow, perhaps in part through Socrates, Critias has gotten hold of the ideal of *sophrosune* as a supreme form of knowledge, but the manner in which he understands this ideal has been shaped by his own shallow thought, unbridled ambition, and unexamined values—the values of a man concerned with his own advantage and honor, not with justice or truth. The argument and drama of the *Charmides* have shown us what this means in terms of his conception of the Greek ideal of a *sophron* individual. It means an understanding in which self-knowledge is completely separated from moderation and the recognition of epistemic limits, an understanding in the service of Critias' inflated self-image as one of the godlike wise men who deserve to rule—his view of himself as "greater than he is." The dialogue has now also shown us what it means on the political level, where it is related by Socrates to the ideal of a *sophron* society. Critias conceives of such a society as shaped by perfect rule and perfect knowledge, as one in which governance is not subject to law but to the ruler's choice, in which decisions are not arrived at by procedures of rational deliberation but by mere command, and in which the rulers would govern with unlimited power over the many, without regard to their consent to that rule. This vision presupposes the very thing that Socrates' original vision of the *sophron* society did not—that it would be self-evident who did and who did not possess the knowledge needed to justify decision-making authority. This is also the view of a society that is "greater than a city is." Critias is enamored of such a city, because he is enamored of his picture of his own commanding role in it. But he cannot defend the ideal of knowledge and virtue that it requires against Socrates' criticisms. So it must be rejected, as something the *Charmides* teaches us we do not know and do not possess, as involving an image of wisdom that is greater than human beings do or can possess. The dialogue therefore suggests that the reader also learn to reject the "great" ideal of perfect knowledge and virtue, together with its implications of absolute rule, when she discovers that *sophrosune* consists not only in the knowledge of what she knows, but also in the knowledge of what she does not know—a discovery that has profound political as well as personal implications.

SOPHROSUNE AND THE TECHNE OF GOOD AND EVIL

I have argued that the refutations of the definition at 167a1–7, at least through 172c4, apply strictly to Critias' conception of *sophrosune*, not to Socrates' own. But the argument in the last section of the dialogue seems at first to encompass his conception as well. For there he argues that even if self-relational being is possible, and even if knowledge of what one knows and does not know is possible, *sophrosune* would still be of no benefit to someone lacking the knowledge of good and evil, whereas if they possessed that knowledge, it would not be needed, either. This argument has seemed to many scholars to refute the definition at 167a1–7, and to imply that *sophrosune* is the craft-knowledge of good and evil.

I do not believe that the final argument refutes the Socratic interpretation of the definition. I will argue that when we relate the final argument to its dramatic setting, we realize that it is *Critias'* conception of *sophrosune* and Critias' understanding of what is involved in the knowledge of good and evil that are put to the test, and that it is these sophistic notions that are refuted with a final decisiveness, not the Socratic ideal. This is not to say that the last section does not suggest the possibility of a greater form of moral knowledge; but this possibility is introduced in a manner that is sufficiently problematic that we should not allow it to undermine our conviction of the lesser benefits suggested by the Socratic, dialectical ideal.

The final argument in the *Charmides* raises a number of important themes in Socratic philosophy:

1. It extends the discussion, adumbrated at 171d1–172a5, of an ideal society ruled by *sophrosune*, but again ends up criticizing this ideal. These discussions provide a basis for the critical view of such a society in the *Charmides*, as opposed to its positive construction in the *Republic*. (I offer such a comparison in appendix B.)

2. The discussion also introduces the concept of a "guardian moderation" (*sophrosune phulattousa*, 173d2) and emphasizes something only hinted at earlier, that someone might be ruled by moderation, rather than merely use it in the service of her goals. This suggests a different theory of the relationship of free agency and rational virtue than what Critias had assumed.

3. The argument develops an account of the relation of the arts and the knowledge of good and evil that is found in many of the early dialogues, notably the *Laches*, *Euthydemus* and *Gorgias*. This characterization of the nature of the relationship between these two modalities of knowledge is important for understanding the structure of Socratic ethical thought.

4. And it raises the question of the relation of moral knowledge to *sophrosune* in the sense of dialectical wisdom, as well as in the sense that Critias had assigned it. Socrates will get Critias to agree to the destructive dilemma that (a) *sophrosune* cannot be beneficial unless guided by a superordinate craft of moral knowledge, and (b) that it is superfluous, if one has such a craft. But if

this is the case, the Socratic, no less than the Critian conception of *sophrosune* would appear to be refuted. *For the Socratic ideal operates in a moral world in which such a superordinate craft has not yet been found.* It proposes instead a dialectical, self-reflective conception of ethics, which falls short of technical mastery, but is not without moral content. If the only knowledge by which we may be benefited is a perfect *techne* of good and evil, and such knowledge is absent in the world of Socratic thought, we are left with a nihilistic conclusion. If we are to avoid that conclusion, there must be some way in which the final argument is less telling against the Socratic ideal than it seems. Now let us turn back to the dialogue.

The final argument in the inquiry may be divided into three segments: (a) Socrates' "dream" of a life according to the sciences, 172c4–173d7; (b) Socrates' criticism of this ideal, based on the difference between living "according to knowledge" and living in accordance with the knowledge of good and evil, 173d8–174d7; and (c) Socrates' characterization of the knowledge of good and evil as a productive *techne* and his defense of the argument against Critias' counterarguments, 174d8–175b4. I will take up each segment in turn, then discuss Irwin's and Tuckey's interpretations of the final argument, and conclude with a comparison of the ideals of Socratic self-knowledge and moral expertise.

Socrates' Dream (172c4–173d7)

Socrates' dream returns to the hubristic supposition, previously rejected, that the knowledge of knowledge and nonknowledge might provide a "great" benefit, since living by it we ourselves and those ruled by us would live unerringly, with the result that not only individuals, but households and city-states as well would be well-ordered and happy. Now, however, he argues that even if we were ruled by *sophrosune*, such wisdom would not be sufficient to guarantee our happiness. We would not be deceived by a fraudulent pilot or doctor or general or anyone else claiming to be but not really being skilled in their art. Our bodies would be more healthy, our lives would be more secure from physical danger, and all of our equipment and possessions would be better built than they are now. Socrates then concedes the possibility of an art of divination and supposes it also to be subject to the rule of *sophrosune*, but insists that even if we had the accurate knowledge of the future it would provide, such "doing according to knowledge" (*epistemonos prattontes*) would still not allow us to "do well" (*eu prattoimen*) and "be happy" (*eudaimonoimen*) (172c4–174d7).

As Tuckey explains, Socrates' discussion here centers on the meaning of the phrase "do well": "His expression of doubt whether *epistemonos an prattontes eu an prattoimen* ["acting knowledgeably we would also do well"] at once demands the determination of the meaning of *eu*, which, as soon becomes clear, can only denote *moral* as opposed to merely *technical* perfection."[13] Socrates' point is that although we might "do well" in the sense of the correct practice of a technical art, we might not "do well" in the moral sense of bringing about well-being and happiness. This, we recall, was the point at which the earlier discussion of *sophrosune* as "doing good" had floundered (164a1–c4; cf. chapter 2).

There are three modifications made here to the description of the ideal society Socrates had already introduced at 171d1–172a5. The first is the specification that *sophrosune* would "preside" (*epistatousan*) over the other knowledges and function as a "guardian moderation" (*sophrosune phulattousa*). What remains unclear is the manner in which *sophrosune* would do this. It seems natural to suppose that it would preside in the manner of a hegemonic art, such as we have associated most closely with the Critian ideal of self-sufficient rulership. Then it would freely dispose over the other sciences, using their products and services as it saw fit. Socrates will soon go on to show Critias that on this model, *sophrosune* must be identical with another science than mere self-knowledge or self-certainty. On the other hand, if *sophrosune* were to function in relation to knowledge in a different manner, it might still be of protective benefit, if only to guard us against the self-deception of thinking that we possessed a greater knowledge than we really had, and that we were ourselves greater than we really are.

The second modification introduces the idea, only implied earlier, that *sophrosune* would rule us, rather than be something over which we would exercise free dominion. Whereas the previous description, so appealing to Critias, had emphasized the distance between the rulers and the ruled and the identification of himself and Socrates as rulers, this description suggests that the rulers are not simply free, but are ruled by their virtue, that is, that their action is no longer governed by mere "self-certainty" but rather by "rational principle." This implies the subordination of the rulers to their knowledge; they would be free in the sense of being ruled by reason. But this model of agency—of *logos* as ruler, as it were—was also shown to be problematic, when Critias demonstrated that it is possible for someone to refuse to be ruled by his own knowledge, to prefer to *seem* to be knowledgeable, rather than admit that there was knowledge he did not possess. Thus Socrates' dream of a perfectly *sophron* society and perfectly *sophron* individuals does not square fully with what we have already learned from the *Charmides* about the relation of knowledge and virtue, about a person's relation to her own professed ideals. If the true *sophrosune* must protect one not only against cognitive error, but also against the willingness to insist one's knowledge is greater (or lesser) than it is, then it cannot consist in a simple state of reason that rules over us; rather, it must reflect the self-relational nature of the rational self, the fact that *for a self to be ruled by reason, she must also rule herself*.[14] Socrates, who has enacted this truth and witnessed its opposite in Critias, must realize this, even if Critias does not. This again suggests the description of the ideal state is elencticly oriented to Critias' understanding of *sophrosune*, not Socrates' own.

The third modification is the introduction of divination, as a special kind of art which might allow us to be even more capable to do what is beneficial. There is a similar argument in the *Laches*, where Nicias, in response to Laches' suggestion that the soothsayers might know what is fearful and encouraging, insists that such judgments are beyond their ken, since while they would know what events would occur in the future, they would not know in virtue of their mere foresight how to judge the moral value of those events: "The soothsayer ought to know only the signs of things that are about to come to pass, whether it be death or disease or loss of property or victory or defeat in war or in any sort of contest. But whether the suffering or non-suffering of these things will be *best* for a man is a question which is no more for a soothsayer to decide than for anyone else" (195e–196a, my italics).[15] The point of this discussion is the same as that underscored by Tuckey concerning the ambiguity of *eu* in the phrase *eu prattein*, namely the essential difference between the knowledge of human things pertaining to their moral value, and that pertaining to prediction of the events themselves. This division is basic to the overall structure of Socratic ethics, since it reflects the distinction between the moral welfare of the soul or whole person, which is sufficient for and constitutive of happiness, and the goods of the body and of fortune, which are at best secondary to it (cf., e.g., *Apology* 30a, *Crito* 47d–48a, *Gorgias* 469d, 470e).[16] This was the distinction Socrates insisted on in the prologue to the *Charmides*, where he asserted that the entire welfare of the person depended on the state of their soul (156e6–8). But is there a final science of good and evil that will guarantee such felicity? Or might moral well-being rather be found in a lesser state of virtue?

Socrates' Criticism of this Ideal (173c8–174d7)

Critias, confused and frustrated by Socrates' argument, retorts that Socrates will not easily find a better delimitation (*telos*) of doing well if he "dishonors" "[acting] knowledgeably" (*epistemonos*). As Tuckey notes, Critias' puzzlement here may in part be due to his belief that Socrates is once again criticizing what Critias believes Socrates himself upholds, that is, that virtue is knowledge.[17] At any rate, Critias still does not understand what Socrates is driving at, until Socrates asks him in what acting knowledgeably will lead to doing well. They then go through three possibilities: (1) the first is actually a set of possibilities, all of which Critias rejects angrily, including the arts of shoe-making, bronze-working, and in general the shaping of a homogeneous physical material, to which Socrates replies that then they must have been mistaken, for these all seem to "live knowledgeably"; (2) the second is the art of divination, which Critias says *would* be one of two types who would be happy, and this leads to Socrates' supposition of one who would know past, present, and future and "be ignorant of nothing"; (3) the third possibility is based on this supposition, but Socrates wants to know which of his knowledges makes him happy: is it the competitive art of draught-playing (a game like chess or checkers), the art of logistic (previously treated as theoretical, 166a5–11), or the knowledge of health and disease? Critias says the latter is more like what he has in mind. Note that this argument presupposes the existence of someone whose wisdom does not consist in knowing what he knows and does not know, *because there is nothing that he does not know.*

Clearly, Socrates intends to lead Critias again to the contrast between the determinate arts and a wholistic "art of living." It could only be in the latter, comprehensive art concerned with human life as a whole that "acting knowledgeably" could guarantee "doing well" and "being happy." If self-knowledge is concerned merely with technical, not with moral matters, it cannot know whether the ends to which it puts those services are beneficial. This was the point Socrates had made earlier at 164a1–c4, and eventually Critias sees what Socrates is getting at, though it is note-

worthy that Critias is inclined to regard the art of divination—
which might allow one to foresee possible future events so as to
select the path that will lead to good and avoid the path that will
lead to ill fortune—as being on an equal status with the art he will
eventually identify as the knowledge of good and evil. This ambivalence on Critias' part would seem to indicate that he is not really
clear about the sovereignty of the moral over the nonmoral values
in human life and happiness. (Nicias—the representative of
Sophistry in the *Laches*—shows a similar ambivalence.[18])

Finally, Critias reveals the knowledge he has in mind, and it
is Socrates' turn to appear angry, hurling the same term of abuse on
Critias that he had previously hurled at Charmides, calling him a
"wretch" (*miare*, 174b11), and accusing him of concealing the fact
that "it was not living knowledgeably that makes one do well and
be happy, not even if it be with all the other knowledges together,
but with one alone, of the good and bad" (174b11–c3). Because if
one takes this knowledge away, the other arts would still deliver
their products and services, but these products and services would
do us no benefit. But then it seems that it is not the knowledge of
knowledges and nonknowledges, but the knowledge of good and
evil that is beneficial, not the art of *sophrosune* (174c3–d7).

The distinctive element in this argument is Socrates' use of
the *techne*-analogy to suggest, *contrary to the entire previous
movement of the inquiry*, that there is an "craft" of living (or of
benefit) separate from self-knowledge. We recall the discussion at
164a1–c4, where the account of *sophrosune* as "doing good" had
floundered on the question of knowing that what one did was beneficial. Critias might have introduced the idea of *sophrosune* as a
craft-knowledge of good and evil at that point, but he rejected that
model when Socrates suggested it shortly afterward at 165c8–e2,
albeit without becoming clear concerning the relation between the
epistemic/formal and hegemonic/substantive aspects of his own
conception of self-knowledge. Socrates has now exploited this
aspect of Critias' misconception, his substitution of "self-certainty" or mere will for a determinate conception of the good. But
he has done so in a manner that is a regression from the earlier
insights of the dialogue, a reversion to the notion of a kind of moral
wisdom that excludes its self-referential aspect, reducing it to the
model of a science with an external product. I have argued that
those insights, while they had dubious application to Critias'
understanding of the ideal of self-knowledge, were profoundly relevant to the Socratic ideal of dialectical self-knowledge and the

moral principles informing it. If that ideal is not also to be rejected, and if the insights relevant to it achieved in the formulation of the definition from 165c4–167a7 and in the metaphysical and epistemological discussion of it from 167a8–172c4 are to be preserved, there must be something *very* wrong with this argument. But can Critias discern it?

Socrates' Reply to Critias' Counterarguments (174d8–175b4)

Critias does his best to rescue *sophrosune* from Socrates' argument of irrelevance, by suggesting that if it is a knowledge of knowledges, it would preside over all the other knowledges, including this knowledge about the good, and thus it would be beneficial. But Socrates responds that since every knowledge makes only its own product (*ergon*), and since they have "long born witness" that *sophrosune* is a knowledge only of knowledge and of nonknowledge but of nothing else, then just as it cannot also be productive of health, because health was from another art, so it cannot be productive of benefit, because they had just assigned this to another art. He concludes it cannot be beneficial, being the "hand-craftsman" (*demiourgos*) of no benefit (174d8–175a8).

With these remarks, the inquiry reaches its aporetic end. Socrates blames himself for this evidently false conclusion, when what everyone agrees is "most beautiful of all" (*kalliston panton*, 175a11) should appear to them be unbeneficial: "For as it is now, we are everywhere worsted, and we are unable to discover whichever of the things that are that the lawgiver set this name upon, '*sophrosune*.'" (175b2–4.) I will discuss these remarks and Socrates' review of the argument in the next chapter. But first let us consider the last steps in the argument. It is *not* the decisive refutation of the Socratic ideal of moderation and self-knowledge that it first seems to be.

Once again, Plato leaves a hint of this in his choice of terminology.[19] Thus Socrates uses the plural in arguing at 174d4–5 that it is not the knowledge "of knowledge*s* and nonknowledge*s*" (*epistemon je kai anepistemosunon*), but the knowledge of good and evil that has as its work our benefit, and Critias confirms this terminology at 174d9 (albeit characteristically dropping the reference to nonknowledges). Socrates uses the singular, however, in referring at 174e6–7 to the "knowledge of knowledge alone and of non-knowledge" (*epistemes monon . . . kai anepistemosunes episteme*), when he contrasts *sophrosune* to those knowledges that have a concrete product.

These terminological shifts may be explained in the following manner: As we have seen throughout, it is Critias who has been associated with the ideal of a "knowledge of the knowledges," that is, with an ideal of wisdom and self-certainty presiding in some manner over the other knowledges. Socrates' refutation here targets this ideal. For it is Critias who long ago introduced a notion of self-knowledge completely separate from moderation, and Critias who all along has not known how to relate the hegemonic aspect of his notion of a "knowledge of the knowledges" to the aspect having to do with the "knowledge of itself" (i.e., of oneself as opposed to others). But here again, Critias has been led by his moral and intellectual confusion into a series of admissions that both bring out his real beliefs and show the contradictions besetting them. For Critias does not suppose that the "knowledge of good and evil" is a separate and subordinate art to *sophrosune*, as he is led to assert at 174c3–174d7. Rather, he has thought of *sophrosune* all along as involving superior knowledge in this respect, as including self-certainty of godlike men regarding "what counts" and "what really matters," that is, his own benefit. It is Socrates who has cleverly shifted the emphasis in the representation of *sophrosune* to the point where what Critias thought of essentially as a manner of rule by self-superior men has come to be envisioned as a self-concerned habit of testing and examining claims to knowledge—where not the knowledge of itself and other knowledges, but the knowledge of knowledge and especially nonknowledge is regarded as its primary feature. And yet Critias must agree that his ideal includes knowledge of what makes for true benefit and happiness; so he must already dimly recognize that something has gone wrong in the argument, when he suggests that *sophrosune* might preside over the craft of self-advantage, along with the other crafts, at 174d8–e2. The tenuous hold he has on his own conceptions is yet once again made evident, when he accedes to Socrates' representation of moral wisdom as a productive *techne* at 174e3–175a8. For it was precisely this model that he rejected at 165e3–166a2, when he rightly insisted that self-knowledge had an entirely different structure than that of a technical-productive science.

Where has Critias gone wrong? The answer would appear to be at the very beginning of Socrates' final elenchus, at 174a4–6, when Critias agreed to the supposition of someone who possessed knowledge of all the knowledges and "was ignorant of nothing."[20] This supposition—that wisdom consists in a state of absolute and comprehensive knowledge, rather than in a state including the knowledge of ignorance—was the crucial premiss leading to Critias' downfall. But despite the fact that Critias is made here to accept a model of the knowledge of good and evil that is inconsistent with the insights he had expressed earlier, this result is not the result of a mere trick of Socratic dialectic (which would then be mere eristic). On the contrary, Critias' refutation is founded on what we have seen to be his most characteristic trait throughout the dialogue: *his absolute unwillingness to acknowledge epistemic limits.* Critias is strung up on his own petard, confuted by his own willful need to claim to seem "ignorant of nothing." He is led into genuine self-contradiction, whether he acknowledges it or not.

Critias, unable to conceive of a kind of knowledge that is neither merely technical nor merely self-certain (that conceit having been refuted), has been trapped by Socrates into self-contradiction. If there were a *techne* of good and evil, it would have to be the architectonic science, not *sophrosune*. If there is no such *techne*—if *sophrosune* does not preside over it as well as the other *technai*—then how could the superior *sophron* man know that he was "doing good"? Though he does not seem to realize it, Critias has been driven back to the very point where he offered genuine insights into the discussion—the point where he first conceived of *sophrosune* as a form of self-knowledge that did not have an external product or an external object as its subject of concern, but rather was concerned with oneself and one's own relation to knowledge. Now, however, he is exposed as someone who has proven completely unable to provide a rational account of those insights. Thanks to Socrates' narrative of his words and his deeds, we can see that he never made them his own. Instead of pursuing self-knowledge and truth, he preferred to save face and tried to bully his way through. Just as his "perplexity" was the mere image of perplexity, so his insights have been the mere images of insight—beautiful words (poetry), but lacking the substance of reasoned explanation (philosophy).

But what of Socrates and his ideal of *sophrosune*? Is it also refuted? I will complete the discussion of this question by considering first Irwin's, then Tuckey's interpretations of the final argument in the dialogue, and compare them to my own.

Irwin and Tuckey on the Final Argument

Irwin says that Socratic self-knowledge is an "important component" in *sophrosune* (which he translates as "temperance"), but he analyzes the final argument as implying that temperance must be identified with the knowledge of good and evil:

1. Only knowledge of good and evil always benefits us (174b11–c3).
2. Therefore, if temperance is separate from the knowledge of good and evil, it does not always benefit us (174d4–7).
3. But temperance always benefits us (175e2–176a5).
4. Therefore, temperance is the knowledge of good and evil.

(Irwin acknowledges that this last step is not explicit in the *Charmides*, but insists that it must be inferred.)[21]

Irwin's interpretation ignores the dramatic context.[22] As a result, he fails to recognize the basic problematic of the dialogue, namely the incompatibility of Socratic *sophrosune*, as articulated in the definition at 167a1–7, with the technical-productive model of the knowledge of good and evil. It is true that Socrates imports the *techne* model, with Critias' agreement, at the end of the inquiry. But self-knowledge, as was first insisted on at 165e3–166a2 and as we have seen exhibited and articulated throughout this study of the dialogue, has a completely different structure than a craft and cannot simply be a "component" of one.[23] Either we must affirm what we have identified as the Socratic account of self-knowledge in the *Charmides*, or we must agree with the supposition that *sophrosune* is a craft of good and evil; we cannot have it both ways. But if we attend to the dramatic element of the dialogue, and contextualize the arguments in relation to it, we have good reasons to affirm the former, and to interpret the latter within the specific framework of the refutation of Critias. For it was Critias who was led, through his admission of an omniscient knower, into the supposition of a *techne* of good and evil. This supposition is without ground in the drama and argument of the dialogue to that point; it functions in the manner of a deus ex machina to the work, though it does reflect Critias' attraction to the ideal of expertise.[24] If there were a perfect knowledge of good and evil along the lines Socrates suggests at the end of the dialogue, then we like Critias should have to accept the first premise, and the argument would stand. But we have no reason to believe, at the end of the *Charmides*, that there is such a self-certain, productive, teachable science—quite the opposite. The *Charmides* does indeed suggest that *sophrosune*, rightly understood, includes moral knowledge in the sense of a reasoned commitment to moral principles. But that knowledge is of a lesser sort than the craft-knowledge that is conjectured, for the purposes of refuting Critias, at the end.

It is appropriate to close with a few words on Tuckey's reading of the dialogue, which in some respects is closest to my own.

Tuckey argues that the dialogue enters in effect on a long digression at 164c6, when the fourth definition ("doing what is good") is shown to lack a cognitive component, "knowing that it is good." But if this is the case, it seems the true definition of *sophrosune* must consist in the science and practice of virtue. This interpretation correlates nicely with the structure of the dialogue, and with a plausible account of the relation of the aporetic dialogues to the *Republic*. The *Charmides* would end by pointing toward the *Republic* ideal, though the craft of philosophical governance there will be called *dikaiosune* rather than *sophrosune*.[25]

The problem with Tuckey's treatment of the dialogue is that he, too, largely ignores the dramatic element in the work. This leads him to fail generally to appreciate the way in which the ambivalence between the Socratic and Critian conceptions of self-knowledge functions throughout their inquiry; he also typically ignores how the speakers' deeds are used to comment on their words.[26] This criticism applies to his interpretation of the specific discussion at 173d8–175a8 as well. Focusing sharply on the phrases *epistemonos . . . ton allon epistemon* and *epistemonos tautes tes peri ton agathon* at 174b11–c2, and relating these only tangentially to the drama, he argues that these phrases must be translated as "with knowledge *that one knows* the other branches of knowledge" and "with knowledge, that is, recognition, *that one knows* the Good" (his italics).[27] But these translations are patently forced, and while Tuckey notes the crucial textual precisions at 174d8 and 174e6 between the knowledge of knowledges and the knowledge of knowledge and nonknowledge, he does not attempt to relate these distinctions to the different interlocutors and their different ideals of hegemonic self-certainty and rational self-criticism and humility.

Tuckey's account of the final argument is extraordinarily convoluted. He reads it to imply that *sophrosune*, to be beneficial, must be omniscience (including knowledge of the Good), but also that Plato realizes that "it is certainly no such thing and it would be very surprising if it were."[28] One would expect therefore that Tuckey would take this to be a dead end, but instead he imports an entirely new meaning of *sophrosune*, which he suggests is what Socrates has in mind at 172b1–c2, "the ability to think clearly and rationally," and argues that it is *this* conception of *sophrosune* that Plato believes must coincide with the knowledge of the Good. But this argument is clearly mistaken. The "lesser" type of *sophrosune*, which Tuckey associates with clear and rational thinking—and which I have associated with Socratic self-knowledge and dialectic—cannot yield *certain* knowledge of the Good, as Tuckey claims for it.[29] This distinction, however, is exactly what is at stake in the Socratic notion of cognitive moderation and self-knowledge, as opposed to the sophistic idea of moral expertise and the claim that those with such expertise should rule. Tuckey is on the right track, in my view, when he looks askance at the role that omniscience plays in the final steps in the argument. But due to his abstraction from the larger dramatic context he has failed to see how this role is particularly relevant to the refutation of Critias, and thus to the critical light that the *Charmides* casts on the ideal of moral expertise—the light which, as I argued in the last chapter, reveals that such a vision of society would be especially appealing to a tyrannical personality, to someone unable or unwilling to recognize his own epistemic limitations, but not unwilling to give free rein to his own ambition to rule. Tuckey has also failed to see how here, no less than throughout the dialogue, Socratic self-knowledge is characterized precisely by its realization that it does *not* possess certainty—without that limitation implying that it is not virtuous, albeit in a more modest way than a Critias wants to assert.

It is true that the Socratic ideal of moderation and wisdom falls short of moral expertise.[30] If there could be no true harm or benefit without such expertise, the refutation might include it. But this takes the final argument, which relies on the possibility of absolute knowledge (omniscience), with its coordinate idea of a moral handcraft, at face value. If such a notion is revealed to be fanciful, we must regard the final argument very differently.

The *Charmides* does not examine the idea of a *techne* of good and evil directly, but it casts an oblique light on it, by its drama and argument. It does so in its drama by associating that ideal with the figure of Critias and exposing him as a man of tyrannical aspirations. It does so in its argument by the attitude it takes toward *techne* as the form of moral knowledge, and by the critical light it sheds on the utopian ideal of a technocratic society. The second half of the inquiry begins by supposing that there is a higher form of knowledge than that modeled on *techne*—self-knowledge. It shows that this form of knowledge has enormous consequences for how we conceive of human beings and what our model of knowledge should be. The drama motivates and informs that inquiry, by revealing such self-knowledge to be present in the figure of

Socrates. The argument then introduces the ideal of a society run by experts, but it rejects this ideal as a deceptive fantasy, after its leaders are shown to lack moral wisdom. The argument ends by conjecturing, as the chief part of absolute knowledge, a perfect technique of good and evil. This "craft of good and evil" might be thought to replace *sophrosune* as the hegemonic science, but it implies that the one who has it would not need to examine critically her own or others' claims to knowledge. It is Socrates who introduces this latter notion and Critias who is refuted by means of it; but it was Critias who, in the drama of the dialogue, came to be associated with the ideal of absolute knowledge, and Socrates who, by his words and deeds, came to be associated with the insight that the knowledge of ignorance and the self-care and "self-guardianship" arising from such self-knowledge are principal elements of human moral wisdom.

What Critias was not associated with, and indeed was disassociated from, is the conception of *sophrosune* involving the knowledge of ignorance, the limitation of human wisdom. That ideal of rationality we have found embodied in Socrates. It was that ideal that established the possibility—indeed, the necessity—of a rethinking of metaphysics, such that it would allow for the reality of self-relational human being. It was that ideal that we also found relevant to a rethinking of epistemology, such that it might be possible to know, if only provisionally, what oneself or another did or did not know. But now it is that ideal that also must be brought into relation to the idea mooted here of a *techne* of good and evil. Apart from a mere assertion, based on the supposition of absolute knowledge, the *Charmides* offers no good reason to suppose that this ideal of perfect moral expertise is a genuine human possibility.

If the notion of a moral technique is rejected as a hubristic fancy when applied to human beings, then we might suppose that the insights emerging in the ascent to the definition at 167a1–7 are true, that is, that moral knowledge is grounded in a voluntary habit of critical reason and that it takes the form neither of technical-productive, nor of theoretical-objective knowledge, but of self-knowledge in a rational community. Then we will consider that dialectical moderation might be a necessary condition for the highest form of moral knowledge that we, as humans, can have. The benefits of such moderation would be as complex as the beings who enjoyed it. On the negative side, they would relate to those experiences in which one discovered that one did not know what one thought one knew—experiences revealing the possibility of self-deception and moral ignorance, which would force one back, in self-concern, on the path of seeking the good. On the positive side, they would include the enlightening, value-formative consequences of continually extending one's rational capacity to one's own and others' lives and conduct. It is these experiences that give semantic depth to the categories of *psyche, episteme,* and *epimeleia* ("self-care," cf. 173a5) as basic to human life. The benefits of Socratic *sophrosune,* positive and negative, may appear to be modest in the light of the dream of an absolute science of happiness and a life of godlike perfection; but that light may be unnaturally bright and lead to blindness, not discernment.

On the Socratic model, dialectic and moral knowledge are not simply separate, but operate interdependently. Dialectic is the rational, self- and other-testing form of Socratic morality; without it whatever values the person might uphold would be prey to the unwarranted influence of others or retained only through an unwavering resoluteness, which by its very dogmatism would undermine concern for truth. Its field of application is the domain of the moral life; the principles guiding it are constitutive of communicative reasoning as a practice oriented toward the common good of truth and the personal goal of happiness. The result is indeed something less than moral expertise. But this does not imply that it is not beneficial to the person who lives by it, or that it protects her against no harm. The *Charmides* teaches that we go astray if we conceive of moral wisdom as something "greater than it is," if we do not recognize our limits.

EIGHT

⬦

EPILOGUE

One of the things of which Plato tries to convince us is this: that by the use of his method Socrates had the privilege of proving to the Sophists and other fools that that was what they were. Such a claim is out of the question.
—Arthur Schopenhauer

The dialogue ends with Socrates' summary of the argument, followed by an exchange with Charmides concerning whether he does or does not have *sophrosune*. Each part of this final scene is marked by immoderation.

Socrates finishes the inquiry by reminding Critias of his fear, expressed at 166c7–d6, that he might not know how to investigate beautifully. For if he had, what is agreed to be "most beautiful of all" (*kallestaton*, 175b1) would never have appeared to be unbeneficial to them. Socrates goes on to identify the unjustified concessions they made: (1) that the knowledge of knowledge exists (which Critias had not been able to explain conclusively at 167a8–169d1); and (2) that this knowledge recognizes the works of other knowledges, with the result that the *sophron* person might know both what he knows and what he does not know (which they had concluded he must not know at 171c4–10 and 172a7–9). This second point Socrates says was an especially "grandiose" (*megaloprepos*) concession, since it implied that one might somehow know what he does not know at all, than which "nothing might seem more unreasonable" (*oudenos hotou ouchi alogoteron*, 175c7–8). Socrates then says that the inquiry itself—the *Logos*—was also unable to discover the truth, for it "quite offensively" (*hubristikos*) made it seem to them that what they had long agreed to and "fabricated" (*symplattones*, a term that echoes Plato's own name) and set down

147

as *sophrosune* was not beneficial (this presumably referring to the final argument at 172c4–175b4, ignoring the benefit suggested at 172b1–c2).

It is interesting that Socrates begins his summation by taking complete personal responsibility for the inquiry. This absolves Critias, who must be burning with frustration, since he cannot claim the knowledge/superiority he just knows he has! It also shifts our attention to the unproven hypotheses, particularly the hypothesis that knowledge of ignorance is possible. Surely these should be further examined. The entire dynamic of the dialogue has centered on the role of the knowledge of ignorance in the conceptualization of moderation and in the actualization of moral knowledge. The puzzle regarding the possibility of discovering and then knowing what you do not know suggests the paradox posed in the *Meno* (cf. 80d).[1] There it leads Socrates into what is generally taken to be the first representation of the Theory of Recollection. In the context of this dialogue, however, we can understand and resolve the paradox without recurring to that theory. It *is* perfectly unreasonable to suppose one can know what one does not know "at all": Critias, who personifies the vice of immoderation, is unable to recognize that he does not know the virtue, as a result of his own willful blindness. And yet it is also—here is the great illogic, the evident contradiction—perfectly reasonable to conclude that one *can* know what one does not know. Paradoxical as it may be, we have seen how moderation might function in the successful operation of the elenchus, and we have seen the virtue written at large in the person of Socrates: we have seen that it is necessary to choose moderation in order to discover it—it is necessary to be willing to submit to the truth, to give up one's own pride of certainty, to recognize what one does not know, and thus be led into the serious pursuit of moral knowledge, the life of philosophy.

But then why at the end does Socrates personify the *logos*, shifting the blame to it for the false conclusion?

The answer to this question is suggested in the *Charmides'* sibling dialogue, the *Laches*, where Socrates, in order to persuade the refuted old general into persevering in the discussion, invokes a laughing Courage, who would mock them if they quit in their attempt to catch her.[2] Here the *logos* is personified, not the virtue, but the effect is similar. The argument has laughed at the truth (*ten aletheian*) and at them, by leading them to think that *sophrosune* is not beneficial. The *logos* is clearly false, and they must return to the task of inquiry. With these words the reader is made to reconsider the argument, particularly the long last part. What Socrates (and Plato) may be telling us is that what was "fabricated together" ("plate-onized") in the dialogue, that is, the definition of moderation at 167a1–7, is genuinely beneficial, even if the argument does not show it to be. And have we not seen this to be the case?

By means of the summary, the inquiry exhibits a mode of critical, self-relational consciousness. On the one hand, it challenges the reader to reassess the hypotheses it failed to establish, but then presumed as it moved to the final refutation; on the other hand, it suggests to the reader that that final refutation—the one proving the Socratic ideal of *sophrosune* to be unbeneficial—may well have been a mockery of the truth. By means of the summary, the argument declares itself to have been excessive or hubristic in both respects: it took as truth what it could not prove (violating the cardinal principle of science), and it rejected virtue as unbeneficial (violating the cardinal principle of ethics). Thus Socrates and the argument exhibit the virtue of knowing what one does not know, by exposing the erroneous reasons that brought it to its conclusions, and by suggesting that some of it—the final section in particular—was deeply misleading. This is not, as we recall, the first time in the *Charmides* that the summary of an argument has cast a skeptical light back on itself. Such also occured in Socrates' summary of the argument at 160b7–d3. The *Charmides* is a dialogue in which the *logos* is self-critical, and in this way thus invites the reader into the process of thinking through the issues for herself. The arguments are not to be taken as the final word; they even tell us that themselves. The speeches are part of a larger picture, in which action and narrative also have a composing role.

Socrates then turns to Charmides and says that he is less annoyed for his own sake than for the sake of Charmides, if he, having his looks and in addition being in soul most moderate (*sophronestatos*), has no benefit from it. But actually Socrates is most annoyed for his own sake, since then he wasted his time learning the incantation from the Thracian, when it was for something that was worthless. He concludes that this is not the case, but that he is a poor inquirer, that *sophrosune* is a great good, and that, if Charmides has it, he is blessed. But this brings them back to the question with which they began—what does Charmides say now: Does he have it, or is he in need of the incantation?

Charmides responds that, "by Zeus," he does not know

whether or not he has it; how could he, when even the two of them—Socrates and Critias—cannot discover what it is. And yet he is not persuaded by Socrates, and he supposes that he does need the incantation—he would be happy to be chanted to by him, until Socrates says it is enough.

There then follows the curious, ominous ending of the dialogue, in which Critias and Charmides draw apart from Socrates and agree that the boy will be attached to Socrates, and that Socrates will perform his incantation on him. This ending echoes the scene in the prologue, when Charmides casually presumed to order Socrates to give him the incantation, though then he quickly relented (156a4). Now, the two future tyrants decide together to impose their will on Socrates, and they declare themselves unwilling to yield to persuasion. "Will you use violence?" Socrates asks. "You can count on it," Charmides answers, "since he [Critias] is ordering me to do it." Socrates concludes that there is no rational path out of the situation for him, since if Charmides attempts to do something, especially by violence, "no human being will be able to oppose you" (176b5–d5).

This ending puts a series of odd spins on what has gone before. Socrates' quick turnabout concerning his vexation might suggest that he is less annoyed for Charmides' sake than his own, because he has discovered that Charmides' moderation is of a type with his looks, a merely apparent and quasi-natural quality that he will not be able to benefit from anyway; his conclusion that he is himself a poor inquirer makes us think that what he learned may have been worthwhile after all, and wonder again if perhaps it was not logic, but something else about the inquiry that led to the conclusion that *sophrosune* as they plated it together was not beneficial. (Socrates is conspicuously silent throughout his summary as to what role Critias may have had in their coming to such untoward conclusions.)

Charmides' reply that he does not know if he has *sophrosune* has been taken by some readers as a genuine sign of moderation, the realization that, indeed, he does not know.[3] But this inference may be confuted, if we think that he should have no doubt at 176a2 that he lacks it, and that he shows little sign of modesty regarding his own judgment when he presumes to insist, contrary to Socrates' lingering uncertainty, that he can get what he needs from Socrates, if the latter will only chant to him as long as necessary. Note too that it is Socrates who is to chant to him, with Charmides' own role passive; this strongly implies the boy has not understood the manner in which one is to submit to Socrates' charms.

The thought that Charmides' final remarks do not reflect the *sophrosune* that would make him want to inquire for himself is confirmed when Critias, his "Guardian Immoderation" as it were, reenters the discussion and proceeds to support the presumptuous claim his ward has made on Socrates' time. Contrary to Socrates' remarks, they do not "take counsel" or "plot" together (*bouleuesthai*; compare the very different scene at *Crito* 46a). Here, at the very end of the dialogue, Charmides declares his continuing subordination to the wishes of the future tyrant; he affirms what we began to suspect at 161b4–c1, when he ran away from the inquiry and Socrates called him a "wretch": he has accepted a life of moral heterarchy, in which he will remain forever the slave of his guardian master. And what a slave he is, with his charming beauty and seeming moderation, but in fact an erotic tool in the hands of a man who in his craving for honor and power will stop at nothing to get what he wants, not even violence.[4] No, Charmides does not prove to be *sophron* at the end of this conversation, quite the contrary. He reveals, together with Critias, the terrible forces of the human *psyche* with which Socratic philosophy is fated to contend—forces that themselves are the most irrational things, because they refuse to submit to reason.

The reversal is now complete: Charmides, spoiled youthful beauty-appetite incarnate, together with Critias, sophistic-poetic/beautiful willful-tyrannic/ugliness incarnate, join together to force the philosopher to teach them virtue, and the philosopher cannot oppose them; they are in the end too strong. But this implies neither that he will teach them nor that he will serve them; the future is more open. The dialogue ends on a tragic note, with its allusion to Charmides' and Critias' collusion in the Thirty and Socrates' own death at the hands of the city that could not appreciate the difference between the ideal by which he lived and its distorted reflection in the deeds and souls of his most immoderate acquaintances. But philosophy does not live by the measure of tragedy and political history. It lives by another measure, that of the *logos*. And the *logos*, so far from being tragic, embodies the spirit of comedy, as it laughs at our inabilities to see its and our own deficiencies, and complete them by importing the action of life.[5] The drama of the *Charmides*, like its hero, serenely transcends the turmoil of its times.

Appendix A
The Structure of the *Charmides*

The literary structure of the *Charmides* can be analyzed in more than one way. The most evident is simply to break it down in terms of the speakers and what appear to be the "natural joints" in the dialogue, marked by new formulations, or extended speeches, or some other signifying device.[1] Thus:

Pattern I: The overt structure

I. Prologue, which ends with Socrates' question to
    Charmides   153a1–158e5
II. Dialogue, which includes the inquiry to its aporetic
    ending   158e6–175b4
    A. With Charmides, which ends with Critias' brusk
        entry   158e6–162b11
        1. first definition, which ends in refutation   158e6–160d4
            a. formulation
            b. examination/refutation
        2. second definition, which ends in refutation   160d5–161b4
            a. formulation
            b. examination/refutation
        3. third definition, which ends in mockery of
            Critias   161b4–162b11
            a. formulation
            b. examination/refutation

B. With Critias, which ends with Socrates' comments   162c1–175b4
    1. third definition, which Critias abandons   162c1–164d3
        a. formulation and modification by Socrates
        b. examination/refutation
    2. fourth definition, which ends in (apparent)
      refutation   164d3–175b4
        a. formulation   164d3–167a8
        b. examination/refutation
          (i) as to its possibility   167a9–169d2
          (ii) as to its desirability   169d3–175b4
III. Epilogue or closing scene   175b5–176d5

More simply, then, and in terms of the definitions offered, the overt structure is:

Model 1

I. Prologue	153a1–158e5
II. Logoi	158e6–175b4
1. Definition 1: "quietness"	158e6–160d4
2. Definition 2: "shame"	160d5–161b4
3. Definition 3: "to do one's own"	161b4–164d3
4. Definition 4: "self-knowledge"	164d3–175b4
III. Epilogue	175b5–176d5

This analysis can be varied, depending on what are taken to be the definitions in the dialogue.

One variation on the pattern is to split the two different versions of the third definition, the one offered by Critias and the one suggested by Socrates, resulting in five definitions.[2]

Model 2

I. Prologue	153a1–158e5
II. Logoi	158e6–175b4
1. Definition 1: "quietness"	
2. Definition 2: "shame"	
3. Definition 3: "to do one's own"	
4. Definition 4: "to do good things"	
5. Definition 5: "self-knowledge"	
III. Epilogue	175b5–176d5

This variation suggests immediately another (championed by Tuckey and Guthrie), according to which the dialogue is structured by six definitions:

Model 3

I. Prologue	153a1–158e5
II. Logoi	158e6–175b4

    1. Definition 1: "quietness"
    2. Definition 2: "a sense of shame"
    3. Definition 3: "to do one's own"
    4. Definition 4: "to do good things"
    5. Definition 5: "self-knowledge"
    6. Definition 6: "knowledge of the good" (implicit)

III. Epilogue	175b5–176d5

The deficiencies of these models are (1) that the fourth definition, in context, seems to be a variation on the third; and (2) that the sixth definition is not presented in the dialogue as a definition of *sophrosune* at all.

It is also possible to subdivide the account of self-knowledge.[3] This yields another sequence of definitions, with the new feature that the definitions may now be seen to develop in two patterns that roughly correspond to a traditional, behavior-oriented notion of the virtue, and a nontraditional, cognition-oriented ideal:

Model 4

I. Prologue	153a1–158e5
II. Logoi	158e6–175b4

    1. Definition 1: "quietness"   4. Definition 4: "self-knowledge"
    2. Definition 2: "shame"   5. Definition 5: "knowledge of itself and other knowledges"
    3. Definition 3: "do one's own"   6. Definition 6: "knowledge of knowledge and non-knowledge"

III. Epilogue	175b5–176d5

This approach might be combined with the one offered by Tuckey, to yield:

Model 5

I. Prologue	153a1–158e5
II. Logoi	158e6–175b4

    1. Definition 1: "quietness"   5. Definition 5: "self-knowledge"
    2. Definition 2: "shame"   6. Definition 6: "knowledge of itself and other knowledges"

| 3. Definition 3: "do one's own" | 7. Definition 7: "knowledge of knowledge and nonknowledge" |
| 4. Definition 4: "do good" | 8. Definition 8: "know good" |

III. Epilogue   175b5–176d5

Again the pattern would be two-dimensional, as it were, with the first four definitions oriented to behavior, the second four to cognition.[4]

A very different approach to the structure of the dialogue is indicated by the analysis that treats it as an ascent in three stages to the definition and then a descent in three stages from that high point.[5] Thus:

Pattern II: The depth-dialectical structure

The definition of *sophrosune*
167a1–8

Socrates/Critias	metaphysics of self-relation
164d4–166e11	167a9–169d2
Critias	knowledge of knowledge
162c1–164d3	169d3–172c3
Charmides	knowledge of good/evil
158e6–162b11	172c4–175b4
entrance/prologue	conclusion/exit scene
153a-158e5	175b4–176d5

The discussion of the last sections is marked by Critias' weak responses to Socrates' arguments, but the low point is not reached until the allusion to violence at 176c–d. On this model, the dialogic structure reflects the level of dialectical insight achieved in the inquiry, which reaches the high point at 167a1–7, understood as an articulation of the Socratic ideal of rationality, but then falls increasingly away from that level of insight, as Critias' understanding of the ideal comes more and more to dominate the overt *logos*.

An application of this approach and variation on this model that corresponds to the analysis in terms of the definitions, gives:

Model 6

Definition 4: self-knowledge
164d5–167a1–8

Definition 3: do own   metaphysics of self-relation
161b4–164d4   167a9–169d2

Definition 2: shame   knowledge of knowledge
160d5–161b4   169d3–172c3

Definition 1: quietness   knowledge of good/evil
158e6–160d4   172c4–175b4

entrance/prologue   conclusion/exit scene
153a–158e5   175b4–176d5

One very attractive aspect of this analysis is that it corresponds in certain respects to the fourfold pattern of cognition Plato later develops in the Divided Line metaphor.[6] Thus the first definition amounts to a kind of image of an image—Charmides' repetition of what he has been taught *sophrosune* is—whereas the corresponding section of critique thematizes the "dream" or fantasy city of Socrates and Critias (*eikasia*). The second level of definition presents a view oriented to the "trust" (*pistis*) that Charmides might have in his personal experience of the ideal, though it conflicts with the trust the culture has in Homer, and on the corresponding side there is the fact that Critias appears to regard the "recognition" of knowledge from the standpoint of mere perception. The third level of the definition on this interpretation has to do with *dianoia*, the level of analysis and scientific or quasi-scientific cognition, and this is represented in the dialogue, if inadequately, by Critias (cf. the reference to the *phronimos* at 163c7), whereas the aporetic nature of the treatment of self-relation in the discussion of the possibility of self-knowledge at 167a–169d has to do with the failure of the dialogue to appeal to a higher, more complex level of cognition, which somehow escapes the "grammar" of perceptual and mathematical objects. Finally, the definition appears to represent the highest form of thought, reason, which is self-reflexive. This approach would appear to be the most adequate analysis of the structure of the dialogue, though it, too, can be analyzed further.

Thus a final model might add yet another complication, still conceiving of the dialogue as an ascent, but one opening out at the top of the ascent to four interpretations of the final step. This approach would then suggest that there are three perspectives from which the whole of the dialogue should be considered, as an interplay of behavior, cognition, and the interpersonal relations of the examination process in the last half of the inquiry.

Model 7

4th form: knowledge of what one knows and does not know: statement at
167a1–7
3rd form: knowledge of knowledge and of nonknowledge: 166e6–7
2nd form: knowledge of itself and other knowledges: 166c2–3
1st form: self-knowledge: 164d4
Definition 4: self-knowledge
164d5–167a1–8
Definition 3: do own   metaphysics of self-relation
161b4–164d4   167a9–169d2
Definition 2: shame   knowledge of knowledge
160d5–161b4   169d3–172c3
Definition 1: quietness   knowledge of good/evil
158e6–160d4   172c4–175b4
entrance/prologue   conclusion/exit scene
153a-158e5   175b4–176d5

How should the highest level of the fourth definition be conceived? Should it be assimilated into yet another higher level, the comprehensive and apparently unself-critical, absolute knowledge of good and evil, as suggested by Tuckey and Irwin? Or should it rather be interpreted in terms of self-critical moral engagement and as affirming the Socratic ideal of rationality, as I have suggested? My arguments are in the body of the commentary; I leave the conclusion to the reader.

APPENDIX B
THE *CHARMIDES* AND THE *REPUBLIC*

Although the society envisioned by Socrates in the *Charmides* may seem to anticipate the utopian society of the *Republic*, the intellectual worlds of the two dialogues are very different.

The intellectual world of the *Charmides* is bounded by dialectic, not moral and metaphysical science. There is a basic difference between those who seem to be set on the right path, who know themselves (and others) in the light of the goal of truth and the means of self-critical reason, and those who appear to be lost in the darkness of moral/intellectual dependency or self-blinding self-assertion. But there are no moral experts, and there is no epistemic closure of the kind attributed to the philosopher kings and queens of the *Republic*.[1] From the standpoint of the *Charmides*, the true citizens of the *Republic* are like gods, possessing something more than human wisdom.

The transition to the metaphysical world of the *Republic* can be seen to begin in the *Gorgias*.[2] There Socrates adumbrates the kind of teleo-cosmological order that would correspond to his own ethic of the self-sufficiency of virtue and reason, as developed in that dialogue. This redefinition of the metaphysical context of human virtue culminates, in the *Republic*, in the vision of the Forms and the Good to which all human desire aspires, through which reason is oriented, and by which all things, intelligible and sensible, have value and meaning. In the *Charmides*, by contrast, the highest metaphysical distinction is that between (perceptual) objects that correspond to the logic of mathematical relations and identity, and self-relational beings, that is, human selves. *Sophrosune* is represented as a virtue; but it is not a virtue that has the certifying imprimatur of a metaphysical nature.

The psychology of the two dialogues is different also. To some extent the *Charmides* anticipates in its drama the tripartite psychology of *Republic* IV: irrational appetite (to *epithumetikon*) is represented object-projectively by Charmides, irrational social emotion/desire (*thumos*) by Critias, reason (*to logistikon*) and rational love by Socrates. The end of the dialogue presents a social/psychological world in conflict, in which the forces of appetitive *eros* and violent *thumos* in the persons of Charmides and Critias combine, as they do in the formation of the tyrannical character, against Socrates and persuasion.[3] On the theoretical level, however, the *Charmides* assumes the soul to be unitary; physical desire, aggression, and reason are first-order mental powers that may be confirmed or rejected by the self in the second order, primary human process of self-determination and self-articulation. The psychology of the *Republic* projects a drive-theoretical model of the soul, in which unity, in most cases, is superficial and temporary; the psychology of the *Charmides* is more humanistic.

These basic theoretical differences between the *Charmides* and the *Republic* are reflected in their politics and discussions of the concept of moderation. Broadly speaking we must say that the *Charmides* and indeed, all "Socratic," dialectical philosophy has anti-authoritarian implications.[4] In the *Charmides*, this implication is made very clear by the characters and the closing scene as cited above. The lust to rule is represented dramatically not by Socrates, but by his interlocutors, Critias and his ward, and this is a pattern found in many early dialogues (indeed, Critias, ugly as he is, is not the most repulsive of these types; Meno and Anytus vie for that title). The anti-authoritarian implications of Socratic skepticism extend in the *Charmides* to the social level as well: the vision of a society run dictatorily by would-be experts is presented as the unhealthy power-fanasty of a future tyrant. The morally healthy or *sophron* person does not seek to govern, certainly not coercively; rather, she wishes to join in community with others in the path of inquiry, the path of the examined life. Insofar as she is "political," it is solely through persuasion, by means of dialectical inquiry and admonitory concern regarding the goods of the soul.

If we distinguish between the "two cities" of the *Republic*, the "high utopia" of Books V–VII and the "low utopia" of Books II–IV, we may find some parallels between the treatment of the concept of moderation and self-knowledge in the *Charmides* and the true or noble moderation of the philosopher-rulers, and between the treatment of traditional moderation in the *Charmides* and the civic or vulgar moderation of the guards/workers in the *Republic*.[5] The moderation of the intellectual/philosophical types, at least in the course of their educational development, is shown to result primarily as a function of their intellectual interests and the sublimation and symbolic reintegration of the lower energies into the pursuit of knowledge (cf. esp. *Republic* VI, 485d–487a; this perspective is also reflected in the developmental histories of 491a–495c and 537e–539e and in books VIII–IX, 559d–5612a, and 572d–573c). (This is not to deny that it has been morally prepared by the music and sports education of the earlier stages, or that it is not personalized in the crucible of civic and military action.) Though Plato allows his true guardians unrestricted freedom of intercourse after their education is completed (461b–c), there is good reason to believe they would not become libertines. Their intercourse among themselves and with the future rulers is essential; but the Platonic model is one of educational *paiderastia* that culminates in relations of equality and reciprocity, not the conventional, hierarchical type which on the part of the elder lover aimed at carnal satisfaction. The analogy in the *Charmides*, of course, is the representation of Socratic sexual self-control in the prologue, though, as we noted in discussing it in chapter 1, his moderation seems to be intrinsically related to the deficiency-model of his intellectual *eros*, his lack of wisdom. It is not only that Socrates finds his good in rational inquiry; it is that he knows he has not yet attained the greater good he so desires. In the world of the *Charmides*, dominated by the sophistic ideals of wisdom, self-certainty, and self-assertion, the essence of moderation is found in the recognition of moral nonknowledge/nonsuperiority and the corresponding enjoyment of the life of the mind.

There are also parallels to be drawn between the treatment of traditional moderation in the *Charmides* and that of civic moderation in the *Republic*. We noted the fourfold structure of the treatment of traditional moderation, in terms of behavioral rules, the internal social emotions and conscience, the link between social role and identity, and a framing religious-normative consciousness. The traditional ideal corresponded to an uncritical, apolitical world which, as the *Charmides* makes evident, had largely ceased to exist in late fifth-century Athens. It was replaced by a society that presumed, among citizens, the kind of intellectual and political equality found only among the rulers in the "high utopia" of the *Republic*. Of course, the *Charmides* does not explore the possibility of a reformation of moral virtue along traditional lines. But such a model of virtue and social world is recreated in the "low utopia" of *Republic* II–IV, where the guards are infused with an education that in form and content is designed to order desires and emotions, no less than beliefs and values, to noble service to the end ordered by the ruling minds. The arts inculcate the correct models of behavior; guards are trained and selected by the measure of their passions of honor and fear of disgrace; social identity is defined at a caste level in terms of the three estates, with each called "citizen" but the vast majority (artisans and farmers) functioning more like metics; and there is an overarching, normative religiomythical consciousness to justify it all. The apparent aim of the guardian education is to recreate the Spartan ideal of civic/aristocratic moderation through a tightly controlled system of physical training or habituation and moral education or indoctrination, all within the social context of "civic communism." The guards are to be warlike not only against the enemies without, but also against the enemy appetites and impulses within; and like the Spartans, their bravery will be rooted in moderation, their moderation in *aidos*, albeit one more finely ingrained than the crude, Spartan sort.

This is the general picture of civic moderation in the *Republic*; but it is complicated by the vexed question of the relation between the two primary estates of the "city of the armed camp" and the universal or restricted availability of civic education to their young. Plato seems to be divided between two positions: (1) that the education of the guards is sufficient, and the workers are just not very important, since they are easily controlled if the guards are strong; or (2) that all three estates must agree and be in harmony, for justice to obtain. The analogy, on the level of individual virtue, is self-control versus perfect virtue.

In the case of the guards, Plato may well believe that he has given sufficient reason why they would be satisfied in all three dimensions of desire. Their intellects are shaped by theology and political doctrine, moral art and the challenges of strategy; their physical needs are satisfied, albeit in an ascetic/athletic manner (with occasional ecstasies for meritorious achievement); and above all their social selves are feted on mutual recognition and the praise due the "craftsmen of freedom." With all this, it may not seem any more unreasonable that they would give up family relations and property (gaining in exchange the life of a civic hero) than that they would ruthlessly enforce the rulers' laws on the lower class (given their certainty of their justice). But mention of guardian control raises again the question as to which model of moderation is at work, for if the behavior that is beneficial to the whole must be forced on the appetitive class, the society would appear not to embody the full ideal (431e–432a). It is insufficient for governing reason to so structure the honor system as to (coercively) control appetitive impulse; ideally the appetitive impulses themselves will be eager to do what reason wants.

Part of the explanation of how consent might be brought about in the *Republic* must lie in the institutions of family, property, and work; these are surely the primary vehicles, for the productive class, of moral formation, to whatever extent they may also be provided the civic education. The institution of monogamous marriage establishes the basic form/limitation of the erotic impulse, which presumably is sublimated in child-care and familial affection; the institution of money and property, tied to competitive work, establishes the basic form/limitation of the narrowly selfish physical pleasure and luxury impulse, carefully monitored by the rulers; and the institution of work is the central vehicle for the satisfaction of intellectual interests and the attainment of social standing and the monetary means for the satisfaction of personal use/property desires. (Compare Richard Kraut's insightful discussion of the justice in the lower classes.[6]) This is a social/psychological world in which the *oikos*, not the *polis*, and *techne*, not *arete*, is primary. Jonathan Lear has recently suggested another way that Plato might explain how the appetitive level of the soul can be assuaged in the direction of social limitations: the educational/formative vehicle of poetry may enter deep into the *psyche* at the level at which the impulses "think," the level of dream or *phantasia*.[7] Thus poetry of the right moral, religious and aesthetic sort might please the fantasy-mind of the appetites, taming them in the direction of social virtue.

The discussions of Plato's social psychology by Kraut and Lear are very suggestive of ways in which the appetitive class of the *Republic* and the instinctual level of the soul might consent to what would otherwise seem the harsh, authoritarian strictures required for social order and the discipline of higher-level cognitive achievement.[8] But they do not explain how the lower classes could be made to consent to the fact that they are subject to physical violence, if they do not consent to do what the rulers envision and the guards demand. How can they rationally consent to the lack of a right of consent? What kind of freedom do they have, if, when they do not agree to what they are told, they are physically compelled to conform? The answer within the framework of the *Republic* would seem to be that the "citizens" who are not guardians are really not conceived of as "selves" in the sense adumbrated in the *Charmides*. In fact, both the artisans and the nonruler guards are defined in such a way as to represent parts or drives of a psychic whole, not whole persons, capable and needful of rational agency and liberty of choice. This truncated view of human nature is confirmed by the Noble Lie. The lower citizens are not really human beings, and this is reflected in their willingness to surrender their political rights. It is this totalitarian division of "humanity" into fully and less-than-equal human types, as much as the assumption of epistemic closure on behalf of the ruling elite, which accounts for the differences between the moral/intellectual worlds of the two dialogues, and the different representations of moderation found within them. Ironically, the very feature of the *Republic* that finally seems to reflect a measure of genuine political moderation— the idea that even the lowest level of citizens have the right of consent to the norms of their rulers—turns out not to have political meaning. We do not readily find images of the virtue of political moderation by looking to the *Republic*, quite the contrary.[9] We do better looking to Socratic dialogues such as the *Charmides*, which undermine both epistemic and political absolutism. On this point, despite the injustice of his scholarship, Popper would seem to have been right.[10]

Appendix C
Logos and *Ergon* in the *Charmides*

This appendix offers a summary of specific passages that exemplify traditional or Socratic moderation in word or deed. Where relevant, I have also attempted to indicate those passages where speech is intended to be supplemented contextually by the dramatic context.

Immoderate	Moderate
The prologue (153a–158e):	
Chaerophon's running (153b3)	greetings from afar (153b1–2)
Chaerophon's question (153b)	Socrates' answer (153b)
the intensity of battle (153c)	the calm of philosophy (153d)
eros toward Charmides (154bc)	Socrates' response (154bc)
Chaerophon on body (154d)	Socrates on soul (154d; cf. 156e)
Charmides takes a seat (155c)	Socratic conversation (155a)
eros toward Charmides (155c)	Socrates' recovery (155c–156d)
Coercion (156a; cf. 176cd)	Persuasion (156a)
Athenian doctors (156e)	Wholistic doctors (156e–157c)
Critias' boasting (155a, 157d)	Socrates' response (155a, 157e)
Charmides' blush (158c)?	Charmides' blush (158c)?

Inquiry with Charmides (158e-162a):

Socrates' argument (159b–160b)

Socrates' summary (160b–d)

Charmides' flight (161b; i.e., not doing his own)

Charmides' insight (160e; i.e., doing his own)

Each doing everything (161e–162a)

Division of labor (162a)

Charmides' laughter (162b)

Socrates' graceful invitation to

Critias' angry response (162d)

Critias to join the inquiry (162de)

Inquiry with Critias: formulating the definition (162a–167a)

Critias' contempt for artisans (163b)

[Socrates' respect for artisans, cf. *Apology* 21a–23b and in general]

One's own is the good (163c)

Doing good is one's own (163e)

Critias abandons his definition (164c)

Knowing one's own (162d)

Critias' atheism (164d)

Traditional piety (164e)

Critias' separates moderation and self-knowledge (165a)

Apollonian wisdom (165a; cf. Socrates, *Apology* 21a–23b)

Critias' demand for agreement (165b)

Socrates first investigates (165c)

Critias' anger at Socrates' supposed eristic (166cd)

Socrates' account of his dialectical method (166de)

Critias' unwillingness to "let go" of who is being refuted (166de)

Socrates' injunction that he focus on the argument (166e)

Knowledge of itself and the other knowledges (166e)

Knowledge of knowledge and of nonknowledge (166e, 167a)

Critias' inability to conceive of a self-relational being (167d)

Socrates' unwillingness to trust himself to know without

Trusting oneself to know (168b)

investigation (168b)

Inquiry with Critias: is self-relational being possible? (167b-169d)

Critias' "imitation" of perplexity (169c)

Socrates' dialectical perplexity (169c)

Critias' refusal to know himself and acknowledge his ignorance (169cd)

Socrates' reasons for his uncertainty (167b–169b)

The "great man" (169a)?

The "great man" (169a)?

Inquiry with Critias: can one know what one knows? (169e-172b)

Critias' certainty that someone with the knowledge of itself will know himself (169e)

Socrates' agreement that someone with knowledge that knows itself will know himself;

Critias' subsequent failure to distinguish political knowledge from technical knowledge (170ab)	but uncertainty that he will know what he knows and does not know (170a; cf. technical vs. moral knowledge, *Apol.* 23a)
Someone with knowledge of the object only, or with knowledge of knowledge or of nonknowledge only (170be)	Someone with knowledge of the knowledge too, i.e., knowledge of what one/another does or does not know (171ad)
The "greater benefit" of life without error and ruling over others (171d-172a)	The "lesser benefit" of being able to justify what one has learned and to examine others (172bc)

Inquiry with Critias: would self-knowledge be beneficial? (172b–175b)

Socrates' dream (173ad)	Socrates' realization that his dream is through ivory (172c–175b)
Knowledges guarantee happiness (173ad)	Moderation on guard (173d)
The omniscient man (174a)	The man who knows he lacks knowledge of good and evil (174b–175b; cf. Socrates fear below)
Knowledge of knowledges (174de)	Knowledge of knowledge and of nonknowledge (174e)
Critias' confidence and self-assertion (esp. 162c, 164de, 166bc)	Socrates' fear and self-care (esp. 166d, 172e, 173a, 175a)
Socrates' argument (167b–175b)	Socrates' summary (175bd)
The concessions without proof (175bc)	The investigations (167b–169a; 169e–171e) and recognition of the lack of proof (175c)
Claiming one can know what one does not know at all (175c)	To know what you do not know (167a; 175bd)

The epilogue (175d–176d)

The personified *logos* (175d)	The definition "plated together" at 167a [also Socrates' *ergon*]
Sophrosune is not beneficial (175d)	*Sophrosune* is beneficial (175de)
The incantation Socrates learned concerned nothing worthwhile (175e)	This inquiry was somehow mistaken (175e)
Charmides says he (still) does not know if he lacks *sophrosune* (176a)?	Charmides says he does not know if he has *sophrosune* (176a)?

Charmides is not persuaded by Socrates and wants to be chanted to (176b)

Charmides thinks he needs the incantation from Socrates (176b)

Charmides is willing to obey Critias, and to use violence to get what he wants, without allowing discussion (176bd)

Socrates would like a "preliminary inquiry," but will not oppose them with violence of his own (176d)

NOTES

PREFACE

1. Drew Hyland: "Very little has been written in English on the *Charmides*, and what literature there is has failed to do justice to the richness and philosophical sophistication of this 'early' dialogue," *The Virtue of Philosophy*, ix. This was written in 1980, and though it is less true today, the dialogue still receives less attention than it deserves. The most prominent discussions of Socratic philosophy, for example, by Vlastos, Irwin, Reeve, Gomez-Lobo, and Brickhouse and Smith, treat the *Charmides* only sparingly, and give most of their attention to the *Apology*, *Crito* and *Gorgias*.

2. Paul Shorey: "The dialogue involves so much metaphysical subtlety that some critics have pronounced it late, some spurious, and many feel the same distaste for it that they do for the subtler parts of the *Theaetetus*." *What Plato said*, 103. This confusion is due primarily to the second half of the inquiry, where Socrates examines the definition at 167a. The dialogue is generally assigned to the "early middle" dialogues: later than works such as the *Ion* and *Crito*, but before the *Phaedo*, *Republic* and *Symposium*. See Leonard Brandwood's summary essay, "Stylometry and Chronology," in Richard Kraut, ed., *Plato*, 90–120, or the more complete discussion in his *The Chronology of Plato's Dialogues*.

3. T. G. Tuckey: "No better introduction to Plato's thought could be devised; the *Charmides* forces its reader to study the historical background of the early dialogue . . . ; it shows us Plato's political and educational

thought in formation . . . ; it helps us to see the origins of those logical and metaphysical theories which Plato later constructed to provide a framework for his ethical doctrine; above all, it forces us to think hard and analyse meanings with care and precision, compelling clear thought by the form of its argument as well as advocating it by its content," *Plato's Charmides*, 105. I shall attempt to provide further substantiation to this claim in the course of this study.

4. For an excellent overview of the debate concerning methodology in reading Plato, see Charles Griswold, ed., *Platonic Writings/Platonic Readings*, especially 1–18. See also E. N. Tigerstedt, *Interpreting Plato;* Gerald Press, ed., *Plato's Dialogues: New Studies and Interpretations*, especially 1–13; Francisco Gonzalez, ed., *The Third Way: New Directions in Platonic Studies*, especially 1–22. I have addressed the issue in greater length in my *On Manly Courage: A Study of Plato's Laches*, chapter 2, "The Literary Form," 27–54.

5. Rosemary Desjardins, "Why Dialogues? Plato's Serious Play," in Griswold, ed., *Platonic Writings/Platonic Readings*, 110–25. The interpretation I offer also conforms to the "pedimental" model of the structure of the Platonic dialogues, as interpreted by Holger Thesleff, "Looking for Clues: An Interpretation of Some Literary Aspects of Plato's 'Two-Level Model'" in Press, ed., *Plato's Dialogues*, 17–45, though I read the "upper level" of the dialogue somewhat differently than does Thesleff, 32.

6. See Desjardins, "Why Dialogues?," 113, 119. The theme of irony in the *Charmides* is also addressed in the fine overview of the dialogue by Jacob Klein in his *A Commentary on Plato's Meno*, 20–27.

ACKNOWLEDGMENTS

1. See Hans-Georg Gadamer, *Truth and Method*, 235–341.

2. My "Socratic Moderation and Self-Knowledge" was one of many published works originally written as a paper for a Vlastos Socrates seminar.

3. The two commentaries in English are by T. G. Tuckey, *Plato's Charmides*, published in 1951, and Drew Hyland, *The Virtue of Philosophy*, published in 1981. Tuckey's is preferable, but it suffers from a failure to appreciate the relation of the drama to the interpretation of the arguments. For comments on Hyland's work, especially note 3, chapter 3; on Tuckey, see especially chapter 5, note 3, chapter 6, and chapter 7. There are also commentaries in German by Thomas Ebert, *Meinung und Wissen in der Philosophie Platons*, E. Martens, *Das selbstbezuegliche Wissen in Platons Charmides*, and Bernd Witte, *Die Wissenschaft von Guten und Boesen.*

4. I have benefited most from Seeskin's account of the elenchus in *Dialogue and Discovery*; O'Brien's treatment of the historical background in *The Socratic Paradoxes and the Greek Mind*; Roochnik's discussions of the *techne*-analogy in "Socrates' Use of the Techne-Analogy" (republished in Benson, ed., *Essays in the Philosophy of Socrates*, 295–310; references will be to this location); Hans-Georg Gadamer, *Plato's Dialectical Ethics*; and Vlastos' many studies, especially "The Socratic Elenchus" and "The Disavowal of Knowledge," found in *Socratic Studies* 1–37, 39–62 (references will be to this location), and "Socrates: An Introduction," in his edition of *The Philosophy of Socrates*, 1–21.

5. See works cited under their names in the Bibliography.

6. Plato, *Charmides*, translated by Thomas West and Grace Starry West. Regarding the translation of *sophrosune*, see the quotation by Edith Hamilton cited at the beginning of chapter 2, which is taken from her preface to the *Charmides* translation in the Hamilton and Cairns edition of Plato, *The Collected Dialogues*, 99.

CHAPTER 1: PROLOGUE

1. Thus Tuckey devotes less than two pages to discussing the prologue, and Taylor, Guthrie, and even Friedlaender give it only a cursory glance. See T. G. Tuckey, *Plato's Charmides*, 18–19; A. E. Taylor, *Plato*, 49–50; W. G. F. Guthrie, *History of Greek Philosophy*, vol. 4, 164; and Paul Friedlaender, *Plato*, vol. 2, 68–70. Drew Hyland, *Virtue of Philosophy*, treats it in two chapters in which he notes some important details, but he acknowledges that he is "continually raising issues without really elaborating on them" (p. 32).

2. It is difficult to establish a precise dramatic date for the dialogue (which may have been intentional on Plato's part). According to Thucydides, there was a big battle in 432, and another, smaller battle in 429. (Compare the account in Donald Kagan, *The Outbreak of the the Peloponnesian War*, 273–85.) The first date does not conform to the impression left by Socrates that he had been away from the city for an extended period of time; but there are also problems with the second. Socrates performed heroically in the campaign, according to Alcibiades, *Symposium* 220d–e.

3. As Paul Friedlaender notes, this physical setting suggests the theme of physical and moral health, and the juxtaposition of the quest for physical well-being to the quest in the dialogue for wholistic well-being, cf. *Plato*, vol. 2, 68. Hyland speculates that the reference to the location of the gymnasium ("temple of the body") opposite the temple of Basile (153a4), who was a goddess in charge of the dead, "may symbolize a forthcoming relation between *sophrosune* and human finitude," *Virtue of Philosophy*, 30.

4. The view that a plague was due to *hubris* or impiety was a commonplace of ancient religion, beginning with the opening scene in Homer's *Iliad*. As Bernard Knox has shown, Sophocles' *Oedipus Tyrannus* treats the same theme, associating Oedipus with Pericles and Thebes with Athens; cf. *Oedipus at Thebes*, 53–106. The plague first struck in 429. It is appealing to think of the plague as part of the historical context of this dialogue, which thematizes the ideas of moral health and disease. Socrates indicates in the *Symposium* that Diotima's presence in Athens forestalled the plague for ten years.

5. Chaerophon was one of Socrates' best-known companions, and the man who Socrates said asked the oracle about his wisdom, *Apology* 21a–23b. He was also a leading democrat, who died fighting in the revolution against the Thirty. Hyland suggests his presence is "a vivid proof that the teachings of Socrates do not necessarily lead to tyranny," *Virtue of Philosophy*, 23. Charmides' behavior—Socrates calls him "mad" (*manikos*, 153b2)—would also appear to demonstrate that those teachings do not necessarily lead to moderation/self-restraint.

6. Hyland suggests that there is "a certain coldness" to Socrates' behavior in this regard, and that this implies that *sophrosune* "can be taken to excess," *Virtue of Philosophy*, 28. Obviously, I cannot accept this evaluation; Socrates immunity to the war-fever here and in other dialogues is a sign of excess only in the sense that virtue is an excess.

7. Friedlaender notes this point, *Plato*, vol. 2, 69.

8. Helen North, *Sophrosyne*, 101–114. Compare the discussions in Eliza Wilkins, *"Know thyself" in Greek and Latin Literature*, 33–41, Victor Ehrenberg, *"Polupragmosune,"* A. W. H. Adkins, *"Polupragmosune* and 'Minding your own business,'" and Tuckey, *Plato's Charmides*, 17.

9. Thucydides, *History of the Peloponnesian War* II.39–40. See the discussion in Lowell Edmunds, *Chance and Intelligence in Thucydides*, 57–70.

10. Thucydides, *History* I.120–24, III.10, also II.63; Knox, *Oedipus at Thebes*, 60–61; Leo Strauss, *The City and Man*, 145–54.

11. See North, "A Period of Opposition to *Sophrosune*," and Edmunds, *Chance and Intelligence*, 92–97, 115. See also note 14 below.

12. Socrates says that Charmides' father's family "has been handed down to us as distinguished for its beauty and virtue and in the rest of what is called happiness" (cf. 157e4–158a2). The phrases "has been handed down to us" and "what is called" underscore Socrates' ironic distance from this judgment. (See notes 33–34 below and note 4, chapter 2.)

13. A contrasting narrative is found at *Symposium* 217e–219e, where Alcibiades recounts how Socrates, when Alcibiades was also in the bloom

of his youth, showed no desire toward him at all. But the *Charmides* narrative is unique in the dialogues for its interior, subjective representation of Socratic *eros*. (It has been suggested to me that Socrates may be ironically exaggerating his erotic response to his unknown auditor for pedagogical reasons; that he had attained moderation, not mere self-control, as the passage in the *Symposium* indicates. But I see no reason from the text to question Socrates' veracity.)

14. Moderation also functioned as something less than a "manly virtue" within the Athenian convention of *paiderastia*, thematized in the *Symposium* and *Phaedrus* and discussed by Kenneth Dover, *Greek Homosexuality*, 81–91, 153–70, and David Halperin, especially in "Platonic Eros and What Men Call Love." I am also indebted for discussion of this theme to Morris Kaplan, "Historicizing Sexuality: Greek Pederasty and the Social Constructionist Controversy," in his *Sexual Justice*. For the thesis that the Greek, especially Athenian attitude was chauvenistic or "phallocentric," see Eva Keuls, *The Reign of the Phallus: Sexual Politics in Ancient Athens*.

15. On the theme of the beloved's possible tyranny, compare *Lysis* 206a–d, *Meno* 76d and *Phaedrus* 233a–d. The tyrant in the *Republic* also exploits his parents' love, *Republic* 572c–574d.

16. The passage at 156a1–3 shows that Charmides, despite his reputation for conventional *sophrosune*, has a touch of the "proud beauty." He reveals more than a mere touch of it at the end of the dialogue, 176a–d.

17. Note that Socrates considers himself the fawn, Charmides the lion in this situation. See Levine, "Plato's *Charmides*," 46. This has sometimes been transposed, as by Gregory Vlastos, *Socrates, Ironist and Moral Philosopher*, 39.

18. This connection has been overlooked by most commentators, but it is clearly an important theme, and it will prove very important later in the dialogue; cf. chapter 5. For contemporary discussions of self-control and identity, cf. especially Harry Frankfurt, "Freedom of the Will and the Concept of the Person," 81–95, and Charles Taylor, "Responsibility for Self," 110–126, in Gary Watson, *Free Will*. Compare the discussion in Christopher Bruell, "Socratic Politics and Self-Knowledge," 146.

19. This is thematically prepared at 154b7–e7. It is the point of the contrast between Chaerophon's concern for Charmides' body and Socrates' concern for his soul, 154d1–e1. Cf. on the same matter Socrates' remark to Alcibiades that he alone cared for Alcibiades' true self, his soul, not his body, in the possibly spurious *Alcibiades I*, 131e, and the discussion in North, *Sophrosyne*, 153, 168–69, and Dover, *Greek Homosexuality*, 153–70.

20. Socrates does not reject these desires as simply external to him, in the manner of a St. Paul; but he does not embrace them as "his own,"

because they do not conform to his will. This is why he says he was himself "rekindled" at 155d2–3. Compare the discussion of Pauline self-alienation in Gareth Matthews, "It is not I that do it . . . ," and of first and second order desires in Harry Frankfurt, "Freedom of the Will and the Concept of a Person."

21. For the concept of social types or characters, see Alasdair MacIntyre, *After Virtue*, 28–29. MacIntyre argues that the defining characters of contemporary American society are the aesthete, the manager, and the therapist. The corresponding predominant characters in Athenian society, I suggest, would be the young gentleman, the public or political person (i.e., the politically active citizen; "politician" in modern representative democracy has different connotations than *polites* had in ancient participatory democracy), and the Sophist. The Laconist, as the Old Oligarch and Callicles' remarks in the *Gorgias* (515e) suggest, was also a public type, but because of his pro-Spartan leanings was not politically influencial for most of latter half of the fifth century, during which time Athens was more or less continually at war with Sparta.

22. Tuckey, *Plato's Charmides*, 17; Friedlaender, *Plato*, vol. 2, 67. It is surprising how many commentators have failed to recognize the negative aspects of Plato's portrait of Critias in the dialogue. Even Tuckey at one point says of him and Charmides: "Clearly Plato had been intimate with them and had felt considerable affection for them. In the dialogue, there is no hint of their later enormities; both are human and sympathetic," *Plato's Charmides*, 4. (His later remarks are more discriminating, 15–17.) See also the account by A. E. Taylor, *Plato*, 49, that the Critias of the dialogue is "simply a young man of parts but with a touch of forwardness and self-confidence," and by Guthrie, *History of Ancient Greek Philosophy*, vol. 3, 299, that Plato shows Critias "only as an intimate member of the Socratic circle, with no hint that he was worse than the rest, and every indication of a genuine interest in philosophy . . . Though writing years after his death, Plato still thinks of his uncle Critias with respect and affection." These misreadings, I suggest, are due to the failure to consider carefully the *logos/ergon* theme, and they contribute to some very serious misunderstandings of the dialogue.

23. Dawson, *Cities of the Gods*, 26–29; cf. also Diels, *The Older Sophists*, 241–70 and the discussions in Rankin, *Sophists, Socratics and Cynics*, 70–74, Kerferd, *The Sophistic Movement*, 52–53, and Guthrie, *History of Greek Philosophy*, vol. 3, 243–44.

24. Euripides is also sometimes mentioned as the author of the *Sisyphus*, but it was attributed to Critias in ancient times. See Guthrie, *History of Greek Philosophy*, vol. 3, 243–44.

25. Tuckey, *Plato's Charmides*, 15.

26. See Ellen and Neal Wood, *Class Ideology and Ancient Political Theory*, 81–118, and I. F. Stone, *The Case Against Socrates*, 9–19. (The latter's "case" was demolished by Julia Annas in *New York Times Review of Books*, February 7, 1988, 7, and also by Myles Burnyeat, *New York Review of Books* 35:12, March, 1988.)

27. Dawson, *Cities of the Gods*, 59.

28. Hyland suggests this is due to his having started drinking too much, *Virtue of Philosophy*, 41, but there is no textual evidence to support this claim. It does allow Plato to suggest that he is "weak in the head," that is, in thought (157c7–d1).

29. The pretense comes from Critias, not Socrates, 155b5–6. Thus from the start it is not clear whether the image of Socratic philosophy as moral-intellectual therapy is to be taken altogether seriously. Socrates' self-description as a psychic healer is part of a ruse that he adopts at Critias' instigation in order to draw Charmides into philosophical dialogue; it is a mask, a pretense. Socrates knows that he does not know what he may seem to know, whether the others also know this or not. The distance established by his self-knowledge here is characteristic of the role of irony in the dialogue as a whole. Nevertheless, the theme of Socrates as moral/intellectual physician runs deep in the Socratic dialogues, as the *Gorgias* makes evident. Part of my aim in this essay is to show how the analogy functions in the *Charmides*.

30. The crucial idea is the notion of logotherapy. See the discussions in chapter 4. (My treatment of this theme is very different from that of P. Lain Entralgo, *The Therapy of the Word in Classical Antiquity*, who discusses the prologue to the *Charmides*, 106–134.)

31. For the claim that he does possess a moral *techne*, see Laszlo Versenyi, "Virtue as a Self-Directive Art." Terence Irwin discusses the *techne*-analogy extensively in his *Plato's Moral Theory*. His treatment has been criticized by George Klosko, "The Technical Conception of Virtue" and David Roochnik, "Socrates' Use of the Techne-Analogy."

32. See Benardete, "On Interpreting Plato's *Charmides*," 17.

33. See 157d9–158c4, which must be put in the context of the overall opposition of moral versus nonmoral goods emphasized at 156d6–157b1. Socrates' ironic praise of Charmides' father's family, mentioned in note 12 above, emphasizes their reputation for wealth, beauty, and the things of fortune, not for political or intellectual achievement. Contrast the misreading by John Burnet, *Greek Philosophy, Part I: Thales to Plato*, 208, that "The opening scene of the *Charmides* is a glorification of the whole [family] connexion," cited in Guthrie, *History of Greek Philosophy*, vol. 4, 11.

34. On the theme of appearance versus reality in the prologue, see Friedlaender, Plato, vol. 2, 79, and Martens, *Das selbstbezuegliche Wissen*, 18.

CHAPTER 2: TRADITIONAL MODERATION

1. See Helen North, *Sophrosyne*, 1–31, 95, 100–114, also Wilkins, *"Know Thyself" in Greek and Latin Literature*, 33–40, 52–59.

2. Gerasimos Santas, "Socrates at Work on Virtue and Knowledge in Plato's *Charmides*," in Lee, Mourelatos and Rorty, eds., *Exegesis and Argument*, 110.

3. Compare Santas, "Socrates at Work on Virtue and Knowledge in Plato's *Charmides*," 112–17. Santas acknowledges the relevance of the historical context in a note, 107, but his interpretation ignores it.

4. For this theme, which began as noted in the prologue (notes 33–34, chapter 1), see again Martens, *Das selbstbezuegliche Wissen*, 29. Note the emphasis on appearance in the prologue at 154b10–c1, 156e6–157a3, 157e1–158a6, 158a7–b4, and in the examination of the first definition at 159a10–b6, 159d4, 160b5, 160c2 (contrasted to being at 160c4), and 160d3.

5. Several commentators ignore the larger historical context, including Santas, Hyland, Friedlaender, and on this point, even Tuckey.

6. The quote is taken from *Odyssey* XVII.347 and is resonant in several respects: Socrates is often compared by Plato to Odysseus; he is also compared famously by Alcibiades in the *Symposium* to a Silenus, appearing very different on the outside than within; and Odysseus' forwardness, set in the context of an inverted social world where the true aristocrat has been displaced, is regarded very differently than that of Thersites in the *Iliad*, who is seen as an upstart and is sharply punished by Odysseus. The quote hearkens back to *Odyssey* III.14, where Athena herself advises Telemachus not to be shy in pursuit of his goal. Cf. also Socrates' use of the quote *Laches* 201a, which is relevant here too.

7. E. R. Dodds, *The Greeks and the Irrational*, 18.

8. Compare Gabrielle Taylor, *Pride, Shame and Guilt*, 53–84. For shame in Greek culture, see Dodds, *Plato and the Irrational*, 1–17, North, *Sophrosyne*, 5–7, and Bernard Williams, *Shame and Necessity*, 75–102. On the convergence of morality and social rules in Homeric ethics, see Alasdair MacIntyre, *A Short History of Ethics*, 5–13.

9. Does Charmides blush because he is embarrassed by Socrates' suggestion that he might have *sophrosune*, or has Socrates uncovered his con-

ceit that he really does have it, as the others say? I am inclined to think the latter, though perhaps he is merely embarrassed by his pleasure at the praise.

10. See especially *Apology* 28b–30b and *Republic* 610a f. For the contrasting educational values of philosophy versus poetry, see Gadamer, *Dialogue and Dialectic*, 39–72, a point also discussed recently in Jonathan Lear's essay, "Inside and Outside the *Republic*."

11. See my "Socrates' Practice of Elenchus in Plato's *Charmides*," 107–108; and now Thomas Brickhouse and Nicholas Smith, *Plato's Socrates*, 12–13, 17–18.

12. Robinson, *Plato's Earlier Dialectic*, 16.

13. As per the quote by Dodds cited earlier, it was the "strongest moral force" in his universe. This traditional perspective is represented by the title character in the *Laches*, incidentally; cf. *On Manly Courage*, 100–101, 118–26.

14. Socrates *contrasts* his attitude to that of Achilles: whereas the latter cares about his reputation, Socrates finds his honor/shame in relation to doing what is right. See *Apology* 28b–30b.

15. However, as suggested in the next section and at note 22 below, it might also have come from Socrates. Then we would have, in Charmides' representation, an image of an image of the original.

16. See the discussion of this notion in Bruno Snell, *The Discovery of the Mind*, 158–60, Jaeger, *Paideia*, vol. 1, 7–9, and Wilkins, *"Know Thyself,"* 33–40.

17. Bruno Snell, *The Discovery of the Mind*, 159; also the MacIntyre discussion cited in note 8 above.

18. The concluding scene of the dialogue suggests that this will be his role throughout his life; cf. especially 176b9–c9 and the discussions in chapter 4 and chapter 8. Charmides' failure reflects the essential weakness of "natural" or traditional moderation: its lack of courage in pursuit of the good, its unwillingness to die for the sake of truth.

19. Heterarchy being the state in which someone is governed not by herself, but by another. A person may be autarchic in the sense that she enjoys negative freedom and exercises unimpaired most of the normal powers of a rational agent, and yet also heteronomous in the sense of lacking critical perspective on her society's or peer group's customs, habits, or values. For a nuanced discussion of the concept of freedom in relation to negative freedom, rational self-direction, autarchy and autonomy, see John Gray, *Mill on Liberty*, 73–81.

20. North, *Sophrosyne*, 12–19; Wilkins, *"Know Thyself,"* 33–40; also Tuckey, *Plato's Charmides*, 5–14.

21. Aristotle did not invent the distinction, which was basic to Greek self-understanding: cf. Werner Jaeger, *Paideia*, vol. 1, 111–13, and the philosophical discussion in Hannah Arendt, *The Human Condition*, 175–207, 220–30.

22. Socrates uses the phrase *to heautou prattein* as a formula for justice at *Republic* 434a. This is dramatically much later than the *Charmides*, but it is conceivable that Critias had heard Socrates discuss the phrase as a definition for moderation (even in the *Republic*, the accounts of justice and moderation are difficult to distinguish). We know that some formulas used as definitions of the virtues are mooted by Socrates early in his career, such as that of courage, "the knowledge of what is to be feared and dared," which is used by Socrates already in the last argument of the *Protagoras*, a dialogue dramatically even earlier than the *Charmides*. This formula is given by Nicias as his definition of courage in the *Laches*, and he implies he has heard or been led to it by Socrates (194c–e). But Socrates does not acknowledge his patrimony of what Nicias understands by the phrase, attributing it rather to the Sophist, Prodicus (197d). If we imagine Critias to have heard the phrase *ta heautou prattein* discussed by Socrates as well as Prodicus in other contexts, this would be another parallel between the *Laches* and the *Charmides*.

23. It was regarded as hubristic to abuse a person in public. Critias' treatment of his ward is immoderate not only because of its psychological aspect (losing his temper), but also because of its interpersonal aspect (mistreating Charmides). It might be thought that this is only just, given Charmides' mocking laughter at b10–11. But Critias' rebuke is clearly excessive, and also clearly not meant for the boy's good, but to serve himself; cf. Socrates' narrative, 162c1–d6.

24. For discussion, see Pierre Vernant, *Myth and Thought among the Greeks*, 3–32.

25. Wilamowitz: "It is easy to imagine how the radical tyrant intrepreted this exhortation and this virtue. A man should know what he is and what he is for. The humble man should not fancy himself, but should realize and acknowledge his inferiority to the man who is greater than he. 'Cobbler, stick to your last.' A born ruler, however, is called and entitled to rule." Cited in Tuckey, *Plato's Charmides*, 24.

26. That is, as belonging not to himself, but to "others." See Levine, "Plato's *Charmides*," 160.

27. As mentioned in note 22 above, Prodicus is also the assigned source of the sophistic definition in the *Laches*, according to Socrates

(197d). Socrates is here declaring that he is not the source of Critias' ideas, but that they have a sophistic origin.

28. On Jason as a model of *sophrosune* in the sense of radically egoistic prudence, see Helen North, *Sophrosyne*, 73–74, 78.

29. See *Lysis* 219c-e, *Gorgias* 466a–468c; also *Symposium* 205a, *Republic* 382b, 505d–e. For discussion, see Gomez-Lobo, *Foundations of Socratic Ethics*, 80; and Vlastos, *Socratic Studies*, 203–209.

30. The question of technical versus moral benefit is underscored by the use of *ta deonta* at 164b3, 5. The contrast between the good of the artist and that of his client is underscored at 164b1; cf. also the narrowness of the benefit to the artist suggested by the verb *onesesthai* at 164b9. The question whether the *sophron* person knows her own *sophrosune* is thematized via the Socratic theme of not possessing absolute moral knowledge and his avowal of epistemic fear, discussed in chapter 3, chapter 5, and chapter 6. In contrast to Critias, who does not care to, and consequently cannot know what "he himself supposes himself to know," Socrates exhibits and articulates this self-care—this *sophrosune*—at 173a5 (*heautou . . . kedetai*) and at related passages at 156e5, 165b8–c1, 166d1–2, 167e10–168a1, 172e6, and 175a9.

31. His willingness to abandon his definition so readily is another act of not "doing [defending] his own." Some commentators have been misled into thinking he shows grace in acknowledging the relevance of Socrates' criticisms here, but careful reading of 164c7–d3, 165a7–b4 shows that this is not the case. Tuckey has some nice remarks on this, *Plato's Charmides*, 24.

32. This is the longest speech in the inquiry part of the dialogue, and is clearly an effort, by Critias, to offer a rhetorical display of his wisdom.

33. See, for example, Hyland, *Virtue of Philosophy*, 88–93, where he relates it to his existentialist reading of Socratic *sophrosune*; Friedlaender, *Plato*, vol. 2, 73, Guthrie, *History of Ancient Greek Philosophy*, vol. 4, 168–69, and North, *Sophrosyne*, 157, border on misreading it as Plato's view also. Most commentators, Tuckey among them, fail to appreciate the speech's radical implications.

34. On the Apollonian ideal see Wilkins, *"Know Thyself,"* 52–59; North, *Sophrosyne*, 4–5, 9–11; Burkert, *Greek Religion*, 143–49; Martin Nilsson, *A History of Greek Religion*, 197–204; and Tuckey, *Plato's Charmides*, 5–11.

35. He says the inscription was put up "as if" it were the greeting of a god, and that "such was the thinking of the one who put it up." In other words, men invent the sayings of the gods and then pretend that the gods themselves said them. See West, notes 42–45 to his edition, Plato, *Charmides*, 34–36.

36. The phrase "in my opinion" (*houto* or *hos moi dokei*) is found three times, at 164d6, 164e5, and 165a2. While Critias might intend the phrase to function defensively, that is, as "my opinion" it is immune to criticism ("it is my opinion, so I have the right to it"), the repeated emphasis also suggests that Plato is signaling its low epistemic status.

CHAPTER 3: SELF-KNOWLEDGE

1. Tuckey notes that the passage at 167a is "clearly intended to remind us of the historical Socrates," but concludes only that "the determination whether *episteme epistemes* is a Platonic conception or an opponent's must await the further analysis of this conception," 40. Hyland is aware of the tension, and, as I mention in note 3 below, his view is closest to mine, but he does not express the dilemma either. Guthrie, *History of Greek Philosophy*, vol. 4, 170, and Friedlaender, *Plato*, vol. 2, 73, fail to recognize the problem clearly. Kahn, "Plato's *Charmides* and the Protreptic Reading of the Platonic Dialogues," 546, recognizes the dilemma, but fails to resolve it.

2. See the works cited in note 4 to the preface, especially the introductions by Griswold, Press, and Gonzalez to their respective editions.

3. Compare Hyland, *Virtue of Philosophy*, 95–110. This is not to say that our interpretations do not differ in terms of our treatment of the text and our understanding of the ideals in question. Hyland apparently conceives of Socratic self-knowledge as a form of *gnosis*, or intuitive self-awareness, 114, though he wishes to relate such self-knowledge to the Ideas, 47–55, 66–67, 91–93, 107, and he comes to this interpretation to a significant extent through the importation of existentialist doctrine, 3–17, 74, 89–90. Hyland's work has been criticized by David Levine, "The Tyranny of Scholarship," and while I believe his review was unduly harsh, he has a point when he accuses Hyland of often digressing into existentialist philosophy rather than sticking to the Platonic text, 67. Tuckey's work remains the best in English, but it suffers from a failure to appreciate the way in which the drama provides the content for the interpretation of the arguments. This leads him, in my view, to fail to appreciate many parts of the dialogue, as well as its overall teaching.

4. See the discussion in Hyland, *Virtue of Philosophy*, 95–96, Taylor, *Plato*, 53, and Tuckey, *Plato's Charmides*, 30–31, 49–50, 57. Robert Wellman, "The question posed at *Charmides* 165a–166c," takes *episteme* here to mean "know-how" and goes on to argue that "the real question in the *Charmides* is the possibility of an immediate act of knowing being its own object as an actualized immediate act of knowing," 113. Then, if the knowledge that is virtue is a kind of know-how, and such knowledge is only expressed in action, the central question of the dialogue is "whether

a man can ever know that he is virtuous." But this interpretation of knowledge in the *Charmides* is clearly mistaken, if it is essentially mediated by rational examination and justification, as I shall attempt to show is the case.

5. For discussion of the intellectual background, see Michael O'Brien, *The Socratic Paradoxes and the Greek Mind*, 56–82; Lowell Edmunds, *Chance and Intelligence in Thucydides*, 7–88; and Jan Moline, *Plato's Theory of Understanding*, 2–31.

6. This is a point on which I depart from Hyland (and from Tuckey, who also infers that self-knowledge is a form of *gnosis*, *Plato's Charmides*, 38–39, 43–44). This is not to say that Socratic self-knowledge should be conceived as a theoretical science—both that model of self-knowledge and the model of *techne* are rejected—but to insist that it is a discursive, not merely intuitive achievement and state.

7. See Tuckey, *Plato's Charmides*, 32.

8. Terence Irwin, *Plato's Moral Theory*, note 65, 298.

9. David Roochnik, "Socrates' Use of the Techne-Analogy," in Hugh Benson, ed. *Essays on the Philosophy of Socrates*, 186–88, 192–93.

10. Roochnik, "Techne-Analogy," 193.

11. What does Socrates mean by "one's own good"? There are several possible meanings suggested in the dialogue: immortality (156d), moderation and wholeness (156e–157a), the quiet life (160c; cf. discussion in chapter 2), good order (161e), truth (166d), and happiness (171d–172a).

12. See the discussions in chapter 2, note 30 above, and in chapter 4.

13. The art of *logistike* is an intriguing choice. On the relation of practical to theoretical logistic, see Jacob Klein, *Greek Mathematical Thought and the Origin of Algebra*, 17–25, 69–79. Compare the ambiguous status of kingship, as both a practical and theoretical art, at the beginning of the *Statesman*.

14. See the review in Tuckey, *Plato's Charmides*, 33–37; also Annas, "Self-Knowledge in Early Plato," 134; Dyson, "Some problems concerning knowledge in Plato's *Charmides*," 102–106; Ebert, *Meinung und Wissen in der Philosophe Platons*, 65–67; Martens, *Das selbstbezuegliche Wissen*, 40–45; Santas, "Socrates at Work on Virtue and Knowledge," 119, note 12; and Witte, *Die Wissenschaft vom Guten und Boesen*, 110. My approach to this issue has been influenced by comparison of Socratic thought to several contemporary accounts of discursive rationality, including Gadamer's account of dialectic in *Plato's Dialectical Ethics*, Juergen Habermas's understanding of communicative ratio-

nality, for example, as found in *Moral Consciousness and Communicative Action*, trans. C. Lenhardt and S. W. Nicholson, 42–115, Amelie Rorty's treatment of the relation of autonomy and rationality in "The Deceptive Self," *Perspectives on Self-Deception*, eds. B. McLaughlin and A. Rorty, 11–28, and Ernst Tugenthat's *Self-Consciousness and Self-Determiniation*, especially 200–218.

15. Self-knowledge in the *Charmides* does not imply knowledge of one's particular, contingent traits of personality, or of one's unique or particular abilities or interests. For discussion of the emergence of this latter concept of self-knowledge in the ancient world, see Christopher Gill, "Peace of Mind and Being Yourself," in *Decline and Rise of the Roman World* 36, 7 (1994): 4599–4640. For Critias' explanation of his view, see also 169d9–e5.

16. Cf. especially the phrase *auto to auto*, "the self itself" (*Alcibiades I* 129b, 130c–d). For discussion of the role of the rational or cognitive self in the *Alcibiades I*, see Julia Annas, "Self-knowledge in Early Plato," especially 130–33; also Lloyd Gerson, "Plato on Virtue, Knowledge and the Unity of Goodness," and Guthrie, *Socrates*, 147–53. Annas does not believe this notion has a significant role in the *Charmides*, however; she indicates at the beginning of her essay, 111, that the discussion of it in the dialogue "is itself baffling, appears maginal to Plato's main concerns, and seems to spring philosophically out of nowhere."

17. "Clearly love of antithesis has led him into a dubious if not false affirmation." Tuckey, *Plato's Charmides*, 39.

18. This reading is confirmed by Critias's later embrace of *sophrosune* as such a "ruling science" at 171d f., 173a f.

19. I owe the phrase "epistemic absolutism" to Levine, "Plato's *Charmides*," 208. This concept, opposed to the correlative Socratic ideal of critical rationality, must not be confused with the Platonic ideal of wisdom. For discussion of whether Plato abandoned the Socratic position, see the discussions by Gadamer, *The Idea of the Good in Platonic-Aristotelian Philosophy*, 63–103 and Gill, "Dogmatic Dogma in *Phaedrus* 276–7?" in L. Rossetti, ed., *Understanding the Phaedrus*.

20. See chapter 2, and note 22, chapter 2 above.

21. See the discussion in Reeve, *Socrates in the Apology*, 37–53.

22. See the treatment of this theme in Rosamund Sprague, *Plato's Philosopher-King*, especially xiii–xvi and 29–42.

23. Compare the accounts of Vlastos, "Socrates' Disavowal of Knowledge" and *The Philosophy of Socrates*, 1–21; Seeskin, *Dialogue and Discovery*, 37–43, 139–45; and Reeve, *Socrates in the Apology*, 53–62.

24. In addition to the Vlastos article cited in the preceeding note, see my "Socratic Conception of Courage," 118.

25. See Hyland, *Virtue of Philosophy*: "Socrates denies that we can straightforwardly disjoin self-examination as helping oneself and the examination of others as helping them . . . Socrates somehow believes that examining others contributes to the same result as examining himself." This is also the implication of the passage from the *Alcibiades I* cited at the beginning of the chapter, which states that it is by means of examining another in dialogue that one comes to know oneself: in the Socratic dialectic the self tests and explores and examines itself—its rational commitments of value—in a process which tests the other, but is oriented to the meaning of the ideal. This process is not predetermined or static, but dynamically open and potentially transformative of the interlocutor himself; see chapter 4.

26. See the discussion of dialectic and rational community in chapter 4.

27. On the difference between Plato and Rorty, see also Charles Griswold, Jr., "Plato's Metaphilosophy," in *Platonic Writings, Platonic Readings*, 143–67, especially 166–67; on the difference between Plato and Davidson, see also Thomas Scaltsas, "Socratic Moral Realism," in *Oxford Studies in Ancient Philosophy* 7 (1989), 129–50. For Davidson's intersubjectivist notion of dialectic in the dialogues (where truth is identified with agreement), see his "Plato's Philosopher," *London Review of Books*, 1 August 1985, 15–17. On the Platonic notion of thinking as itself inherently dialogical, see Arendt, *Life of the Mind*, vol. 1, 179–93.

28. Christopher Gill, "Afterword," in his edition, *Form and Argument in Late Plato*, 283–311, especially 284–86, and his *Personality in Greek Epic, Tragedy and Philosophy*.

29. Gill has also discussed the question of the terminus of dialectic in the middle and late Platonic dialogues in his illuminating study, "Dogmatic Dogma in *Phaedrus*, 276–7?" (cited in note 19 above). The status of the moral truth discovered dialectically in the early dialogues would appear to be of a different character than the comprehensive truth said to be revealed through dialectic in such passages as *Republic*, 534b–d, *Symposium*, 212a and *Seventh Letter*, 344b. As I suggest in appendix B, the open, dialectical boundary of the *Charmides* contrasts to the apparently closed metaphysical world of the *Republic*. (Or is Plato too fluid to admit such easy oppositions? For a very different, antidoctrinal view of the *Republic*, see Diskin Clay's reader-response approach to it in his "Reading the *Republic*" in the Griswold volume, *Platonic Writings, Platonic Readings*, 19–33.)

30. Compare the discussion of virtue and knowledge in Lorraine Code, *Epistemic Responsibility*, 37–67.

31. Compare "Socratic Moderation and Self-Knowledge," 345, and *On Manly Courage*, 128–29.

32. Socrates is willing to employ this ameliorative technique, to keep an inquiry going when the fear of refutation might cause it to break down; compare *Protagoras* 338b–c. But he soon makes it clear once again that it is the interlocutor's beliefs that are under examination, and that for the elenchus to operate correctly in relation to the interlocutor, the latter must say what he believes. (See the discussion in chapter 4, and the references in note 9, chapter 4 below.) Does the dialectic examine propositions or beliefs? If the answer to this question is principally the latter, interpretation of the teaching of the dialogues must rely more heavily on the relation of the arguments to the dramatic context than is generally done in the scholarly literature on Plato. Vlastos has made much of the theme of the personalization of the elenchus versus impersonal inquiry, particularly in "The Socratic Elenchus," 17–29. But he has not carried through the interpretation of speech in relation to action as much as is necessary, if the approach I have taken here is correct. For discussion of the personal aspects of the elenchus, see also Richard Robinson, *Plato's Earlier Dialectic*, 15–17, Thomas Brickhouse and Nicholas Smith, *Plato's Socrates*, 12–13, 17–18, and my "Socrates' Practice of Elenchus in Plato's *Charmides*," 107–108.

33. Many commentators have been puzzled by Socrates' obscure remark at 169e6–8. His point here, however, seems to be that it is not sufficient to know what you know (when you know it); it is also necessary to know what you do not know (when you do not know it). This was the characteristic failure of those among his fellow citizens who really did possess technical knowledge, cf. *Apology* 22c–d. It is also the failure Critias is about to display, in his inability to distinguish the kind of knowledge that is involved in medicine and music from political self-knowledge.

34. Gadamer: "Plato saw that knowledge of the good cannot be understood using *techne* as a model . . ." *The Idea of the Good in Platonic-Aristotelian Philosophy*, 33; also 35–36, 42–43.

35. It is the task of the drama/*erga* to adumbrate and clarify these ambiguities in particular, after the manner suggested in the preface.

36. See Sprague, *Plato's Philosopher-King*, 36–37, and the brief discussion in Tuckey, *Plato's Charmides*, 39–40. Tuckey does not exploit this point, however, and his analysis of the description ignores its ambiguities (as does Hyland).

CHAPTER 4: THE SOCRATIC IDEAL OF RATIONALITY

1. O'Brien, *The Socratic Paradoxes and the Greek Mind*, 22–82.

2. Lowell Edmunds, *Chance and Intelligence in Thucydides*, 7–88.

3. G. B. Kerferd, *The Sophistic Movement*, 24–41; Jan Moline, *Plato's Theory of Understanding*, 3–51. On the theme of Pericles and the Sophists, see also Knox, *Oedipus at Thebes*, and Edward Schiappa, *Protagoras and the Logos*, 3–16, 168–89.

4. See David Roochnik, "Socrates' Use of the Techne-analogy," 298–300, 305–307, also Klosko, "The Technical Conception of Virtue," 102; C. D. C. Reeve, *Socrates in the Apology*, 37–62; and Gadamer, *The Idea of the Good in Platonic-Aristotelian Philosophy*, 33–62.

5. Laszlo Versenyi draws out similarities between Socrates and the Sophists in his *Socratic Humanism*, going so far as to call Socrates "the greatest Sophist," 69. In fact, one may trace a division among Plato scholars since Grote and Zeller in the nineteenth century, between those who have seen him more in company with or more in contrast to the Sophists. Whatever the truth about the historical Socrates may be, Plato clearly means to contrast him to the Sophists and their progeny, especially in the early dialogues.

6. Compare Nietzsche, *The Birth of Tragedy and the Genealogy of Morals*, 72–96.

7. For the "standard form," see Vlastos, "The Socratic Elenchus," 11–17.

8. This point is not sufficiently recognized in the scholarly literature. See my "Socrates' Practice of Elenchus in Plato's *Charmides*," 143, and *On Manly Courage*, 90, 101.

9. Vlastos, "The Socratic Elenchus," 7–11; Seeskin, *Dialogue and Discovery*, 1–4, 32–35; Gadamer, *Plato's Dialectical Ethics*, 35–44; and Robinson, *Plato's Earlier Dialectic*, 15–17. Truthfulness in dialectical moral inquiry thus functions in a similar manner to truthfulness and trust in everyday life: the very practice of communicative reason breaks down without it. It is not that the speech of the interlocutor cannot be examined, but the integrity of the speaker and his speech is violated, on the one hand—so he runs the risk of self-deception—and the epistemic and moral community is disrupted; on the other—so the principle of a common commitment to the truth discovered is given up. Compare the discussion of trust among the Ik in Code, *Epistemic Responsibility*, 178–89.

10. This is not to say that the other premises to which Socrates secures agreement are not also fully accepted by the interlocutor, for example, Euthyphro's agreement at 10d that the gods love an act or person because it is pious, Laches' agreement at 193b that raw courage unfortified by technical advantage is more noble than with it, Charmides' assumption at 161a of the authority of Homer. These premises are also important parts of the cultural belief system the interlocutor conveys, but at the center of

their particular convictions is the specific virtue ideal with which they personally identify.

11. This is true both of Vlastos' discussion, and most recently of Thomas Brickhouse and Nicholas Smith, *Plato's Socrates*, in which almost two thirds of all citations are to the *Apology*, the *Crito*, or the *Gorgias*, and but few to the *Charmides*.

12. Cornford discusses the relation of the concept of the true self to the arguments of the *Gorgias* in his *Before and after Socrates*, 51; on the same notion, see now Brickhouse and Smith, *Plato's Socrates*, 101–102.

13. Vlastos, "The Socratic Elenchus," 17–29.

14. Compare the discussion in Hans-Georg Gadamer, *Plato's Dialectical Ethics*, 44–51.

15. Plato, *Sophist*, translated by H. N. Fowler, in the Loeb edition, 315.

16. See Brickhouse and Smith, *Plato's Socrates*, 12–13, 17–18; also my "Socrates' Practice of Elenchus in the *Charmides*."

17. On the relation of autonomy and thinking for oneself, see *On Manly Courage*, 125–30; also Hannah Arendt's insightful essay on Socrates, "Thinking and moral considerations," revised and reprinted in *The Life of the Mind*, vol. 1, 166–93; William Frankena, *Ethics*, 1–9; Stephen Nathanson, *The Ideal of Rationality*, 3–16; Vlastos, "The Paradox of Socrates," in his edition, *The Philosophy of Socrates*, 1–21; and Kant's classic essay, "What Is Enlightenment?" found in Carl Friedrich's edition, *The Philosophy of Kant: Immanuel Kant's Moral and Political Writings*, 132–39.

18. Kenneth Seeskin, *Dialogue and Discovery*, especially 81–92.

19. Myles Burnyeat, "Socratic Midwifery, Platonic Inspiration," 7–16, 12.

20. The fact that all are equal members in the epistemic community of the dialectic does not imply that one may be not called on to play the role of teacher as well as inquirer. Socatic self-knowledge would thus include not only quietness in the subtle sense hinted at in the summary, and shame in the sense of fear of error and humility before the truth, but also knowledge of one's role in the interactive community of the dialectic—of leading or of openly, reflectively being led.

21. On Alcibiades and *akrasia* in the early dialogues, see my "Socratic Moderation and Self-Knowledge," 145–47; also Seeskin, *Dialogue and Discovery*, 145–48.

22. Vlastos, "The Socratic Elenchus," 17–29; Reeve, *Socrates in the Apology*, 45–62; Seeskin, *Dialogue and Discovery*, 73–90, 144–45; also Nehamas, "Eristic, Antilogic, Sophistic, Dialectic," and Gomez-Lobo, *Foundations of Socratic Ethics*, especially 138–39.

23. For the primacy of the good of truth, cf. *Charmides* 166d4–6; on the necessity of moral courage and intellectual humility, see *Charmides* 160e2–5 and 169c6–d1 (compare *Laches* 194d and *Gorgias* 487b–d, 492d, 505e); on dialectical fairness and concern for others, see 166c7–d6; on applying reason to conduct, see 155c5–156d3, and compare *Crito* 46b, *Gorgias* 488a. Socrates implies his willingness to be refuted at *Charmides* 166d8–e2; compare *Gorgias* 458a. For discussions of these values in the elenchus, see the works by Burnyeat, Seeskin, and myself cited in notes 8–9, 12, 16 above, and compare the account of ethics in contemporary critical theory, for example, Juergen Habermas, "Discourse Ethics," *Moral Consciousness and Communicative Action*, 42–115.

24. See Nicholas Rescher, *Dialectic*, 46–60, also Nehamas, "Eristic, Antilogic, Sophistic, Dialectic," 7–9.

25. See Gadamer, Plato's *Dialectical Ethics*, 51–65; also Nehamas, "Eristic, Antilogic, Sophistic, Dialectic," 10–11.

26. See Benardete, "On Interpreting Plato's *Charmides*," 13.

27. Compare Nietzsche: "*The great majority of people* lacks an intellectual conscience. I mean: does not consider it contemptible to believe this or that and to live accordingly, without first having given themselves an account of the final and most certain reasons pro and con, and without even troubling themselves about such reasons afterward. But what is good-heartedness, or refinement, or creativity to me, when the person who has these virtues does not account *the desire for certainty* as his inmost craving and deepest distress?" *The Gay Science*, para. 2, trans. Walter Kaufmann (Vintage, 1974), 76. Later in the same work Nietzsche considers the possibility that the idea of truth is itself a vital lie: "We godless anti-metaphysicians still take our fire, too, from the flame which is also the faith of Plato, that God is the truth, that truth is divine. But what if this should become more and more incredible . . . what if God himself [Truth] should prove to be our most enduring lie?" *Gay Science*, para. 344, 283. For discussion of the difference between the Nietzschean and Socratic conceptions of truth, see chapter 3 and notes 27–29 to that chapter.

28. See the discussion in Hannah Arendt, "Thinking and moral considerations," 438–46, and *The Life of the Mind*, vol. 1, 188–93.

29. Compare Stephen Darwell, *Impartial Reason*, 101–102: "Rationality consists, at least partly, in our capacity to make our ends and preferences the object of our rational consideration, and to revise them in

accordance with reasons we find compelling." As Darwell points out, this is a richer conception of what it means to be a rational person than is found in contemporary decision theory.

30. Vlastos, "Socrates," in *The Philosophy of Socrates*, 9–15, 20. See also my "Socratic Moderation and Self-Knowledge," 144–45. From a Socratic point of view, the otherwise illuminating account in John Kekes, *The Examined Life*, 114–28, appears to give insufficient attention to the role of critical moral dialogue in the development of self-knowledge.

31. The relation between intellectual and interpersonal relations is thematized in the *Lysis, Phaedrus*, and *Symposium*.

32. The *eromenos* may serve as representative of sexual appetite, insofar as he is conceived of as actively seductive. Cf. Socrates' reference to Charmides as the lion who might devour him, 155e1–2, and Agathon's speech in praise of Eros qua seductive young beloved in the *Symposium* 194e–197e. Xenophon, incidentally, represents Charmides as a somewhat jaded hedonist in his *Symposium*; cf. especially II.19, III.1, and IV.27.

33. On the role of this concept of the self and self-determination in the *Charmides*, see especially the discussions in chapter 1, chapter 2, chapter 4, and chapter 5.

34. See the discussions cited in note 33 above and the model of the self in *Republic* 437a–c. Compare the accounts in Frankfurt, "The Freedom of the Will and the Concept of the Person," and Tugendhat, *Self-Consciousness and Self-Determination*, especially 200–218.

35. See the discussion of the "objectivist-participant" outlook described in chapter 3, the discussion of the dialogic community in this chapter, and the treatment of this theme in Gill, *Personality in Greek Epic, Tragedy and Philosophy*, chapters 1, 6.

36. I take up this theme again in chapter 7, and in appendix B.

CHAPTER 5: METAPHYSICS

1. One pattern is: Definition of *sophrosune*

Socrates/Critias	metaphysics of self-relation
Critias	knowledge of knowledge
Charmides	knowledge of good/evil
entrance/prologue	conclusion/exit scene

The discussion of the last sections is marked by Critias' weak responses to Socrates' arguments, but the low point is not reached until the allusion to violence at 176d. For further discussion of the structure of the dialogue, see appendix A.

2. Compare the reader-response approach recommended for the reading of utopian literature in Peter Ruppert, *Reader in a Strange Land*, especially chapters 1 and 7, 11–25, 150–66. The dialogic approach I have taken here may be compared in general to reader-response theory in contemporary literary theory. On this view, Plato was an early author of "modernist" literature, insofar as his goal was not simply to represent a fictional world and personal message, but to evoke creative interaction with his text on the part of the reader. For further discussion of Plato's art of writing, see my *On Manly Courage*, chapter 2, "The Literary Form," 27–54.

3. Tuckey, for example, completely misreads this section, failing to see the import not only of Socrates' allusion to heat heating itself at 168e10, but also of Critias' choice not to know his ignorance at 169c3–d1. Friedlaender, Taylor, Santas, McKim—all fail to relate *logos* to *ergon* and thus fail to appreciate the important teaching that Plato is adumbrating in this section. Hyland does better with it, though he again digresses into existentialist doctrines, *Virtue of Philosophy*, 121–22.

4. On Critias' name, see Friedlaender, *Plato*, vol. 2, 67; also West, *Plato's Charmides*, note 55, 44.

5. Bruell, "Socratic Politics and Self-Knowledge," 173–76; cf. also Hyland, *Virtue of Philosophy*, 114–17.

6. cf. Aristotle, *On the Soul* III.2. For discussion, see especially Bruell, "Socratic Politics and Self-Knowledge," 173–76.

7. *Gorgias* 466d–468e, *Protagoras* 340b; also *Lysis* 218d–220b.

8. For discussion of this principle, see Gomez-Lobo, *Foundations of Socratic Ethics*, 7–8.

9. On the contrast of first and second order knowledges, see Sprague, *The Philosopher-King*, xiii–xvi, 29–42; on first and second order desires, see Frankfurt, "Freedom of the Will and the Concept of a Person," and Tugendthat, *Self-Consciousness and Self-Determination*, cited in note 34, chapter 4; also Charles Taylor, "Responsibility for Self" in Gary Watson, ed. *Free Will*, 111–26.

10. This particular section is discussed minimally by Tuckey, *Plato's Charmides*, 41 and Hyland, *Virtue of Philosophy*, 118.

11. Tuckey dismisses the claim by Von Arnim that this passage "clearly implies that the Theory of Ideas had already been worked out," 41–42. But Tuckey does not acknowledge the striking relevance of the passage to the Ideas and the problem of their self-predication. It is this kind of "metaphysical subtlety" which led some critics to place the *Charmides* in the vicinity of the *Theatetus* among the dialogues. On Kahn's approach, it would be viewed as a striking instance of prolepsis.

12. A Great greater than itself and other greaters, though not as such greater than their lessers, might be linked to *sophrosune* itself: cf. the discussion of the "greater" versus "lesser" benefits of *sophrosune* at 169d–172c in chapter 6, and the remarks at the end of chapter 7, opening section. I owe this point to Martin Andic.

13. On the mathematical and ontological background to this section, see Jacob Klein, *Greek Mathematical Thought and the Origin of Algebra*, 69–99.

14. Levine notes this in "Plato's *Charmides*," 245.

15. Compare Tuckey, *Plato's Charmides*, 46–47.

16. But these several points have been overlooked, to my knowledge, in the scholarly literature, even by Kahn in his discussion of "Plato's *Charmides* and the Proleptic Reading of the Platonic Dialogues."

17. *Republic* 509d–511e. For discussion of the Line, see Klein, *A Commentary on Plato's Meno*, 115–25.

18. This is a dominant theme of Plato's later writing, especially the *Sophist* and *Seventh Letter*. In the *Seventh Letter*, Plato envisions the essence of the philosophical task as explicating the relation among names, essences, knowledge, Forms and their relations—the relations among the levels being characterized in terms of image and original. For a discussion of Plato's metaphysics in terms of this relation, see Richard Patterson, *Image and Reality in Plato's Metaphysics*. For discussion of the *Seventh Letter*, see Gadamer, "Dialectic and Sophism in Plato's *Seventh Letter*," *Dialogue and Dialectic*, 90–123.

19. T. M. Robinson, *Plato's Psychology*, 8. Robinson does not remark on the ambiguity of the representation of the relation of body and soul in the prologue in the *Charmides*.

20. There is a noticeably "Kantian" aspect to this view of the *Charmides*. There is also a "Hegelian" element in the dialogue, in its emphasis on the relation of the self and of rationality to community, as sketched in chapter 3 and chapter 4.

21. These remarks should not be read to claim that the *Charmides* fully reflects the Theory of Forms or the *symploke eidon* of the *Sophist*, as claimed by some critics. (These critics are cited in Guthrie, *History of Ancient Greek Philosophy*, vol. 4, note 3, 169.)

22. Gould, *The Development of Plato's Ethics*, 39, ignores the conditional character of Socrates' remarks at 169a7–b3, where he says "I don't trust myself . . . *until* I investigate" (my italics).

23. Hyland sees this point: "Plato wants to remind us forcefully that Critias at this point really is muddled, that he is in *aporia* far more than

Socrates, but he does not realize it," *Virtue of Philosophy*, 122. Tuckey merely remarks that "Critias is naturally embarrassed by this [his inability to prove that self-relational knowledge is possible,]" *Plato's Charmides*, 48.

24. *Republic* 382b–c: "Falsehood in the most vital part of themselves, and about their most vital concerns, is something that no one willingly accepts . . . essential falsehood, then, is hated not only by gods but by men."

25. Thus the *Charmides*, and the phenomenon of dialectical *akrasia* in general makes it evident, contrary to the statements of *Republic* 382b–c, that Plato *does* allow the possibility of self-deception "in the most vital part of themselves, and about their most vital concerns." It should be noted that the psychology of *Republic* II–IV is superseded by later developments, especially the discussion of the relation of reason, *thumos* and appetite at 439e–440b by the social psychology of *Republic* VIII–IX. The model of self-relation in terms of first- and second-order desires is implicit already at 437a–c, however.

26. See the discussions of the paradox of self-deception in Herbert Fingarette, *Self-Deception*; David Hamlyn, "Self-knowledge" in T. Mischel, ed., *The Self*, 170–202; and Amelie Rorty, "The Deceptive Self," in B. McLaughlin and A. Rorty, eds., *Perspectives on Self-Deception*, 11–28.

27. See L. Jonathan Cohen, *An Essay on Belief and Acceptance*, especially 133–60.

28. Aristotle, *Nicomachean Ethics* VII.iii.8, 1147a19–24, discusses *akrasia* in terms of the actor/speaker distinction.

29. There is really no figure comparable to Eumaios, Odysseus' pious and happy swineherd, in the Platonic dialogues. Even Cephalus, who might seem a comparable type of religiously content man, is motivated by anxiety about the afterlife. The idea of religious wisdom, acquired through experience or revelation, is not presented as a viable alternative to the quest for rational insight concerning the good and meaning of human life in relation to the whole. (The idea of mystical experience as a culminating moment in that quest is present in the account of the ladder of love in the *Symposium*, however.)

30. For treatment of the relation of the reciprocal influence of individual and society, see now Jonathan Lear, "Inside and Outside the *Republic*."

Chapter 6: Knowledge of Knowledge

1. Plato, *Charmides*, West edition, note 57, 45.

2. The interpretations of "the knowledge of knowledge" in the scholarly literature are diverse: Bruell, "Socratic Politics," relates it to self-con-

sciousness; Martens, *Das selbstbewusstliche Wissen*, and Sprague, *Plato's Philosopher King*, 36–37, to Socrates in the *Apology* 21a–23b; Sprague also to the ideal of a ruling art, 39–42; Santas, "Socrates at Work on Knowledge and Virtue," 119–24, and Taylor, *Plato*, 54, to epistemology. Hyland, *Virtue of Philosophy*, 95, and Tuckey, *Plato's Charmides*, 39, both recognize that the meaning of the phrase is insufficiently determined at 167a.

3. See Gould, *The Development of Plato's Ethics*, 37–41; O'Brien, *The Socratic Paradoxes and the Greek Mind*, 123–24; Tuckey, *Plato's Charmides*, 60–61.

4. As indicated in chapter 3, I follow Hyland's lead here, though our interpretations differ significantly. See note 3, chapter 3. Hyland offers an existentialist reading, which does not thematize the different epistemological models.

5. The "that which" refers to a sticky point of translation/interpretation. In fact, the Greek phrase *hoti* at 170b11 would normally be translated as "that," but the context clearly calls for "what." West leaves it as "that," but this renders Socrates' argument unintelligible. Lamb translates it as "what" in the Loeb edition.

6. See the argument in Schofield, "Socrates on Conversing with Doctors," 122–23.

7. McKim argues that Socrates' point is that while the doctor would know the healthful, he would not know that his or another's knowledge of the healthful was knowledge without the knowledge of knowledge, "Socratic Self-Knowledge and 'Knowledge of Knowledge' in Plato's *Charmides*," 68–69. This implies that one might examine someone who claimed to be a doctor and (1) determine that he knew everything relating to the diagnosis and cure of illness and restoration of health, including why one should say what he said about such matters and do what he did; but (2) still be ignorant of whether he possessed *iatrike*, medical knowledge— which is absurd. It is part of the knowledge of medicine to be able to know itself qua medicine, part of the knowledge of the doctor to know himself (or another) as a doctor. The problem comes in primarily where people lack genuine knowledge, or think they possess knowledge not only in their own field, but in other matters as well, notably moral and political matters, as Socrates says at *Apology* 21a–23b. The physician does not need dialectic to examine another physician for knowledge of medicine; but he needs it, if he is going to test a physician's (or his own) claim to knowledge of what is best for the patient or society in the larger sense of benefit.

8. Tuckey notes the discrepancies, but does not relate them to the dramatic context, *Plato's Charmides*, 58–59.

9. Most commentators—for example, Friedlaender, Hyland, Santas, Shorey, Tuckey, Taylor—fail to note the oddity of this example.

10. See especially *Protagoras* 319a–320c; in contrast to Socrates, the Sophist does regard it as such. See also *Apology* 21a–23b. Socrates' remarks at *Gorgias* 508e6–509a1 that his position is "clamped down with arguments of steel and adamant" have to be taken in the context of the earlier remarks, especially 506a3–4, as Vlastos has shown.

11. Schofield, "Socrates on Conversing with Doctors," 122.

12. Schofield, ibid., 122–23.

13. For two reasons: (1) he can test for contradiction in the professed expert's factual knowledge; (2) he has empirical knowledge relevant to the professed science, for example, he could know that a builder who claimed to make houses of straw was a fake, or a physician who sought to cure weak sight by stabbing the eye with a sword. (This is one reason why it is relevant for Plato to later distinguish the slavish and free physicians at *Laws* 720b–e.)

14. See especially 156b1–c6. I am assuming Socrates presents himself as one who can induce "mental health"/*sophrosune*. Certainly, this is how he comes to be taken. For discussion of the problem of whether his treatment can guarantee results, see chapter 4.

15. Cf. the account of the arts in *Gorgias*, especially 465a, and note 13 above.

16. Even at the end of the dialogue, Critias avers the art of medicine is most like the one they seek. The statesman's art is a form of psychic medicine in the *Gorgias*, 464b–466a. In Aristotle, too, ethics is compared to a medical model; cf. the survey by Werner Jaeger, "Aristotle's use of medicine as a model of method in his ethics," *Journal of Hellenic Studies* 77 (1957), 54–61.

17. The exegetical problem is how to account for *any* benefit, given what he has argued. Tuckey notes the problem, but his solution seems to me inadequate, for the reasons I indicate. Hyland does not seem to appreciate the problem in his discussion in *The Virtue of Philosophy*, 126–29, nor does Friedlaender in *Plato*, vol. 2, 56, Santas in "Socrates at Work on Virtue and Knowledge in Plato's *Charmides*," 124–29, or Taylor in *Plato*, 55–56.

18. Tuckey, *Plato's Charmides*, 66–67, 69.

19. Tuckey, ibid., 68.

20. Note the "I see" (*horo*) again, 172a9. See the discussion in chapter 5.

21. Compare the loose discussion in Hyland, *Virtue of Philosophy*, 126–29. Tuckey is sensitive to many of the perplexities of the text at

170a–172c, but he is misled, in my view, by his failure to be sufficiently aware of the *logos/ergon* theme; thus he takes Socrates' introduction of politics as a *techne* at 170b at face value, and fails to see how it exemplifes the very failure Socrates is talking about (the failure to know the difference between productive or purely theoretical, as opposed to moral knowledge); and he fails to appreciate the very different epistemology of the second discussion, reflected in the emphasis on testing the knowledge-claimant and in the introduction of the possibility of combining knowledge in a given area with the knowledge of knowledge.

22. See the discussion of this passage in Vlastos, "Socrates' Disavowal of Knowledge," especially 59 f.

CHAPTER 7: UTOPIA, DYSTOPIA, AND KNOWLEDGE OF THE GOOD

1. Irwin, *Plato's Moral Theory*, 1, also 71–77.

2. Tuckey, *Plato's Charmides*, 87.

3. Robert Elliott, *The Shape of Utopia*, 101. In this connection, there is a memorable passage in which Francis Cornford, asserting a philosophical difference between Socrates and Plato, compares Plato to the Grand Inquisitor, Socrates to his prisoner; see *The Unwritten Philosophy*, 67.

4. This is a view with which Popper, of course, would agree. See *The Open Society and Its Enemies*, vol. 1, 195. Popper also notes the ambiguity of Socrates' teaching: "The moral intellectualism of Socrates is a two-edged sword. It has its equalitarian and democratic aspect, which was later developed by Antisthenes. But it also has an aspect which may give rise to strongly anti-democratic tendencies. Its stress upon the need for enlightenment, for education, might easily be interpreted as a demand for authoritarianism. . . ." *The Open Society*, 114. For a very different interpretation of the *Republic*, see the article by Diskin Clay, cited in note 29, chapter 3 above. Might Plato himself have had a sympathetic view of what Socrates calls the "most beautiful" regime? Strauss argues for this possibility in *The City and Man*, 131.

5. Compare West, in his edition of Plato, *Charmides*, 5–6.

6. This point is unclear. It is puzzling that he appears to allow for households in the city, given the rule that all knowledge would be turned over to the one who knows. Is he simply expressing the basic idea incompletely, appealing perhaps to Critias as the head of a household in which Charmides is one of his dependents? Compare the treatment of this issue at *Lysis* 207d–210d and *Republic* 332d–333e.

7. This term, like *eunomia* and *eukosmia*, had a class or ideological meaning in the Dorian world; cf. North, *Sophrosyne*, 9, 15, 25, 113.

8. The reference is to *Odyssey* XIX, 564–67, where Penelope refers to the two gates in the underworld whence dreams come, some deceiving, some revealing. The acknowledged ambiguity of Socrates' "dream" continues the theme of ambiguity and enigma announced earlier, cf., for example, 161c, 162a, 164e.

9. Plato, *Charmides*, West edition, 5–6.

10. For discussion of the democratic Socrates, see Gregory Vlastos, *Socrates, Ironist and Moral Philosopher*, 18, and his "The Historical Socrates and Athenian Democracy," *Political Theory* 11 (1983), 495–515 (republished in *Socratic Studies*, 87–108). This article is criticized by Ellen and Neal Wood, "Socrates and Democracy," *Political Theory* 14 (1986), 55–83. For further discussion sympathetic to a democratic view of Socrates, see J. Peter Euben, "Democracy and Political Theory," in Euben, Wallach, and Ober, *Athenian Political Thought and the Reconstruction of American Democracy*, 198–226, and Richard Kraut, *Socrates and the State*, 194–244.

11. Compare Vlastos, *Socratic Studies*, 103–105, Euben, "Democracy and Political Theory," 208, 217, 222. Cf. also the discussion in chapter 4. The same idea is found in Sartre's *bon mot*: "When Socrates stopped to talk with a slave about geometric patterns, it was as if he said, 'This slave is as capable as I of being a member of the Council.'" In "Legend de la Verite," *Bifur VIII* (Paris, 1931), 86.

12. This point underscores the relevance of the fact that the leaders in Socrates' original characterization of the city possessed knowledge both of what they did *and* what they did not know—in marked contrast to Critias's would-be omniscient rulers.

13. Tuckey, *Plato's Charmides*, 74.

14. The term "self-control" is ridiculed at *Republic* 430e–431a, but cf. especially 437b–c, where the model is in terms of first and second order desires, the latter "affirming" or "denying" what the former intends.

15. For further discussion of this quote, see my *On Manly Courage*, 140–41.

16. Tuckey, *Plato's Charmides*, 73–76. On this distinction and its place in Socratic ethics, see the discussions in Vlastos, *Socrates, Ironist and Moral Philosopher*, 200–232; Brickhouse and Smith, *Plato's Socrates*, 103–36; Gomez-Lobo, *Foundations of Socratic Ethics*, 7–10, 33–44, 82–87; and Versenyi, *Socratic Humanism*, 75–86.

17. Tuckey, *Plato's Charmides*, 76.

18. This comes out under examination by Socrates, not in the initial discussion with Laches. See *On Manly Courage*, 151–58, 163, 165.

19. See Tuckey, *Plato's Charmides*, 84, who, however, does not relate this point to the dramatic context, and its relevance to Socrates' regressive re-introduction of the idea of moral expertise in the argument.

20. Tuckey, *Plato's Charmides*, 79, notes that the rulers in Socrates' first portrait of the ideal society were not omniscient, but he does not relate this point to the dramatic context of the discussion and fails to appreciate that it is *Critias'* presumption of the connection between self-knowledge and omniscience that is undergoing refutation here.

21. Irwin, *Plato's Moral Theory*, 88. Richard McKim takes Irwin to task for relying on an implicit conclusion to the argument, "Socratic Self-Knowledge and the 'Knowledge of knowledge' in Plato's *Charmides*," note 28, 78. But he does not take into account Irwin's remarks explaining why he draws the inferences.

22. This is a common error, as noted by McKim, "Socratic Self-Knowledge and the 'Knowledge of knowledge' in Plato's *Charmides*," note 2, 60. For discussion of McKim's own interpretation, see chapter 6, note 7 above.

23. If *sophrosune* were a craft, it would have to be the hegemonic, master-craft; but this is to ignore, as Critias has done throughout, the "Socratic addition," which concerns the knowledge of ignorance. That second element can be no mere subordinate craft, but must function as the self-critical/self-moderating form of the moral life.

24. This discussion must be related to the treatment in chapter 3 of the use of the *techne* analogy in the *Charmides*.

25. *Plato's Charmides*, 86.

26. Tuckey fails to appreciate the dramatic significance not only of Socrates' acts of self-knowledge and moderation at 154b–c, 155c–156d, 165b–c, 166c–d, 175a–d, but also Critias's failures of self-knowledge and moderation at 162c–d, 169c–d, and 176c–d. As a result, his treatment largely ignores the fundamental role that knowledge of ignorance plays in the Socratic, as opposed to Critian intepretation of *sophrosune* and the definition at 167a, and thus he also fails to systematically relate this distinction to his interpretation of the definition and subsequent arguments.

27. Tuckey, *Plato's Charmides*, 78.

28. Tuckey, ibid., 86.

29. Tuckey: "It follows that no man can acquire knowledge of the Good, that is, *certain* as opposed to *fancied* knowledge without this same ability . . . *sophrosune* . . . will be this *certain* knowledge of the Good," *Plato's Charmides*, 87 (italics in original).

30. Gadamer: "Knowledge of the good is exactly what is not asked about in the *technai* and by the *technites* . . . [Socrates'] awareness of this fact is the basis of his superior 'ignorance.' Knowledge of the good would seem to be different in kind from all familiar human knowledge. Hence, if measured against such a concept of specialized expertise, it could indeed be called ignorance," *The Idea of the Good in Platonic-Aristotelian Philosophy*, 23, and again at 33: "Plato himself saw that knowledge of the good cannot be understood using *techne* as a model, although—or better said, precisely because—Socrates continually uses this *techne* model in his critique and refutation of the views of his partners in discussion."

CHAPTER 8: EPILOGUE

1. For discussion of the paradox, see Klein, *A Commentary on Plato's Meno*, 88–92.

2. *Laches* 194a. For discussion, see *On Manly Courage*, 126–31.

3. Thus Shorey, *What Plato Said*, 105, Rutherford, *The Art of Plato*, 93, Friedlaender, *Plato*, vol. 2, 73. Hyland, *Virtue of Philosophy*, 146–47, and West, Plato, *Charmides*, 56, note 68, realize this is not the case.

4. In the account of the genesis of the tyrant in the *Republic*, too, it is not merely the predominance of lawless *eros*, but the willingness of the tyrant to resort to violence, and perhaps the taste he acquires for it, that characterizes the decisive moment in his self-formation; cf. especially *Republic* 565e–566a.

5. Compare the discussion of the personified *logos* in Kuhn, "The True Tragedy," *Harvard Studies in Classical Philology*, vol. 42, 1–41, vol. 43, 37–88.

APPENDIX A: THE STRUCTURE OF THE *CHARMIDES*

1. Compare the analysis in the West edition of Plato, *Charmides*, 7–8.

2. See Tuckey, *Plato's Charmides*, vii. Tuckey adds a sixth definition, the knowledge of good and evil, 87.

3. See R. B. Rutherford, *The Art of Plato*, 90.

4. Friedlaender also offers a complex and interesting two level interpretation of the structure, distinguishing the Charmides level from the Critias level, and dividing the latter both in terms of the distinction between the individual and society, on the one hand, and outward and inward modes of being, on the other. See his *Plato*, vol. 2, 79. On the idea of a 'Two-Level Model' in relation to the Platonic dialogues, see the essay by Holger Thesleff, "Looking for Clues" in Press, *Plato's Dialogues*, 17–45, referred to in note 5 of the preface.

5. So far as I know, this approach to the structure of the dialogue has not been offered previously in the scholarly literature.

6. Compare the discussion of the relation of the Divided Line to the structure of the *Laches* in my *On Manly Courage*, 45–48.

APPENDIX B: THE *CHARMIDES* AND THE *REPUBLIC*

1. On the question of epistemological closure in Plato, see the works by Christopher Gill and H. G. Gadamer cited in note 19, chapter 3; also Gadamer's "Dialectic and Sophism in Plato's *Seventh Letter*," *Dialogue and Dialectic*, 90–123, 121: "The labor of dialectic in which the truth of what is finally flashes upon us is by nature unending and infinite."

2. Gomez-Lobo, *Foundations of Socratic Ethics*, especially 102–11.

3. See note 4 to chapter 8, above.

4. See the references cited in notes 10–11 to chapter 7 above.

5. On "high" versus "low" utopias, see Doyne Dawson, *Cities of the Gods*, 3–11, 77–91.

6. Kraut, "Reason and Justice in the *Republic*," in *Exegesis and Argument*, edited by E. Lee, A. Mourelatos and R. Rorty, 207–24.

7. Lear, "Inside and Outside the *Republic*," 208–15.

8. Compare Freud, *Civilization and Its Discontents*, 18–27, 47–51, 76–89.

9. For the view that the *Republic* contains no politics at all, see Leys, "Was Plato Non-Political?" in Vlastos ed., *Plato*, vol. 2, 166–73, the criticism by F. E. Sparshott at 174–83, and Leys' response, 183–86. For the view that the *Republic* should not be read in a didactic, but rather in an dialogic manner, see the article by Clay cited in note 29 to chapter 3.

10. For discussion of the Popper/Plato debate, see the essays in Renford Banmbrough, *Plato, Popper and Politics*, the summary of the debate in Dawson, *Cities of the Gods*, 62–70, and the article by Clay mentioned in the note above.

BIBLIOGRAPHY

Adkins, A. W. H. *Merit and Responsibility*. Oxford: Clarendon Press. 1960.

——— . "*Polupragmosune* and 'Minding Your Own business,'" *Classical Philology* 71 (1976), 301–28.

Anderson, Robert J. *A Commentary on Plato's Theaetetus*. Unpublished manuscript.

——— . "The Theory of Perception in Plato's *Theaetetus*." In *Plato, Time and Education: Essays in Honor of Robert S. Brumbaugh*, edited by Brian Hendley. Albany: State University of New York Press, 1987.

Annas, Julia. *An Introduction to Plato's Republic*. Oxford: Clarendon Press, 1981.

——— . "Self-Knowledge in early Plato." In *Platonic Investigations*, edited by Dominic O'Meara. Washington, D.C.: Catholic University of America Press, 1985.

Arendt, Hannah. *Between Past and Future*. New York: Viking Press, 1954.

——— . *Life of the Mind 1: Thinking*. New York: Harcourt Brace Jovanovich, 1971.

——— . "Thinking and Moral Considerations." *Social Research* 38/3 (1971): 418–46.

Aristotle. *Nicomachean Ethics*. Translated by H. Rackham. Cambridge: Harvard University Press, 1926.

————. *On the Soul*. Translated by W. S. Hett. Cambridge: Harvard University Press, 1975.

————. *Politics*. Translated by H. Rackham. Cambridge: Harvard University Press, 1932.

Arrowsmith, William. "Aristophanes' *Birds*: Fantasy Politics of *Eros*." *Arion* 1 (1973): 119–67.

Austin, Scott. "The Paradox of Socratic Ignorance (How to Know That You Don't Know)." *Philosophical Topics* 15 (1987): 23–34.

Bambrough, Renford, ed. *Plato, Popper and Politics*. Cambridge: Cambridge University Press, 1967.

Ben, N. van der. *The Charmides of Plato*. Amsterdam: B. R. Gruner, 1985.

Benardete, Seth. "On Interpreting Plato's *Charmides*." *Graduate Faculty Philosophy Journal* 11 (1986): 9–36.

Benhabib, Seyla. *Critique, Norm, and Utopia*. New York: Columbia University Press, 1986.

Benson, Hugh H. "A Note on Eristic and the Socratic Elenchus." *Journal of the History of Philosophy* 27 (1989): 591–99.

————. "The Priority of Definition and the Socratic *Elenchos*." *Oxford Studies in Ancient Philosophy* 8 (1990): 19–65.

————, ed. *Essays on The Philosophy of Socrates*. Oxford: Oxford University Press, 1992.

Beversluis, J. "Does Socrates Commit the Socratic Fallacy?" *American Philosophical Quarterly* 21 (1987): 211–23.

————. "Socratic Definition." *American Philosophical Quarterly* 11 (1987): 331–36.

Bonitz, H. "Bemerkungen zu dem Abschnitt des Dialogs *Charmides* 165–172." *Platonische Studien*. Hildesheim: Georg Olms Verlag, 1886.

Brandwood, Leonard. *The Chronology of Plato's Dialogues*. Cambridge: Cambridge University Press, 1990.

————. "Stylometry and Chronology." In *The Cambridge Companion to Plato*, edited by Richard Kraut. Cambridge: Cambridge University Press, 1993.

Brickhouse, Thomas C. and Nicholas D. Smith. *Plato's Socrates*. Oxford: Oxford University Press, 1994.

Bruell, Christopher. "Socratic Politics and Self-Knowledge." *Interpretation* 6 (1977): 141–203.

Brumbaugh, Robert S. *Plato for the Modern Age*. New York: Crowell Collier, 1962.

———. "Plato's *Meno* as Form and as Content." *Teaching Philosophy* 1 (Fall, 1975): 107–115.

Burger, Ronna. "Belief, Knowledge and Socratic Knowledge of Ignorance." *Tulane Studies in Philosophy* 30 (1981): 1–23.

Burkert, Walter. *Greek Religion*. Translated by John Raffin. Cambridge: Harvard University Press, 1985.

Burnyeat, Myles. "Socratic Midwifery, Platonic Inspiration," *Bulletin of the Institute of Classical Studies* 24 (University of London): 7–16.

Butler, Joseph. *Sermons*. New York: Robert Carter & Brothers, 1986.

Casey, John. *Pagan Virtue*. Oxford: Clarendon Press, 1990.

Chance, Thomas. *Plato's Euthydemus: Analysis of What Is and What Is Not Philosophy*. Berkeley: University of California Press, 1992.

Claus, David. *Toward the Soul*. New Haven: Yale University Press, 1981.

Clay, Diskin. "Reading the *Republic*." In Griswold, Charles, ed. *Platonic Writings/ Platonic Readings*. New York: Routledge Chapman & Hall, 1988.

Cohen, Joshua. "Procedure and Substance in Deliberative Democracy." Paper presented at The Chapel Hill Colloquium in Philosophy, October 27, 1995.

Cooper, John. "The Psychology of Justice in Plato." *American Philosophical Quarterly* 14, 2 (1977): 151–57.

Darwell, Stephen L. *Impartial Reason*. Ithaca: Cornell University Press, 1983.

Davidson, Donald. "Plato's Philosopher," *London Review of Books*, 1 August 1985, 15–17.

Davies, J. K. *Athenian Propertied Families*. Oxford: Clarendon Press, 1971.

Dawson, Doyne. *Cities of the Gods*. Oxford: Oxford University Press, 1992.

Desjardins, Paul. "The Form of Platonic Inquiry." Ph. D. dissertation, Yale University, 1958.

Desjardins, Rosemary. *The Rational Enterprise*. Albany: State University of New York Press, 1990.

———. "Why Dialogues? Plato's Serious Play" in Griswold, Charles, ed. *Platonic Writings/Platonic Readings*. New York: Routledge Chapman & Hall, 1988.

Devereux, George. "Greek Pseudo-Homosexuality and the 'Greek Miracle.'" *Symbolae Osloenses* 42 (1967): 69–92.

Diels, Hermann. *The Older Sophists*. Edited by Rosamund Kent Sprague. Columbia: University of South Carolina Press, 1972.

Dilman, Ilham. *Morality and the Good Life*. New York: Barnes & Noble, 1979.

Dodds, E. R. *The Greeks and the Irrational*. Berkeley: University of California Press, 1951.

Dover, Kenneth. *Greek Homosexuality*. Cambridge: Harvard University Press, 1978.

Dyson, M. "Some problems concerning knowledge in Plato's '*Charmides*.'" *Phronesis* 19 (1974): 102–11.

Ebert, Thomas. *Meinung und Wissen in der Philosophie Platons: Untersuchungen zum "Charmides," "Menon" und "Staat."* Berlin, 1974.

Edmunds, Lowell. *Chance and Intelligence in Thucydides*. Cambridge: Harvard University Press, 1975.

Ehrenberg, Victor. "*Polypragmosyne.*" *Journal of Hellenic Studies* 67 (1947): 46–67.

Elliott, Robert C. *The Shape of Utopia*. Chicago: University of Chicago Press, 1970.

Entralgo, P. Lain. *The Therapy of the Word in Classical Antiquity*. Translated and edited by L. Rather and J. Sharp. New Haven: Yale University Press, 1970.

Euben, J. Peter. "Democracy and Political Theory: A Reading of Plato's *Gorgias*." In *Athenian Political Thought and the Reconstruction of American Democracy*, edited by J. Peter Euben, John R. Wallach, and Josiah Ober. Ithaca: Cornell University Press, 1994.

Evans, Joseph C. "Socratic Ignorance—Socratic Wisdom." *Modern Schoolman* 67 (1990): 91–110.

Everson, Stephen, ed. *Companions to Ancient Thought 1: Epistemology*. Cambridge: Cambridge University Press, 1990.

Fingarette, Herbert. *Self-Deception*. London: Routledge Kegan Paul, 1969.

Foucault, Michel. *The History of Sexuality: The Use of Pleasure*. Vol. 2. Translated by Robert Hurley. New York: Random House, 1990.

Frankena, William. *Ethics*, 2nd edition. Englewood Cliffs, N.J.: Prentice Hall, 1973.

Frankfurt, Harry G. "Freedom of the Will and the Concept of a Person." *Journal of Philosophy* 68 (1971), 5–20. Reprinted in *Free Will*, edited by Gary Watson. Oxford: Oxford University Press, 1982.

Freud, Sigmund. *Civilization and Its Discontents*. Translated by James Strachey. New York: Norton, 1962.

Friedlaender, Paul. *Plato*. Vol. 1–2. Translated by Hans Meyerhoff. New York: Bollingen Foundation, 1964.

Gadamer, Hans-Georg. *Dialogue and Dialectic*. Translated by Christopher Smith. New Haven: Yale University Press, 1980.

——— . *The Idea of the Good in Platonic-Aristotelian Philosophy*. New Haven: Yale University Press, 1986.

——— . *Plato's Dialectical Ethics*. Translated by Robert M. Wallace. New Haven: Yale University Press, 1991.

——— . *Truth and Method*. New York: Seabury Press, 1975.

Gerson, Lloyd. "Plato on Virtue, Knowledge and the Unity of Goodness." Paper presented at Society for Ancient Greek Philosophy, New York, 1984.

Gill, Christopher. "Afterword: Dialectic and the Dialogue Form in Late Plato." In *Form and Argument in Late Plato*, edited by Christopher Gill and Margaret McCabe. Oxford: Oxford University Press, 1996.

——— . "Dogmatic Dogma in *Phaedrus* 276–7?" In *Understanding the Phaedrus, Proceedings of the II Symposium Platonicum* edited by L. Rossetti. St. Augustine, 1992.

——— . "Peace of mind and Being Yourself: Panaetius to Plutarch." *Decline and Rise of the Roman World* 36, 7 (1994): 4599–4640.

——— . *Personality in Greek Epic, Tragedy, and Philosophy: The Self in Dialogue*. Oxford: Oxford University Press, 1996.

Goffmann, Erving. *The Presentation of Self in Everyday Life*. Garden City: Doubleday, 1959.

Gomez-Lobo, Alfonso. *The Foundations of Socratic Ethics*. Indianapolis: Hackett, 1994.

Gonzalez, Francisco, ed. *The Third Way: New Directions in Platonic Studies*. Lanham, Md.: Rowman & Littlefield, 1995.

Gould, J. *The Development of Plato's Ethics*. Cambridge: Cambridge University Press, 1955.

Gourevitch, Victor. "Philosophy and Politics II." *Review of Metaphysics* 22, 2 (1968): 281–329.

Gray, John. *Mill on Liberty: A Defense*. London: Routledge & Kegan Paul, 1983.

Griswold, Charles L., Jr. "*Politike episteme* in Plato's *Statesman*." In *Essays in Ancient Greek Philosophy*. Vol. 3. Edited by John P. Anton and Anthony Preus. Albany: State University of New York Press, 1989.

———. *Self-Knowledge in Plato's Phaedrus*. New Haven: Yale University Press, 1986.

———, ed. *Platonic Writings/Platonic Readings*. New York: Routledge, Chapman & Hall, 1988.

Grote, George. *Plato and the Other Companions of Sokrates*, 2nd ed. Vol. 1–3. London: J. Murray, 1875.

Gulley, Norman. *The Philosophy of Socrates*. London: MacMillan, 1968.

Guthrie, W. K. C. *A History of Greek Philosophy*. Vols. 3 and 4. Cambridge: Cambridge University Press, 1969, 1975.

Habermas, Juergen. *Moral Consciousness and Communicative Action*, trans. C. Lenhardt and S. W. Nicholson. Cambridge: MIT Press, 1990.

Halperin, David. "Platonic Eros and What Men Call Love." *Ancient Philosophy* 5 (1985), 161–204.

Hamlyn, David W. "Self-Knowledge." In *The Self*, edited by Theodore Mischel. Totowa, N.J.: Rowman & Littlefield, 1977.

Hyland, Drew. "*Eros, Epithymia*, and *Philia* in Plato." *Phronesis* 13 (1968), 32–46.

———. *The Virtue of Philosophy*. Athens: Ohio University Press, 1981.

Irwin, Terence. "Coercion and Objectivity in Plato's Dialectic," *Revue Internationale de Philosophie* 40 (1986): 49–74.

———. *Plato's Moral Theory*. Oxford: Clarendon Press, 1977.

———. "Socrates and Athenian Democracy." *Philosophy and Public Affairs* 18 (1989), 184–205.

Isenberg, Arnold. "Natural Pride and Natural Shame." *Philosophy and Phenomenological Research* 10 (1949): 1–24.

Jaeger, Werner. "Aristotle's Use of Medicine as Model of Method in His Ethics." *Journal of Hellenic Studies* 77 (1957), 54–61.

——— . *Paideia*. Vols. 1–3. Translated by Gilbert Highet. Oxford: Oxford University Press, 1939.

Kagan, Donald. *The Outbreak of the the Peloponnesian War*. Ithaca: Cornell University Press, 1969.

Kahn, Charles. "Did Plato Write Socratic Dialogues?" *Classical Quarterly* 31 (1981): 305–20.

——— . "Drama and Dialectic in Plato's *Gorgias*." *Oxford Studies in Ancient Philosophy* 1 (1983): 75–121.

——— . "Plato's *Charmides* and the Proleptic Reading of Socratic Dialogues." *Journal of Philosophy* 85/10 (1988): 541–49.

Kant, Immanuel. "What Is Enlightenment?" in *The Philosophy of Kant: Immanuel Kant's Moral and Political Writings*. Edited by Carl Friedrich. New York: Modern Library, 1949.

Kaplan, Morris. *Sexual Justice*. New York: Routledge, 1997.

Kerferd, G. B. *The Sophistic Movement*. Cambridge: Cambridge University Press, 1981.

Keuls, Eva. *The Reign of the Phallus: Sexual Politics in Ancient Athens*. New York: Harper & Row, 1985.

Klein, Jacob. *A Commentary on Plato's Meno*. Chapel Hill: University of North Carolina Press, 1965.

——— . *Greek Mathematical Thought and the Origin of Algebra*. Translated by Eva Brann. Cambridge, Mass.: MIT Press, 1968.

Klosko, George. *The Development of Plato's Political Theory*. New York: 1986.

——— . "The Technical Conception of Virtue." *Journal of the History of Philosophy* 19 (1981), 95–102.

Kosman, L. A. "Platonic Love." In *Facets of Plato's Philosophy*, edited by W. H. Werkmeister. Assen, Holland: Van Gorcum, 1976.

——— . "*Sophrosune* as Quietness." In *Essays in Ancient Greek Philosophy*, Vol. 2, edited by John P. Anton and Anthony Preus. Albany: State University of New York Press, 1983.

Knox, Bernard. *Oedipus at Thebes*. New Haven: Yale University Press, 1957.

Kraut, Richard. "Reason and Justice in Plato's *Republic*." In *Exegesis and Argument*, edited by E. N. Lee, A. P. D. Mourelatos, and R. M. Rorty. Assen, Holland: Van Gorcum, 1973.

———. *Socrates and the State*. Princeton: Princeton University Press, 1984.

Krentz, Peter. *The Thirty at Athens*. Ithaca: Cornell University Press, 1982.

Krueger, Gerhard. *Einsicht und Leidenschaft*. Frankfurt: Klostermann, 1939.

Kuhn, Helmut. *Sokrates: Versuch ueber den Ursprung der Metaphysik*. Munich: Koesel-Verlag, 1959.

Lachterman, David. "Plato's *Charmides*." B. A. Thesis, St. John's College, Annapolis, Md., 1965.

Lear, Jonathan. "Inside and Outside The *Republic*." *Phronesis* 37/2 (1992), 184–215.

Levine, David L. "Plato's *Charmides*," Ph.D. dissertation, Pennsylvania State University, 1976.

———. "The Tyranny of Scholarship." *Ancient Philosophy* 4 (1984): 65–72.

Leys, Wayne. "Was Plato Non-Political?" and "Afterthought." In *Plato: A Collection of Critical Essays*, vol. 2, edited by Gregory Vlastos. Garden City, N.Y.: Doubleday, 1971.

Luckhurst, K. "Note on Plato's *Charmides* 153b." *Classical Review* 48 (1934): 207–208.

MacIntyre, Alasdair. *After Virtue*. Notre Dame: University of Notre Dame Press, 1981.

———. *A Short History of Ethics*. New York: MacMillan, 1973.

Martens, E. *Das selbstbezuegliche Wissen in Platons Charmides*. Munich: Carl Hansen Verlag, 1973.

Matthews, Gareth. "It is no longer I that do it . . ." *Faith and Philosophy* 1 (1984), 44–49.

McKim, Richard. "Socratic Self-Knoweldge and 'Knowlege of Knowledge' in Plato's *Charmides*." *Transactions of the American Philological Association* 115 (1985): 59–77.

Mischel, Theodore, ed. *The Self: Psychological and Philosophical Issues*. Totowa, N.J.: Rowman and Littlefield, 1977.

Moline, Jon. *Plato's Theory of Understanding*. Madison: University of Wisconsin Press, 1981.

Montesquieu, C.-L. de S. *The Spirit of the Laws*. Edited by F. Neumann, translated by T. Nugent. New York: Hafner, 1949.

Morris, T. F. "Knowledge of Knowledge and of Lack of Knowledge in the *Charmides*." *International Studies in Philosophy* 21 (1989): 49–61.

Murdoch, Iris. *The Sovereignty of Good*. New York: Schocken, 1971.

Nathanson, Stephen. *The Ideal of Rationality*. Chicago: Open Court, 1994.

Nehamas, Alexander. "Eristic, Antilogic, Sophistic, Dialectic," *History of Philosophy Quarterly* 7 (1986): 3–16.

———. "Meno's Paradox and Socrates as Teacher." *Oxford Studies in Ancient Philosophy* 3 (1985): 1–30.

Nietzsche, Friedrich. *The Birth of Tragedy and the Geneology of Morals*. Translated by Francis Golffing. New York: Doubleday & Co., 1956.

———. *The Gay Science*. Translated by Walter Kaufmann. New York: Vintage, 1974.

North, Helen. "A Period of Opposition to *Sophrosune*." Transactions of the American Philological Association 78 (1947), 1–17.

———. *Sophrosyne: Self-Knowledge and Self-Restraint in Greek Literature*. Ithaca: Cornell University Press, 1966.

Nussbaum, Martha. *The Fragility of Goodness*. Cambridge: Cambridge University Press, 1986.

Oakeshott, Michael. *Rationalism in Politics*. New York: Basic Books, 1962.

O'Brien, Michael J. *The Socratic Paradoxes and the Greek Mind*. Chapel Hill, N.C.: University of North Carolina Press, 1967.

Pangle, Thomas L. *Montesquieu's Philosophy of Liberalism*. Chicago: University of Chicago Press, 1973.

Parke, H. W. and D. E. W. Wormell. *The Delphic Oracle*. Oxford: Oxford University Press, 1956.

Patterson, Richard. *Image and Reality in Plato's Metaphysics*. Indianapolis: Hackett, 1985.

Plato. *Charmides*. Translated by Thomas G. West and Grace Starry West. Indianapolis: Hackett, 1986.

———. *Charmides, Alcibiades I and II, Hipparchus, The Lovers, Theages, Minos, Epinomis*. Translated by W. R. M. Lamb. Cambridge, Mass.: Harvard University Press, 1927.

———. *Collected Dialogues*. Translated and edited by Edith Hamilton and Huntington Cairns. Princeton, N.J.: Princeton University Press, 1961.

———. *Laches and Charmides*. Translated by Rosamund Sprague. Indianapolis: Bobbs-Merrill, 1973.

———. *Lysis, Symposium and Gorgias*. Translated by W. R. M. Lamb. Cambridge, Mass.: Harvard University Press, 1925.

———. *Opera*. Edited by John Burnet. Oxford: Oxford University Press, 1903.

———. *Republic*. Translated by Richard W. Sterling and William C. Scott. New York: W. W. Norton & Co., 1985.

Plochmann, George Kimball, and Franklin E. Robinson. *A Friendly Companion to Plato's Gorgias*. Carbondale: Southern Illinois University Press, 1988.

Popper, Karl. *The Open Society and Its Enemies 1: The Spell of Plato*. Princeton, N.J.: Princeton University Press, 1962.

Press, Gerald, ed. *Plato's Dialogues: New Studies and Interpretations*. Lanham, Md.: Rowman & Littlefield, 1993.

Rankin, H. D. *Sophists, Socratics and Cynics*. Totowa, N.J.: Barnes & Noble, 1983.

Reeve, C. D. C. *Socrates in the Apology*. Indianapolis: Hackett, 1989.

Rescher, Nicholas. *Dialectics*. Albany: State University of New York Press, 1977.

———. *Rationality*. Oxford: Clarendon Press, 1988.

Robinson, Richard. *Plato's Earlier Dialectic*. Oxford: Clarendon Press, 1953.

Robinson, T. M. *Plato's Psychology*. (1st ed.). Toronto: University of Toronto Press, 1970.

Roochnik, David L. "The Erotics of Philosophical Discourse." *History of Philosophy Quarterly* 4 (1987): 117–29.

———. "Socrates' Use of the Techne Analogy," *Journal of the History of Philosophy* 24 (1986), 295–310, reprinted in Benson, ed., *Essays on the Philosophy of Socrates*, 185–97.

———. *Of Art and Wisdom: Plato's Understanding of Techne*. University Park, Pa.: Pennsylvania State University Press, 1996.

Rorty, Amelie. "The Deceptive Self." In *Perspectives on Self-Deception*, edited by Brian McLaughlin and Amelie Rorty. Berkeley: University of California Press, 1988.

Rosen, Stanley. *Plato's Symposium.* New Haven: Yale University Press, 1968.

———. "*Sophrosyne* and *Selbstbewusstsein.*" *Review of Metaphysics* 26 (1973): 619–42.

———. "Self-Consciousness and Self-Knowledge in Plato and Hegel." *Hegel-Studien* 9 (1974): 109–29.

Ruppert, Peter. *Reader in a Strange Land: The Activity of Reading Literary Utopias.* Athens, Ga.: University of Georgia, 1986.

Santas, Gerasimos. "Socrates at Work on Virtue and Knowledge in Plato's *Charmides.*" In *Exegesis and Argument: Essays in Honor of Gregory Vlastos*, edited by E. N. Lee, A. P. Mourelatos, and R. M. Rorty. Assen, Holland: Van Gorcum, 1973.

———. *Socrates: Philosophy in Plato's Early Dialogues.* London: Routledge & Kegan Paul. 1970.

Sartre, Jean Paul. "Legend de la Verite," *Bifur VIII* (Paris, 1931): 86.

Scaltsas, Thomas. "Socratic Moral Realism" in *Oxford Studies in Ancient Philosophy* 7 (1989): 129–50.

Schiappa, Edward. *Protagoras and the Logos: A Study in Greek Philosophy and Rhetoric.* Columbia: University of South Carolina Press, 1991.

Schliermacher, F. *Introductions to the Dialogues of Plato.* Translated by W. Dobson. Cambridge: Cambridge University Press, 1836.

Schmid, W. Thomas. *On Manly Courage: A Study of Plato's Laches.* Carbondale, Ill.: Southern Illinois University Press, 1992.

———. "Socratic Conception of Courage." *History of Philosophy Quarterly* 2/2 (1985): 113–29.

———. "Socratic Moderation and Self-Knowledge." *Journal of the History of Philosophy* 21 (1983): 339–48.

———. "Socrates' Practice of Elenchus in the *Charmides.*" *Ancient Philosophy* 1 (1981): 141–47.

Schofield, M. "Socrates on Conversing with Doctors." *Classical Review* 73 (1973): 121–23.

Seeskin, Kenneth. *Dialogue and Discovery.* Albany,: State University of New York Press, 1987.

———. "Vlastos on Elenchus and Mathematics" (unpublished manuscript).

Shorey, Paul. *What Plato Said*. Chicago: University of Chicago Press, 1933.

Snell, Bruno. *The Discovery of the Mind*. Translated by T. G. Rosenmeyer. New York: Harperand Row, 1960.

Sparshott, F. E.. "Plato as Anti-Political Thinker." In *Plato: A Collection of Critical Essays*, vol. 2, edited by Gregory Vlastos. Garden City, N.Y.: Doubleday, 1971.

Spiegelberg, Herbert. *The Socratic Enigma*. Indianapolis: Bobbs-Merrill, 1964.

Sprague, Rosamund Kent. *Plato's Philosopher-King*. Columbia, S.C.: University of South Carolina Press, 1976.

Stalley, R. F. "Mental Health and Individual Responsibility in Plato's *Republic*." *Journal of Value Inquiry* 15 (1981), 109–24.

Stone, I. F. *The Case Against Socrates*. Boston: Little, Brown, 1988.

Strauss, Leo. *The City and Man*. Chicago: Rand McNally, 1964.

———. *On Tyranny*. Glencoe, Ill.: The Free Press, 1963.

———. "The Spirit of Sparta or the Taste of Xenophon." *Social Research* 6/4 (1939), 502–36.

Taran, Leonardo. "Platonism and Socratic Ignorance." In *Platonic Investigations*, edited by Dominic O'Meara. Washington, D.C., Catholic University of America Press, 1985.

Taylor, A. E. *Plato: The Man and His Work*. New York: Dial Press, 1936.

Taylor, Charles. "Responsibility for Self," in *The Identities of Persons*, edited by Amelie Rorty. Berkeley: University of California Press, 1976. Reprinted in *Free Will*, edited by Gary Watson. Oxford: Oxford University Press, 1982.

———. *Sources of the Self*. Cambridge: Harvard University Press, 1989.

———. "What Is Human Agency?" in *The Self*, edited by Theodore Mischel. Totowa, N.J.: Rowman and Littlefield, 1977.

Taylor, Gabriele. *Pride, Shame, and Guilt*. Oxford: Clarendon Press, 1985.

Thesleff, Holger. "Looking for Clues: An Interpretation of Some Literary Aspects of Plato's 'Two-Level' Model." in *Plato's Dialogues*, edited by Gerald Press, 17–45. Landham, Md.: Rowman & Littlefield, 1993.

Thucydides. *The Peloponnesian War*. Translated by Richard Crawley and revised by T. E. Wick. New York: Random House, 1982.

Tigerstedt, E. N. *Interpreting Plato*. Uppsala: Almquist & Wiksell International, 1977.

Tuckey, T. G. *Plato's Charmides*. Amsterdam: Adolf M. Hakkert, 1968. Reprinted from the London, 1951 ed., Cambridge University Press.

Tugendhat, Ernst. *Self-Consiousness and Self-Determination*. Translated by Paul Stern. Cambridge: MIT Press, 1986.

Usher, S. "This to the Fair Critias," *Eranos* 77 (1979): 39–42.

Vernant, Jean Pierre. *Myth and Thought among the Greeks*. London: Routledge and Kegan Paul, 1983. First published as *Mythe et pensee chez les Grecs*. Paris: Librairie Francois Maspero, 1965.

Versenyi, Lazlo. *Socratic Humanism*. New Haven: Yale University Press, 1963.

———. "Virtue as a Self-Directed Art." *Personalist* 53 (1972): 274–89.

Vlastos, Gregory. "The Historical Socrates and Athenian Democracy." *Political Theory* 11 (1983): 494–515. Reprinted in *Socratic Studies*.

———. *Platonic Studies*, 2d ed. Princeton, N.J: Princeton University Press, 1981.

———. "Socrates." In *The Philosophy of Socrates*, edited by Gregory Vlastos. Garden City: Doubleday, 1971.

———. "Socrates' Disavowal of Knowledge." *Philosophical Quarterly* 35 (1985): 1–31. Reprinted in *Socratic Studies*.

———. *Socrates, Ironist and Moral Philosopher*. Ithaca: Cornell University Press, 1991.

———. "The Socratic Elenchus." *Oxford Studies in Ancient Greek Philosophy* 1 (1983): 23–58. Reprinted in *Socratic Studies*.

———. *Socratic Studies*. Cambridge: Cambridge University Press, 1994.

———. "Solonian Justice." *Classical Philology* 41 (1946): 65–83.

———. *Studies in Greek Philosophy*. Vol. 1–2. Edited by Dan Graham. Oxford: Oxford University Press, 1995.

———, ed. *Plato: A Collection of Critical Essays*, vol. 2. Garden City, N.Y.: Doubleday, 1971.

Watson, Gary. "Free Agency." In *Free Will*, edited by Gary Watson, 96–110. Oxford: Oxford University Press, 1982.

Wellman, Robert R. "The Question Posed at *Charmides* 165a–166c." *Phronesis* 9 (1964): 107–13.

Wilkins, Eliza Gregory. *"Know Thyself" in Greek and Latin Literature.* New York: Garland, 1979 (reprint from Menasha, Wisc.: G. Banta Publishing Co., 1917).

Wilson, J. F. *The Politics of Moderation: An Interpretation of Plato's Republic.* Washington, D.C.: University of America Press, 1984.

Witte, Bernd. *Die Wissenschaft von Guten und Boesen: Interpretationen zu Platons "Charmides."* Berlin: Walter de Gruyter & Co., 1970.

Wood, E. M. and Neal Wood. *Class Ideology and Ancient Political Theory.* Oxford: Oxford University Press, 1978.

———. "Socrates and Democracy." *Political Theory* 14 (1986): 55–83.

Woodruff, Paul. "The Skeptical Side of Plato's Method." *Revue Internationale de Philosophie* 40 (1986): 22–37.

———. "Plato's Early Theory of Knowledge." In *Ancient Greek Epistemology,* edited by Stephen Everson. Cambridge: Cambridge University Press, 1990.

Xenophon. *Hellenica.* Vols. 1 and 2. Translated by C. L. Brownson. Cambridge: Harvard University Press, 1980.

———. *Memorabilia, Oeconomicus, Symposium and Apology.* Translated by E. C. Marchant and O. J. Todd. Cambridge: Harvard University Press, 1923.

———. "On the Spartan Constitution" in *Scripta Minora.* Translated by E. C. Marchant. Cambridge: Harvard University Press, 1923.

INDEX

L

M